THE PRE-EXISTENCE OF CHRIST
IN THE WRITINGS OF JUSTIN MARTYR

HARVARD THEOLOGICAL REVIEW
HARVARD DISSERTATIONS IN RELIGION

edited by
Caroline Bynum
and
George Rupp

Number 6

THE PRE-EXISTENCE OF CHRIST
IN THE WRITINGS OF JUSTIN MARTYR

by
Demetrius Christ Trakatellis

SCHOLARS PRESS
Missoula, Montana

THE PRE-EXISTENCE OF CHRIST
IN THE WRITINGS OF JUSTIN MARTYR

by
Demetrius Christ Trakatellis

Published by
SCHOLARS PRESS
for
Harvard Theological Review

Distributed by

SCHOLARS PRESS
University of Montana
Missoula, Montana 59812

THE PRE-EXISTENCE OF CHRIST
IN THE WRITINGS OF JUSTIN MARTYR

by

Demetrius Christ Trakatellis
Athens, Greece

Library of Congress Cataloging in Publication Data

Trakatellis, Demetrius Christ.
　The pre-existence of Christ in the writing of Justin
Martyr.

　(Harvard dissertations in religion ; no. 6)
　Originally presented as the author's thesis, Harvard.
　Bibliography: p.
　1. Jesus Christ—Pre-existence—History of doctrines.
2. Justinus Martyr, Saint. I. Title. II. Series.
BT198.T7 1976　　　232　　　76-44913
ISBN 0-89130-098-8

Printed in the United States of America

Edwards Brothers, Inc.
Ann Arbor, Michigan 48104

CONTENTS

ACKNOWLEDGEMENTS

This dissertation is the result of a long and welcome stay at Harvard University. The rich library and excellent research facilities, the high scholarly standards and warm human atmosphere, all have been part of my experience at Harvard University and have in various ways contributed to this dissertation.

My appreciation is particularly extended to the Graduate School of Arts and Sciences and to the Divinity School. In the New Testament Department of the Divinity School where I did my specialized studies, I found an outstanding faculty of scholars who were highly accessible and graciously eager to provide me with advice and assistance. I am deeply indebted to all the members of this faculty: Dean Krister Stendahl and Professors Helmut Koester, John Strugnell, Dieter Georgi and George MacRae. Professor Helmut Koester was my adviser for this dissertation, indeed more than an adviser, a friend and colleague. Dean Krister Stendahl was a friend and adviser throughout my graduate studies at Harvard. To both I am especially grateful.

I am also grateful to the Examining Committee for granting the honor of distinction to the present dissertation and to the New Testament Department for recommending the dissertation for publication in the new Harvard Dissertations in Religion series.

Many others offered valuable assistance as well. My friend and colleague Dr. Theodore Stylianopoulos read the entire manuscript and corrected my many infelicities in English. Professor George Williams kindly put at my disposal

his exhaustive bibliography on Justin. Dr. Maria Grossman,
Peter Oliver and Charles Woodbury of Andover-Harvard Library
at the Divinity School were extremely useful in my research.
Camilla Sieveking, Doris Carlin, and Penelope Konstantinidis
gave decisive assistance with typing, re-typing and other
technical work. To all these and many others I am greatly
indebted.

Athens, Greece   Demetrius Trakatellis
                                            Bishop of Vresthena

ABBREVIATIONS

Ap.	Justin's First Apology
App.	Justin's Second Apology
Dial.	Justin's Dialogue with Trypho

For the ancient texts I follow the
abbreviations used by the *Theological
Dictionary of the New Testament*.

INTRODUCTION

1. The pre-existence of Christ in a divine status prior to his incarnation is stated in various texts of the New Testament, e.g., Phil. 2,6-11, John 1,1-14, Hebr. 1,1-12, Col. 1,15-20.[1] In all of these instances the statement of the pre-existence of Christ does not appear isolated but integrated in a chain of christological affirmations. In most of the cases, this chain seems to follow a certain pattern frequently called "humiliation and exaltation" christological pattern.[2]

If one studies the concept of the pre-existence of Christ, in the Apostolic Fathers and the Apologists of the second century A.D., one will be especially impressed by the writings of Justin Martyr. In his texts the concept of the pre-existence of Christ occurs in an astonishingly high frequency and within the most diversified contexts. This fact raises a number of questions: why this striking difference in frequency of occurrence between Justin and the New Testament? Is the concept of the pre-existence of

---

[1]For a list of all the possible New Testament occurrences see Fred B. Craddock, *The Pre-existence of Christ in the New Testament* (Nashville, 1968), p. 14. Cf. also P. Benoît, "Préexistence et Incarnation," *Revue Biblique* 77 (1970), 5-29.

[2]The expression "humiliation and exaltation" is a reflection of the phrase ἐταπείνωσεν ἑαυτόν . . . διὸ καὶ ὁ θεὸς αὐτὸν ὑπερύψωσεν of Phil. 2,8-9. The main work on the humiliation and exaltation Christology in the New Testament is Eduard Schweizer's *Erniedrigung und Erhöhung bei Jesus und seinen Nachfolgern* (Zürich, 1955). English translation, with revision by the author, under the title *Lordship and Discipleship* (London, 1960). My references are to the English translation, unless otherwise stated.

Christ in Justin's texts still a part of the humiliation
and exaltation pattern as in the New Testament? If yes,
to what extent and in what manner? If not, why not? And in
that case, how does the concept of pre-existence function
theologically?

The attempt to answer these questions is worth
undertaking. The answers contribute to the study of the
christological patterns and their function within the
christian literature of the first two centuries A.D.[3] They
provide also significant clues for the understanding of
Justin's Christology and particularly its relationship to the
tradition.

It is apparent that in order to arrive at these
answers one should make a thorough examination of the concept
of Christ's pre-existence in the Justinian texts. This is
precisely what I have tried to do in the present dissertation. For reasons of efficiency, I have centered my investigation around the following three problems:

a) What are the sources behind Justin's
various formulations that affirm the pre-existence of Christ?

b) What is the theological function of the
pre-existence of Christ in Justin's texts?

c) Does the concept of Christ's pre-existence
in the Justinian writings belong to a humiliation and exaltation pattern or to any other christological schema, or does
it stand alone and autonomous?

2. Before proceeding into some other introductory
matters I should like to make two basic clarifications. They
pertain to the terms "the pre-existence of Christ" and
"humiliation and exaltation pattern" respectively.

a) The word pre-existence could have various

---

[3]Helmut Koester's papers, "Γνῶμαι διάφοροι: The
Origin and Nature of Diversification in the History of Early
Christianity," *Harv. Theol. Rev.* 58 (1965), 279-318, and
"One Jesus and Four Primitive Gospels," *Harv. Theol. Rev.*
61 (1968), 203-247, have shown the possibilities of such an
enterprise. (These papers could be found also in the book
just published by J. M. Robinson and H. Koester, *Trajec-
tories through Early Christianity* [Philadelphia, 1971], pp.
114-157 and 158-204.)

meanings[4] which may cause confusion if the term is used without having been defined. On the other hand, an arbitrary
definition might impose an artificial frame on the material
under investigation. In order to avert both dangers, I use
the word pre-existence in terms of its usage in the writings
of Justin. To be sure, he does not employ the noun προ-
ὕπαρξις to which pre-existence corresponds. He uses, however,
the verb προϋπάρχειν in a definitely christological way. As
a typical formulation one could quote Dialogue 48,1: προϋπάρχειν θεὸν ὄντα πρὸ αἰώνων τοῦτον τὸν Χριστὸν, εἶτα καὶ
γεννηθῆναι ἄνθρωπον γενόμενον (also, Dial. 48,2-3; 87,2).
Here the pre-existence of Christ is defined by two basic
categories: (a) the status of being God (θεὸν ὄντα) and
(b) the actual existence prior to creation (πρὸ αἰώνων)
with a definite "terminus" at incarnation (εἶτα καὶ γεννηθῆναι etc.). So the phrase pre-existence of Christ,
according to Dialogue 48,1 and parallels,[5] designates Christ's
actual existence in a status of God from incarnation backwards
indefinitely.[6] This Justinian designation of the term pre-
existence of Christ is presupposed in my usage of the same
term throughout the present dissertation.

    b) By "humiliation and exaltation" christo-
logical pattern I mean the creedal formulation which:

    (1) holds Christ as pre-existing in a divine status
before becoming incarnate;

---

[4]See F. Craddock, *op. cit.*, pp. 16-19.

[5]I shall return to these passages for a detailed
analysis in Chapter 1. The presentation here is provisional
and strictly limited to an initial working definition.

[6]F. Bosse *Der präexistente Christus des Justinus
Märtyr*, Greifswald, 1891, p. 11, was correct when he concluded that the pre-existence of Christ in Justin means
*"das göttliche Dasein Christi vor seiner geschichtlichen
Erscheinung als Mensch"* (the italics are Bosse's), and
that "über den Anfang dieses Daseins ist damit an sich
nichts ausgesagt. . . . Der Beziehungspunkt für das προ-
[i.e. of προϋπαρξις], ist auch für Justin durchaus die
Inkarnation." The last point explains why J. T. Brothers,
"The Interpretation of παῖς θεοῦ in Justin Martyr's
Dialogue with Trypho," *Studia Patristica* IX (Berlin, 1966),
p. 129, uses the term "pre-incarnate" Christ as a substitute for the phrase "pre-existing" Christ.

(2) presents the incarnation as humiliation, apparently because of the transition to an immensely inferior status, and because of the sufferings and the death of Jesus; and

(3) declares that the humiliated Christ was exalted by God, and given by him all power in heaven and on earth.[7]

Eduard Schweizer has argued that the humiliation and exaltation schema in the New Testament follows the model of the suffering and exalted righteous one in Judaism.[8] Such a model alone, however, cannot account for all the New Testament cases. Phil. 2,6-11, for example, has been viewed by several scholars as patterned after the most diversified models.[9] Schweizer does not seem to take sufficiently into account the Old Testament hypostatization process related, mainly, to the figure of Wisdom.[10] Such a process runs primarily through Prov. 8, Wisd. 6-9, Sir. 1 and 24 down to the intertestamental literature and to Philo, and, I believe, plays a fundamental role in the configuration of the humiliation and exaltation pattern in the New Testament.

---

[7]The passage Phil. 2,6-11 is the clearest indicator for the existence of the humiliation and exaltation pattern in the New Testament, together with the Epistle to the Hebrews (especially chs. 1 and 2 and 5,5-10), the Gospel of John (esp. 1,1-14) and Col. 1,15-20.

[8]E. Schweizer, *op. cit.*, pp. 32 ff.

[9]A survey of the relevant literature and the pertinent hypotheses advanced by scholars such as Cerfaux, Cullmann, Georgi, Käsemann, Krinetzki, A. D. Nock and others, is to be found in R. P. Martin's book *"Carmen Christi," Phil. 2,5-11 in recent interpretation etc.* (Cambridge, 1967), pp. 74-95. For something comparable to the work done on Phil. 2,6-11, this time with respect to Col. 1,15-20, see N. Kehl, *Der Christushymnus im Kolosserbrief* (Kol. 1,12-20), (Stuttgart, 1967). Cf. also J. T. Sanders, *The New Testament Christological Hymns* (Cambridge, 1971).

[10]For the impact of the figure of wisdom on the New Testament Christology see the recent books by A. Feuillet, *Le Christ Sagesse de Dieu* (Paris, 1966), and Felix Christ, *Jesus Sophia, die Sophia-Christologie bei den Synoptikern* (Zürich, 1970). See also P. E. Bonnard, *La Sagesse en personne annoncée et venue: Jesus Christ* (Lectio Divina 44) (Paris, 1966); C. Larcher, *Etudes sur le livre de la Sagesse,* Etudes Bibliques (Paris, 1969); H. Koester, "The Structure

When, therefore, I employ the phrase "humiliation and exaltation pattern" I mean basically the schema consisting of points (1), (2), and (3) without connecting it necessarily to the specific model that Schweizer posits.

3. Many have dealt with Justin's Christology and consequently touched upon his concept of the pre-existence of Christ, especially since the publication of M. von Engelhardt's significant book.[11] Actually every major work on the history of dogma contains a section on the Justinian Christology.[12] The same is true for works that grapple with special christological problems.[13] In these cases, however, the treatment is general and does not contribute much to our specific study.

Things are different with works dedicated exclusively to Justin's theology. An important book in this category is E. R. Goodenough's *The Theology of Justin Martyr* which deals with problems that relate to our subject. In the course of our presentation, we will have the opportunity to discuss basic opinions of Goodenough.[14]

---

and Criteria of Early Christian Beliefs," in J. M. Robinson and H. Koester, *op. cit.*, pp. 219-223.

[11]*Das Christentum Justin des Märtyrers, Eine Untersuchung über die Anfänge der katholischen Glaubenslehre* (Erlangen, 1878).

[12]Cf. A. von Harnack, *Lehrbuch der Dogmengeschichte*, Vol. I (Tübingen, 1909[4]), pp. 496-550 (esp. 507-513, 542-545); F. Loofs, *Leitfaden zum Studium der Dogmengeschichte* (Halle, 1906[4]), pp. 114-129; R. Seeberg, *Text-Book of the History of Doctrines*; E. T. by C. E. Hay, Vol. I (Philadelphia, 1905), pp. 109-118; J. Turmel, *Histoire des Dogmes*, Vol. II (Paris, 1932), pp. 48-73; J. Lebreton, *Histoire du Dogme de la Trinité*, Vol. II (Paris, 1928), pp. 405-484 (esp. 428-471) and pp. 663-677 etc.

[13]Cf. for instance A. Grillmeier, *Christ in Christian Tradition*, E. T. by J. S. Bowden (New York, 1965), pp. 105-111; S. Agourides, "The Christology of the Apologists," *Kleronomia* I (Thessalonike, 1969), pp. 39-62 (in Greek, with a summary in French, pp. 62-64).

[14]Two other relevant books published during the last decade are L. W. Barnard, *Justin Martyr, his Life and Thought* (Cambridge, 1967), and A. Theodorou, *The Theology of Justin the Philosopher and Martyr and its Relationship to the Greek Philosophy* (Athens, 1960), (in Greek).

6

Our research has been facilitated by studies on the relationship between Justin's theology and the philosophical and ideological currents of his time.[15] We profited, however, much more from a special category of works which are directly connected to general or particular problems of the present thesis. The most significant among them are the dissertations by F. Boose[16] and B. Kominiac,[17] the papers by C. Andresen,[18] R. Holte[19] and J. H. Waszink,[20] and the monographs by H. Koester,[21] P. Prigent[22] and W. A. Shotwell.[23] In the following chapters we will cite and discuss these works.[24]

---

[15]One should mention here J. Daniélou, *Message Evangélique et Culture Hellénistique aux IIe et IIIe siècles* (Tournai, 1961); H. Chadwick, "Justin Martyr's Defence of Christianity," *Bull. J. Ryl. Libr.* 47 (1964-65), 275-297; N. Hyldahl, *Philosophie und Christentum*, Eine Interpretation der Einleitung zum Dialog Justins (Kopenhagen, 1966).

[16]*Der präexistente Christus des Justinus Märtyr: Eine Episode aus der Geschichte des christologischen Dogmas* (Greifswald, 1891).

[17]*The Theophanies of the Old Testament in the Writings of St. Justin* (Washington, D.C., 1948).

[18]"Justin und der mittlere Platonismus," *ZNW* 44 (1952-53), 157-195. Cf. also his book, *Logos und Nomos, die Polemik des Kelsos wider das Christentum* (Berlin, 1955) esp. ch. IV: Kelsus und Justin, pp. 308-400).

[19]"Logos Spermatikos, Christianity and Ancient Philosophy according to St. Justin's Apologies," *Studia Theologica* 12 (1958), 109-168.

[20]"Bemerkungen zu Justins Lehre vom Logos Spermatikos," in *Mullus* (Festschr. Th. Klauser, Münster, 1964), pp. 380-390. See also his paper "Bemerkungen zum Einfluss des Platonismus im frühen Christentum," *Vigiliae Christianae* 19 (1965), 129-162.

[21]*Septuaginta und Synoptischer Erzählungsstoff im Schriftbeweis Justins des Märtyrers* (Habilitationsschrift) (Heidelberg, 1956).

[22]*Justin et l'Ancient Testament*, Etudes Bibliques (Paris, 1964).

[23]*The Biblical Exegesis of Justin Martyr* (London, 1965).

[24]The foregoing brief survey implies that only

4. As we have said already, there is a great number
of cases where Justin makes statements that contain the concept of the pre-existence of Christ. A more careful examination, however, shows that there are definite and clearly
distinguished poles around which the great majority of
relevant passages may be grouped. One could suggest four
such groupings:

(a) Texts which speak of the pre-existence of Christ
prior to creation.

(b) Passages which relate the pre-existing Son to
the Old Testament theophanies and divine manifestations in
general.

(c) Texts where the pre-existing Logos is related to
pagan people or to pagan individuals (Socrates, Musonius and
others).

(d) Many texts where the pre-existence of Christ is
connected with its "terminal" viz. the incarnation.

These four groupings will be investigated con-
secutively in the four chapters of this dissertation.

The examination is undertaken with attention to the
three basic problems regarding the pre-existence of Christ,
i.e., its sources, its theological function and its relationship to the humiliation and exaltation pattern.

The major areas in which, during the exegetical work,
I have tried to trace any elements which possibly occur also
in Justin are: The Old Testament (mostly Septuagint), the
Philonic writings, the New Testament, the Apostolic Fathers,
the Apologists (mainly the Greek), the gnostic accounts in
Irenaeus and Hippolytus as well as Clement's Excerpta ex
Theodoto, texts of Stoic and Platonic[25] philosophers, and the

---

F. Bosse's book deals exclusively with the problem of the
pre-existence of Christ in Justin Martyr. This book, however, covers the Justinian texts only in part, is poor in
background material and dogmatically, not exegetically
oriented. Works such as Holte's paper, on the other hand,
although exegetically rich, address themselves to a particular aspect and not to the entire problem of the pre-existence
of Christ, which is in the periphery of their enterprise.
Thus, within the Justinian bibliography there is no work
that examines thoroughly the idea of pre-existence.

[25] I have paid special attention to the Middle-Platonic

Corpus Hermeticum.

5. The detailed discussion of the literary and textual problems related to Justin's works is not decisive for the present study. I should like only to say that in this dissertation:

a) I limit myself to the First Apology, the Second Apology and the Dialogue with Trypho which are generally accepted as authentic writings of Justin.[26]

b) I follow the text edited by E. Goodspeed,[27] but in many instances I have also consulted that edited by J. C. T. Otto.[28]

---

philosophers, because their importance for the Justinian research has been widely accepted since the publication of the relevant works by Andresen, Holte, Danielou, etc. The designation Middle-Platonic philosophers is not yet clearly and uniformly defined. For practical purposes I use it in the sense of C. Tull, *The Theology of Middle-Platonism*, Unpublished Dissertation, Union Theological Seminary, New York, 1968, who classifies as Middle-Platonic philosophers Albinus, Apuleius, Atticus, Celsus, Maximus of Tyre and Plutarch. These are the authors who are primarily quoted by Andresen too.

[26]There have been in the past doubts concerning the authenticity of the Dialogue and the Apologies as well. J. Wetstein was the first to question the genuineness of the Dialogue (*Novum Testamentum Graecum*, Tom. I 1751, Prolegomena p. 66), but it was E. Preuschen who presented the most elaborate argument against its authenticity ("Die Echtheit von Justins Dialog gegen Trypho," *ZNW* 19 [1919-20], 102-127). Today, nevertheless, there seems to be no serious argument against the Justinian authorship of the Dialogue and the two Apologies.

[27]*Die ältesten Apologeten* (Göttingen, 1914).

[28]*Corpus Apologetarum Christianorum saeculi secundi*, Editio Tertia, Vol. I (Jena, 1876), Vol. II (Jena, 1877). It should be noted that the text of Justin's works is in poor condition. See more in G. Archambault, *Justin Dialogue avec Tryphon*, Texte Grec, Traduction fraçaise, Introduction, Notes et Index, Vol. I (Paris, 1909), pp. XII ff.; A. L. Williams, *Justin Martyr, the Dialogue with Trypho*, Translation, Introduction and Notes (London, 1930), pp. XVII ff.; W. Schmid, "Die Textüberlieferung der Apologie des Justin," *ZNW* 40 (1941), 87-138; *idem*, Frühe Apologetik und Platonismus, *Hermeneia* (Festschr. Regenbogen, 1952), pp. 163 ff.

c) I use the term Second Apology (abbr.: App.) as an established title. Whether the Second Apology is a separate work or an appendix to the First Apology does not have a substantive impact on my research.

CHAPTER ONE

THE PRE-EXISTENCE OF CHRIST
PRIOR TO CREATION

Justin is not interested in speculating about what happened within the deity before creation. However, because of his apologetic purposes, he is compelled to deal with the problem of the pre-existent Son and his relationship to the Father before the world came into being.

There are several passages in the two Apologies and in the Dialogue where Justin touches upon that problem. In most of them there is an explicit reference to the pre-creational status of the Son. In some, the reference is implicit. We are going to investigate both categories as they appear in isolated passages or in groups of passages that use similar material or comparable terminology.

A. *The Son* θεὸς προϋπάρχων

1. Justin speaks of Christ as pre-existing in the status of God on many occasions.[1] In two basic passages, viz. Dial. 48,1-3 and 87,2, he uses the term θεὸς and the verb προϋπάρχειν in order to denote this pre-existence in the divine status. He says in Dial 48: προϋπάρχειν θεὸν ὄντα πρὸ αἰώνων τοῦτον τὸν Χριστόν (v. 1), and προϋπῆρχεν υἱὸς τοῦ ποιητοῦ τῶν ὅλων θεὸς ὤν (v. 2). Similarly in Dial. 87,2 he states: Χριστόν . . . καὶ θεὸν αὐτὸν προϋπάρχοντα.

The verb προϋπάρχειν has been used by Justin only in the above passages. It occurs in the Septuagint and in the

---

[1]E.g. Ap. 63,15; Dial. 48,1-3; 87,2; 126,2; 127,4; 128,1 etc.

11

New Testament but only as a word denoting a situation which was before something else or which was already existing when something happened.[2] In all these instances προϋπάρχειν does not seem to have any specific theological meaning.[3]

Philo offers two passages where the verb προϋπάρχειν acquires a new dimension because of the context. In *Op. Mund.* 129, when commenting on Gen. 2,4-5, he argues that the ἀσώματοι καὶ νοηταὶ ἰδέαι are σφραγῖδες τῶν αἰσθητῶν and, therefore, exist prior to them.[4] Philo returns to the same biblical text, viz. Gen. 2,4-5, in *Leg. All* I, 22 and uses again the verb προϋπάρχειν: ὥσπερ τοῦ ἐπὶ μέρους καὶ ἀτόμου νοῦ προϋπάρχει τις ἰδέα ὡς ἂν ἀρχέτυπον καὶ παράδειγμα τούτου. In both Philonic passages the emphasis lies on the priority of ideas over against the created things. Because of such priority and also of the reference to a "time" before the creation of heaven and earth, the verb προϋπάρχειν obtains a nuance of pre-eminence both in terms of essence and time. Here one could trace an approximation to the Justinian usage of προϋπάρχειν.

There are, however, two other texts which might be illuminating. The first belongs to Hippolytus. In his *Ref.* VI, 18 he quotes a passage from the book *Apophasis (megale)* ascribed by him to Simon Magus. In this quotation the verb προϋπάρχειν appears twice in conjunction with one of the two δυνάμεις which have no beginning nor end.[5] The

---

[2] See for instance Job 42,18; Lk. 23,12; Acts 8,9.

[3] Both the Septuagint and the New Testament usage of προϋπάρχειν follow that encountered also in Plato (e.g. *Prot.* 317D: ἐκεῖ γὰρ προϋπῆρχε τὰ βάθρα), Aristotle (e.g.*Rhet.* 1419b: ἡ τῶν σωμάτων αὔξησις ἐκ προϋπαρχόντων ἐστί), the Stoics (apud J. v. Arnim, *Stoicorum Veterum Fragmenta*, Vol. III, p. 51). Plutarch exhibits the same usage (e.g. *Apophth. Lac.* 225F; *Pyth. Or.* 404F; *Mus.* 1141C). Cf. also Josephus, *Ant.* IV, 125: ἅ τε καὶ προϋπῆρξεν ἐν τοῖς ἔμπροσθεν χρόνοις.

[4] Cf. *Op. Mund.* 130: ἐκάστου τῶν ἄλλων ἃ δικάζουσιν αἰσθήσεις τὰ πρεσβύτερα εἴδη καὶ μέτρα, οἷς εἰδοποιεῖται καὶ μετρεῖται τὰ γενόμενα, προϋπῆρχε.

[5] Hippolytus, *Ref.* VI, 18: οὗτός ἐστιν ὁ ἐστώς, στὰς στησόμενος . . . δύναμις κατὰ τὴν προϋπάρχουσαν δύναμιν . . .

context suggests that προϋπάρχειν carries a theological
meaning. It is likely that Justin knew Simon's work since
he mentions him[6] and particularly in Ap. 26 where he also
refers to his own book *Against All Heresies* (Ap. 26,8).

The second text appears in the account concerning
the Ebionites given by Eusebius (*Hist. Eccl.* III, 27). In
this report Eusebius describes two groups of Ebionites. The
first one insisted that Jesus Christ was conceived and born
in a completely human manner. The second group opposed this
idea and confessed Christ as born from the Virgin Mary and
the Holy Spirit but agreed with the first group that Christ
was not θεὸς προϋπάρχων.[7] Eusebius' passage is strikingly
close to Dial. 48 and Dial. 87 as regards the usage and the
meaning of προϋπάρχειν.[8] It is noteworthy that in both Dial.
48 and 87 Justin has Trypho introducing the προϋπάρχειν
terminology. This, in connection with the Eusebian report,
might indicate that the προϋπάρχειν language in Justin
emerged from his confrontation with the Jewish teachings which
refer to the Messiah.[9]

Ἔχων γὰρ ἐν ἑαυτῷ αὐτὴν [ἐπίνοιαν] ἣν μόνος, οὐ μέντοι
πρῶτος, καίπερ προϋπάρχων.

[6]Ap. 26,2,4; 56,2; App. 15,1; Dial. 120,6. I do not
mean to imply that *Apophasis megale* is a work whose authentic
author is Simon Magus. The authorship of this book is still
an open question. See more in J. M. A. Salles-Dabadie,
Recherches sur Simon le Mage, I. l'"Apophasis megalé," (Paris,
1969), p. 9 and p. 143. Dabadie seems to accept Simon Magus
as the authentic author of *Apophasis megale* (*ibid.* p. 143).
I assume that it is not improbable that Justin might have
known the book as a work of Simon Magus.

[7]Eusebius, *Hist. Eccl.* III, 27: ἐκ παρθένου καὶ ἁγίου
πνεύματος μὴ ἀρνούμενοι γεγονέναι τὸν Κύριον, οὐ μὴν ἔθ'
ὁμοίως καὶ οὗτοι προϋπάρχειν αὐτὸν θεὸν λόγον ὄντα καὶ σοφίαν
πατρὸς ὁμολογοῦντες, τῇ τῶν προτέρων περιετρέποντο δυσσεβείᾳ.

[8]There is even a verbatim agreement:

Eusebius, Hist. Eccl. III, 27	Justin, Dial. 48,1
προϋπάρχειν	προϋπάρχειν
αὐτὸν	
θεὸν	θεὸν
λόγον	
ὄντα	ὄντα

[9]Cf. Bosse, *op. cit.*, p. 14.

14

Two characteristics are easily distinguishable in
Dial. 48,1-3 and 87,2:

a) Justin does not speak about a mere pre-
existence of the Messiah before he appeared among men.
Neither does he understand προϋπάρχειν in the sense in which
the rabbinic literature applied the notion to the Torah.[10]
For Justin Christ is pre-existent because he is God or by
being God: προϋπάρχειν θεὸν ὄντα (Dial. 48,1); προϋπῆρχεν
υἱὸς τοῦ ποιητοῦ τῶν ὅλων θεὸς ὤν (Dial. 48,2).[11] The
emphasis obviously is on the divine status, not on the
priority in time.

b) Christ is declared θεὸς προϋπάρχων but this
affirmation does not stand isolated or loose. In all cases
it is accompanied by a statement which asserts Christ's incarnation, sometimes in an emphatic way:

Dial. 48,1: προϋπάρχειν	εἶτα καὶ γεννηθῆναι
θεὸν ὄντα πρὸ αἰώνων	ἄνθρωπον γενόμενον
	ὑπομεῖναι.
Dial. 48,2: προϋπῆρχε . . .	καὶ γεγέννηται
θεὸς ὤν	ἄνθρωπος διὰ τῆς παρθένου.
Dial. 48,3: ὁ Χριστὸς	καὶ γεννηθῆναι ἄνθρωπος
ὁ τοῦ θεοῦ προϋπῆρχε	ὁμοιοπαθὴς ἡμῖν σάρκα
	ἔχων ὑπέμεινε.
Dial. 87,2: θεὸν αὐτὸν	καί . . . σαρκοποιηθέντα
προϋπάρχοντα	διὰ τῆς παρθένου γεγεννῆσ-
	θαι ἄνθρωπον.

In Dial. 48,1-3 the statement about incarnation seems
to be necessary because the point of the argument lies in the
contradistinction between the divinity and the humanity of

---

[10]Cf. *Pesahim* 54a: "Seven things were created before
the world was created, and these are they: the Torah etc."
See more, especially with reference to the Philonic Logos,
in K. Schubert, "Einige Beobachtungen zum Verständnis des
Logosbegriffes im frührabbinischen Schrifttum," *Judaica* 9
(1953), 65-80. Cf. also H. A. Wolfson, *The Philosophy of
the Church Fathers*, Vol. I (Cambridge, Mass., 1956), pp.
157 ff.

[11]Cf. F. Bosse, *op. cit.*, p. 18, n. 8: "So oft im
Dialog das προϋπάρχειν vorkommt, ist die Subjektsbezeichnung
θεὸς in der Nähe. *Ibid.* p. 19: ". . . es sich ihm [i.e.

Christ. This, however, is not the case with Dial. 87,2.
Moreover, one might argue that even in 48,1-3 Justin was not
compelled to use terms like ὑπομεῖναι or ἄνθρωπος ὁμοιοπαθὴς ἡμῖν which have a humiliation nuance. Do we have then
here elements of a humiliation and exaltation pattern?[12] Or
do those expressions simply serve anti-docetic purposes,
and this is the reason why they occur in Dial. 48 and 87?
We will discuss the matter at the end of the present chapter.

2. The attribute θεὸς for the pre-existing Christ
has already been encountered in John 1,1 (καὶ θεὸς ἦν ὁ
λόγος), Phil. 2,5 (ὃς ἐν μορφῇ θεοῦ ὑπάρχων), Ignatius
(*Tral.* 7,1 θεὸς ᾽Ιησοῦς Χριστός; *Eph.* and *Rom.* prologue
᾽Ιησοῦς Χριστὸς ὁ θεὸς ἡμῶν). But there is an apparent difference between the New Testament and the Ignatian texts on
the one hand, and the Justinian statements on the other.
Justin in Dial. 48 and 87, for example, is consciously and
purposely arguing for the pre-existence of Christ in the
status of God. It is his theme, his focal point.

W. Bousset contends that this confession of the
deity of Christ in Justin is a fruit of the cult, namely,
that "for Justin deity and worship belong together."[13] The
observation might hold true for John 1,1 and Phil. 2,5,
especially since these two passages belong to a hymnic context and possibly to a liturgical-creedal setting. But as
regards Justin, Bousset's remark should be received with
strong reservations. There are reasons to believe that the
worship of the Church gave a solid basis to our Apologist

Justin] nicht um das farblose προϋπάρχειν, sondern um das
προϋπάρχειν θεὸν ὄντα handelt."

[12]An indirect evidence could be found in Eusebius
*De Eccles. Theol.*I, 14 (Migne, P. Gr. 24.852C). In this
passage Eusebius uses the verbs προϋπάρχειν and ὑπομένειν in
a Justinian fashion within a statement patterned after Phil.
2,6-11: καὶ τὴν ἔνσαρκον ὑπέμεινε οἰκονομίαν, προὼν μὲν
αὐτῆς καὶ προϋπάρχων, θεότητι πατρικῆς δόξης τετιμημένος·
οὐ μὴν ἁρπαγμὸν ἡγούμενος τὸ εἶναι ἴσα θεῷ, ἑαυτὸν δ᾽οὖν
κενώσας . . . ἐταπείνωσεν ἑαυτόν.

[13]W. Bousset, *Kyrios Christos*, English translation
by J. E. Steely (Nashville, 1970), p. 323.

16

for the confession of the divinity of Christ.[14] But the discussion in Dial. 48,1-3 and 87,2 goes far beyond this basis. It is theological, and with definite apologetic purposes. Hence the terminology of Christ as pre-existing God in the Justinian texts shows more freedom and flexibility than the one encountered in the New Testament.[15]

That Justin moves with apparent ease when speaking of the Son as pre-existing God, could be seen in a sampling of passages:

Ap. 63,15: υἱὸς τῷ πατρί . . . ὃς καὶ λόγος πρωτότοκος ὢν τοῦ θεοῦ καὶ θεὸς ὑπάρχει.

Dial. 113,4: ἅτε οὐ Χριστὸς ὁ θεὸς ὢν οὐδὲ υἱὸς θεοῦ.

Dial. 125,3: θεοῦ δὲ ἐκ τοῦ εἶναι τέκνον πρωτότοκον τῶν ὅλων κτισμάτων.

Dial. 126,2: αὐτὸν εἶναι θεὸν τοῦ μόνου καὶ ἀγεννήτου καὶ ἀρρήτου θεοῦ υἱόν.

Dial. 127,4: καὶ θεὸν ὄντα υἱὸν αὐτοῦ.

Dial. 128,1: Χριστὸς καὶ θεὸς θεοῦ υἱὸς ὑπάρχων.

The passages just quoted do not belong to the same context. Yet they contain the same affirmation that the Son is God. A closer look at them leads to the following observations:

a) The vocabulary of the passages is limited and simple. Along with the title θεός used for the Son we find the titles υἱός, λόγος, πρωτότοκος. All of them have been already employed by the basic humiliation and exaltation texts of the New Testament (John 1,1-14; Col. 1,15-20; Hebr. 1,1-9), but they have been used separately (e.g. Logos is missing from Hebrews and Colossians). Justin has all of them

---

[14]In the chapters that follow we shall report instances where Justin seems to be influenced by liturgical concepts and terms. Suffice it to note here the term προσκυνητὸς, in the phrase καὶ Χριστὸς καὶ θεὸς προσκυνητός (Dial. 126,1. Cf. Dial. 38,1; 68,3), which is considered by W. Bousset an unmistakable indication of the connection between worship and proclamation of Christ's divinity.

[15]The formulations in Ignatius (*Rom.* and *Eph.* prol. Ἰησοῦς Χριστὸς ὁ θεὸς ἡμῶν) are still of a stereotyped nature, possibly of liturgical provenance. With *Tral.* 7,1 (θεὸς Ἰησοῦς Χριστός), however, Ignatius seems to move into a direction which is perhaps more personal.

together and sometimes in one passage as, for instance, in
Ap. 63,15. This is an indication that here we are at a stage
where various terminologies about pre-existence blend together. Does Justin initiate this process or is he a witness
of its existence? It is hard to know. One thing is certain,
however, and this is Justin's apparent freedom in employing
the pre-existence terminology and, particularly, the title
θεός. In the passages under discussion, despite the limited
vocabulary, the statement "the Son is God" does not appear
in a stereotyped form awkwardly inserted into the text, but
it is usually formulated "on the spot" as an integral part of
the context, organically connected. One might argue that
here an important change is already traceable: the pre-
existence terminology, which in the New Testament texts
appears mostly within hymnic-creedal formulations, is
encountered in Justin as a main component in large segments
of theological deliberations.

     b) Justin does not seem to observe the distinc-
tion between the terms θεὸς and ὁ θεός. Both apply equally
to the Father as well as to the Son. Some scholars have
argued to the contrary. G. Archambault, for instance, commenting upon Dial. 58,9 (θεὸς καλεῖται καὶ θεὸς ἔστι καὶ
ἔσται) and Dial. 56,10 (εἷς τῶν τριῶν ἐκείνων καὶ ὁ θεὸς
ἐστὶ καὶ ἄγγελος καλεῖται), contends that Justin, because of
his subordinationist tendencies, used θεος without the
article for the Logos and ὁ θεὸς for the Father.[16] J. C. T.
Otto, the first to advance such an idea, was, however, more
cautious in drawing general conclusions.[17] The evidence
brought forward by Otto--which is repeated, but drastically
abbreviated by G. Archambault and A. L. Williams--seems rather
unconvincing. In the first place Otto already notes that
"Supremus deus, τῷ ὄντι θεὸς (c. 55) sive ὁ ὄντως θεὸς (Apol.
I c. 13), a Iustino mox ὁ θεὸς mox θεὸς vocatur."[18] So then

---

[16]*Op. cit.*, vol. I, p. 273, n. 9. Similarly A. L.
Williams, *Op. cit.*, p. 122, n. 2.

[17]*Op. cit.*, Vol. II, p. 190, n. 20. Cf. also Vol.
I, p. 33, n. 13.

[18]*Op. cit.*, Vol. I, p. 190, n. 20.

there is no such thing in Justin as the usage of ὁ θεός for
the Father. In many instances he employs simply the term
θεός and this fact seriously damages half of the argument.
If we now turn to the Son we will see that he is called ὁ
θεος in Dial. 56,10: εἷς τῶν τριῶν ἐκείνων καὶ ὁ θεὸς ἐστὶν
καὶ ἄγγελος καλεῖται. In Dial. 113,4 we encounter even a
reversal of appellations: ἅτε οὐ Χριστὸς ὁ θεὸς ὤν οὐδὲ
υἱὸς θεοῦ. Here ὁ θεὸς is applied to Christ, and the plain
θεὸς to the Father!

Under these circumstances it is incorrect to explain
Justin's attitude towards the terminology of ὁ θεὸς and θεὸς
from Philo, as Otto and Archambault have done. Philo, in *De
Somniis* I, 227-230, after citing Gen. 31,13 makes the remark
μὴ παρέλθῃς δέ τὸ εἰρημένον, ἀλλ᾽ ἀκριβῶς ἐξέτασον εἰ τῷ
ὄντι δύο εἰσὶν θεοί. He then answers the question this way:
ὁ μὲν ἀληθείᾳ θεὸς εἷς ἐστιν, οἱ δ᾽ἐν καταχρήσει λεγόμενοι
πλείους . . . Διὸ καὶ ὁ ἱερὸς λόγος ἐν τῷ παρόντι τὸν μὲν
ἀληθείᾳ διὰ τοῦ ἄρθρου μεμήνυκεν [ὁ θεός] . . . τὸν δ᾽ἐν
καταχρήσει χωρὶς ἄρθρου [θεός]. . . καλεῖ δέ θεὸν τὸν πρεσβύτατον αὐτοῦ λόγον. Philo makes a clear-cut distinction
which eventually leaves only one real God on the stage.
Justin on the contrary fights for the divinity of the Son and
ultimately this is his real point of disagreement with his
Jewish opponents for whom Trypho is the spokesman. The
hypothesis that our Apologist follows the Philonic distinction
between ὁ θεὸς and θεὸς and applies it to the Father and the
Son is not supported by the texts.[19]

c) In Justin the title θεὸς for the pre-
existing Christ is usually accompanied by the term υἱός. The
six passages quoted at the beginning of this section are an
ample illustration of the point (in the case of Dial. 125,3
we have τέκνον). One might suggest that υἱός is the qualifica-
tion "par excellence" for the term θεὸς used for the son.
The Son is God by being God's son. The phrase "καὶ θεὸς
θεοῦ υἱὸς ὑπάρχων" (Dial. 128,1) is a typical formulation of

---

[19]An author like Justin who speaks about θεὸς ἕτερος
. . . ἀριθμῷ (Dial. 56,11) and καὶ θεὸν καλεῖ καὶ ἀριθμῷ
ἕτερόν τι ἐστὶν (Dial. 128,4) with reference to the Son,
would hardly abide by distinctions like the Philonic one.

such a fundamental thought.[20] Another wording of the same
idea is met in Dial. 125,3 "θεοῦ δὲ ἐκ τοῦ εἶναι τέκνον
πρωτότοκον τῶν ὅλων κτισμάτων." In the last case one might
discern a likely impact of Justin's christological presuppositions on his use of a passage like Col. 1,15.[21] The phrase
πρωτότοκος πάσης κτίσεως of Colossians, slightly modified, is
used by Justin as a proof of the divinity of the son: the
son is God because he is πρωτότοκος τῶν ὅλων κτισμάτων.[22]
The sonship of the Son as a fundamental reason for his divinity is a central point in Justin's thought.[23] One should,
however, note that in the etiological connection between sonship and divinity we have already the beginning of a differentiation between the concept θεός applied to the Father and
the same concept applied to the Son.

B. *The Son* κυρίως υἱὸς
συνὼν καὶ γεννώμενος

Among the Justinian passages, which have to do with
the prior-to-creation existence of the Son, App. 6,3 reveals

---

[20]Here one might discern Justin's adherence to Scripture as well as to the early Christian tradition. The term
υἱὸς appears in Ps. 2,7, which is a Psalm often quoted by
Justin. It appears also in the New Testament texts utilized
by our Apologist. A diametrically different attitude is
shown by Tatian who does not use the term υἱὸς even once! Cf.
M. Elze, *Tatian und seine Theologie* (Göttingen, 1960), p. 74.

[21]The evidence is not negligible that Justin knew Col.
1,15. He uses the phrase πρωτότοκος πάσης κτίσεως of the
Colossian passage verbatim in Dial. 85,2 and Dial. 138,2.
Dial. 84,2, Dial. 100,2 and Dial. 125,3 offer plausible variants of the same phrase. Cf. Bosse, *op. cit.*, pp. 27-28.

[22]The difference between Col. 1,15 and Dial. 125,3
lies not so much in the relationship of πρωτότοκος to κτίσις
or κτίσματα as Bosse thinks (*op. cit.*, p. 28), but in the
function of the whole phrase "πρωτότοκος etc." within its
context in the two passages.

[23]Sometimes Justin's statements like the one in Dial.
129,1 (ὡς πατὴρ καὶ θεός, αἴτιός τε αὐτῷ [Χριστῷ] τοῦ εἶναι
καὶ δυνατῷ καὶ κυρίῳ καὶ θεῷ) might be echoes of Middle-
Platonic formulations (e.g. Albinos, *Didasc.* 10: πατὴρ δέ
ἐστι τῷ αἴτιος εἶναι πάντων καὶ κοσμεῖν τὸν οὐράνιον νοῦν
καὶ τὴν ψυχὴν τοῦ κόσμου). Justin, nonetheless, always

aspects of particular importance. The text reads: ὁ δὲ υἱὸς
ἐκείνου, ὁ μόνος λεγόμενος κυρίως υἱός, ὁ λόγος πρὸ τῶν
ποιημάτων καὶ συνὼν καὶ γεννώμενος, ὅτε τὴν ἀρχὴν δι' αὐτοῦ
πάντα ἔκτισε καὶ ἐκόσμησε, Χριστός . . .

1. The first point of discussion is the expression
"ὁ μόνος λεγόμενος κυρίως υἱός." Κυρίως in the sense of
"properly and fully" does not occur in the New Testament nor
in the Septuagint. None of the Apostolic Fathers or the
Apologists employ it. Justin uses it here and (in the form
of an adjective) in Dial. 11,2 with reference to Christ as
διαθήκη κυριωτάτη πασῶν. The term in itself does not reveal
anything specific. It is extensively used by various authors
outside the early christian literature. Justin, however, is
the first to speak of the son as κυρίως υἱός. That this is a
conscious usage could be verified by the fact that Justin in
other instances introduces adverbs synonymous to κυρίως in
connection with the Son and his begetting. Such are the
terms ἰδίως and τῷ ὄντι.[24] There is an obvious similarity,
for example, between App. 6,3 ὁ μόνος λεγόμενος κυρίως υἱὸς
and Ap. 23,2 μόνος ἰδίως υἱὸς τῷ θεῷ.

The closest terminological parallel to the Justinian
ὁ μόνος κυρίως υἱὸς seems to be the Philonic ὁ μόνος καὶ
ἀγαπητὸς υἱός.[25] The Apologist might have known the passage
from Philo which in addition to the phrase just quoted
presents some further similarities to App. 6,3, namely:
(1) it contains the verb συνεῖναι in exactly the same form
συνὼν and (2) it deals with the creation of the world.
Furthermore *Ebr.* 30 is directly linked to Prov. 8,22 (*Ebr.*
31), a text which is often used by Justin (Dial. 61,3-5;
129,3 etc.). If our author knew the Philonic passage, then
his formulation in App. 6,3 could be an indirect refutation

---

includes in his formulations the concept of Son. This fact
shows that our Apologist is biblically oriented.

[24]E.G. Ap. 23,2: καὶ Ἰησοῦς Χριστὸς μόνος ἰδίως υἱὸς
τῷ θεῷ γεγέννηται; Dial. 62,4: τοῦτο τὸ τῷ ὄντι ἀπὸ τοῦ
πατρὸς προβληθὲν γέννημα.

[25]Philo, *Ebr.* 30: . . . ἐπιστήμην ἢ συνὼν ὁ θεός . .
ἔσπειρε γένεσιν. Ἡ δέ . . . τὸν μόνον καὶ ἀγαπητὸν αἰσ-
θητὸν υἱὸν ἀπεκύησε τόνδε τὸν κόσμον.

of it by firmly and exclusively asserting the uniqueness of
the sonship of Christ over against any other alleged sonship.

The term ἰδίως in connection to μονογενής appears in
Excerpta ex Theodoto.[26] This is the only passage, as far as
I know, next to the Justinian ones, where the adverb ἰδίως
has been used in conjunction to a pre-existence christological statement within the Christian literature of the second
century A.D. It is, however, problematic whether or not we
have here positive traces of a literary relationship between
Ap. 23,2 and *Exc. ex Theod.* 10.

Attention should be drawn to the fact that Justin in
App. 6,3 and Ap. 23,2 utilizes the adjective μόνος together
with κυρίως (and ἰδίως). A study on the usage of μόνος in
Justin's works shows that the Apologist understands this word
as a carrier of the concept of uniqueness and exclusivity, not
isolation.[27] Within such frame of reference Justin employs
μόνος for the Father of all,[28] and for Christ.[29] It is,
therefore, significant that in both Ap. 23,2 and App. 6,3 we
find Justin using not only the strong and self-sufficient
μόνος in conjunction to υἱός but also the adverbs κυρίως and
ἰδίως. This might reveal how central is for our author the
concept of the sonship of Christ as a unique attribute of his
pre-existence status.

---

[26]*Exc. ex Theod.* 10: ὁ μὲν μονογενής καὶ ἰδίως
νοερὸς ἰδέα ἰδίᾳ καὶ οὐσίᾳ ἰδίᾳ κεχρημένος . . . καὶ προσε-
χῶς τῆς ἀπὸ τοῦ πατρὸς ἀπολαύων δυνάμεως. Note also the
similarity between μόνος ἰδίως (Ap. 23,2) and μονογενής καὶ
ἰδίως (*Exc. ex Theod.* 10).

[27]For a study of the word μόνος in connection to εἷς
with reference to God and Christ, see the monograph by Erik
Peterson, *Eis Theos: Epigraphische, formgeschichtliche und religionsgeschichtliche Untersuchungen* (Göttingen,
1926), especially pp. 5, 15-18, 20, 23, 28-29, 78.

[28]Dial. 5,4: μόνος γὰρ ἀγέννητος καὶ ἄφθαρτος ὁ
θεός; D. 55,2: τῶν νομιζομένων θεῶν ὁ τῷ ὄντι θεὸς ὁ τὰ
πάντα ποιήσας κύριος μόνος ἐστιν. Cf. also Dial. 68,4;
Dial. 126,2; Ap. 16,7.

[29]Dial. 110,6: σὺν τῷ δικαιοτάτῳ καὶ μόνῳ ἀσπίλῳ
καὶ ἀναμαρτήτῳ Χριστῷ; Dial. 17,3: τοῦ μόνου ἀμώμου καὶ
δικαίου φωτὸς τοῖς ἀνθρώποις πεμφθέντος; Dial. 97,4: εἰ μὴ
μόνος οὗτος ὁ Χριστός.

22

2. The second point of discussion pertains to the phrase δι' αὐτοῦ πάντα ἔκτισε καὶ ἐκόσμησε (App. 6,3). The wording follows the line of the traditional formulae[30] "δι' οὖ τὰ πάντα" (1 Cor. 8,6), "τὰ πάντα δι' αὐτοῦ καὶ εἰς αὐτὸν ἔκτισται" (Col. 1,16), "δι' οὖ καὶ τοὺς αἰῶνας ἐποίησεν" (Hebr. 1,2) with one difference: Justin presents a new component, namely, the verb ἐκόσμησε. The New Testament and the Old Testament cannot be the source of Justin's formulation. Besides, Justin himself points to the source when he affirms that "τῷ λέγειν ἡμᾶς ὑπὸ θεοῦ πάντα κεκοσμῆσθαι καὶ γεγεννῆσθαι Πλάτωνος δόξομεν λέγειν δόγμα."[31]

Plato uses the verb κοσμεῖν frequently in a cosmological context in order to denote (a) the fashioning of the world out of the ἄμορφος ὕλη, (b) the adorning of the world so that it be beautiful, and (c) the restoring of the world and its keeping from falling into chaos and dissolution.[32] Justin probably knows the cosmological concept expressed in case (a), as one could gather from Ap. 10,2[33] (cf. also Ap. 59,1), and presumably employs κοσμεῖν in this sense. But he is also aware of the notion of adorning or setting in order which is implicit in the verb κοσμεῖν.

---

[30]For a discussion on these formulae and their background see E. Lohse, *Die Briefe an die Kolosser und an Philemon*, Meyer Kommentar (Göttingen, 1968), pp. 88-92. Cf. E. Norden, *Agnostos Theos*(Leipzig, 1913), pp. 240-250 and 347-348; also B. Gärtner, *The Areopagus Speech and Natural Revelation* (Uppsala, 1955), pp. 155, 201.

[31]Ap. 20,4. Cf. Andresen, *Logos u. Nomos*, p. 314, n. 7.

[32]In Plato's *Polit.* 273 DE we encounter an example of case (c) with elements from cases (a) and (b): διὸ δὴ καὶ τότ' ἤδη θεὸς ὁ κοσμήσας αὐτὸν [κόσμον] καθορῶν ἐν ἀπορίαις ὄντα, κηδόμενος ἵνα μὴ χειμασθεὶς ὑπὸ ταραχῆς διαλυθεὶς . . . τὰ νοσήσαντα καὶ λυθέντα ἐν τῇ καθ' ἑαυτὸν προτέρᾳ περιόδῳ στρέψας κοσμεῖ τε καὶ ἐπανορθῶν ἀθάνατον αὐτὸν καὶ ἀγήρων ἀπεργάζεται.

[33]Ap. 10,2: καὶ πάντα τὴν ἀρχὴν ἀγαθὸν ὄντα δημιουργῆσαι αὐτὸν ἐξ ἀμόρφου ὕλης δι' ἀνθρώπους δεδιδάγμεθα. The passage does not necessarily mean that Justin did not believe in the creation ex nihilo as Andresen seems to imply (*Logos u. Nomos*, p. 335). Danielou, *op. cit.*, p. 112, has shown that ἄμορφος here stands for the adjective ἀκατασκεύ-

This assumption finds support in Dial. 11,1 where we meet
the phrase τοῦ ποιήσαντος καὶ διατάξαντος τόδε τό πᾶν. Here
διατάσσειν corresponds to κοσμεῖν and Justin seems to follow
the usage of the Hellenistic Jewish apologetic as it is
encountered e.g. in Wisd. 11,20 and Philo.[34]

The passage App. 6,3 is a rather rare instance where
the Apologist makes a statement concerning the function of
the pre-existing Christ as an agent instrumental in the
creation of the world. Justin included the cosmological
formulation in App. 6,3 perhaps in order to stress the
Father's transcendence of which he speaks in App. 6,1-2.
Otherwise our author, in spite of the many references to
the pre-existence of the Son, does not speak about him as an
agent in creation.[35] Instead he tirelessly uses the appellation ποιητῆς τῶν ὅλων for the Father.[36] Justin's attitude
might be accounted for by his intention to refute Marcion's
teachings on the one hand, and to persuade his Jewish
opponents on the other. Two cases could be quoted here:

a) In Ap. 26,5 our author reports that Marcion
καὶ νῦν ἐστι διδάσκων τοὺς πειθομένους, ἄλλον τινα νομίζειν
μείζονα τοῦ δημιουργοῦ θεόν . . . καὶ ἀρνεῖσθαι τὸν ποιητὴν

αστος of Gen. 1,2 as it is evidenced from Ap. 59,1-3 and
Hippolytus, *Ref.* VI, 30 (cf. Wisd. 11,17). Tatian (*Or.
Graec.* 5 and 12), later on dissipated any ambiguity by
declaring that the ὕλη was created by God and that it was,
therefore, neither ἄναρχος nor ἰσοδύναμος to him. Cf.
M. Elze, *op. cit.*, p. 80. The most characteristic formulation, however, with easily discernible harmonization tendencies, belongs to Theophilus of Antioch (*Ad Autol.* II, 10):
ταῦτα ἐν πρώτοις διδάσκει ἡ θεία γραφὴ [in Gen. 1,2]τρόπῳ⁓
τινι ὕλην γενητήν, ὑπὸ θεοῦ γεγονυῖαν, ἀφ᾽ ἧς πεποίηκε καὶ
δεδημιούργηκεν ὁ θεὸς τὸν κόσμον.

[34]Wisd. 11,20: πάντα μέτρῳ καὶ ἀριθμῷ καὶ σταθμῷ
διέταξας; Philo, *Migr. Abr.* 182: δύναμιν δι᾽ ἑαυτοῦ καθ᾽
ἣν ἔθηκε καὶ διετάξατο καὶ διεκόσμησε τὰ ὅλα; *Conf. Ling.*
137: δύναμις δὲ καθ᾽ ἣν ἔθηκε καὶ διετάξατο τὰ πάντα.

[35]Cf. Ap. 23,1-3; 63,10,16; Dial. 45,4; 48,1,3;
100,2 etc.

[36]Cf. Ap. 20,2; 26,5; Dial. 38,2; 48,2; 55,1; 56,1,4,
10; 60,2,3; 74,3; 84,2; 117,5 etc. Very often Justin utilizes
also the phrase ὁ ποιήσας τὰ πάντα or a variant of it (e.g.
Dial. 11,1; 56,11; 68,3; 102,6 etc.).

τοῦδε τοῦ παντὸς θεόν, ἄλλον δέ τινα, ὡς ὄντα μείζονα τὰ μείζονα παρὰ τοῦτον ὁμολογεῖν πεποιηκέναι.[37] Against Marcion Justin emphasizes that there is but one δημιουργός, ποιητὴς καὶ πατὴρ τῶν πάντων, and deliberately avoids making frequent references to the Son as an agent in creation.

     b) In Dial. 11,1 Justin addresses himself to Trypho this way: οὔτε ἔσται ποτὲ ἄλλος θεός, ὦ Τρύφων, οὔτε ἦν ἀπ' αἰῶνος . . . πλὴν τοῦ ποιήσαντος καὶ διατάξαντος τόδε τὸ πᾶν. Οὐδὲ ἄλλον μὲν ἡμῶν, ἄλλον δὲ ὑμῶν ἡγούμεθα θεὸν ἀλλ' αὐτὸν ἐκεῖνον τὸν ἐξαγαγόντα τοὺς πατέρας ὑμῶν ἐκ γῆς Αἰγύπτου. The thrust of the thought is clear: there is but one Creator of all who is also the God of Israel and the Lord of Christians. This stress on the identity of God is of distinct apologetic importance for Justin, hence he keeps talking about the ποιητὴς τῶν ὅλων and does not mention the formula δι' οὗ or δι' αὐτοῦ or δι' υἱοῦ in a cosmological sense.[38]

     3. The main question raised by the passage under discussion concerns the expression καὶ συνὼν καὶ γεννώμενος ὅτε etc.[39] K. G. Semisch sees here two stages in the pre-existence of Christ. Obviously connecting "ὅτε τὴν ἀρχὴν etc." to γεννώμενος, he thinks that Justin "adopted the philosophical division of the Logos into immanent and transitive . . . As long as the Logos rested in God, it was essentially identically (sic) with his substance, or rather stood in a relation of a part to the whole; by coming forth from the divine essence, it first attained a personal self-subsistence."[40]

---

[37]A similar statement is uttered in Ap. 58,1, which includes also Christ.

[38]Besides App. 6,3 Justin uses the δι' οὗ phrase in a christological cosmological sense in Dial. 113,5: οὗτος γάρ ἐστιν ἀφ' οὗ καὶ τὸν οὐρανὸν καὶ τὴν γῆν καὶ δι' οὗ ὁ πατὴρ μέλλει καινουργεῖν. Yet here we are in the presence of strong eschatological elements.

[39]A. Theodorou, op. cit., pp. 84-88, gives a brief but substantial report on the pertinent discussion. He seems, however, to overrate the syntactical elements as key factors for the interpretation of the passage.

Goodenough disagrees with Semisch's theory because
it rests on a doctrine of a distinction between λόγος ἐν-
διάθετος and λόγος προφορικὸς which Justin avoided. Furthermore, Goodenough assumes that "Justin has expressly marked
the two words συνὼν and γεννώμενος as parallels by the
double καὶ so that it is quite forced to associate the ὅτε
with the word γεννώμενος alone."[41] After Goodenough,
Lebreton discussing this passage also disagrees with Semisch;
he admits, however, that Justin unconsciously opened the road
to a Christology of λόγος ἐνδιάθετος--λόγος προφορικὸς as
it is evidenced in the case of his disciple Tatian (*Or.
Graec*. 5).[42]

The thesis advanced by Semisch is vulnerable indeed.
In addition to Goodenough's arguments brought against it,
one could mention the fact that Justin in several instances
speaks about the begetting of the Son πρὸ πάντων τῶν κτισμάτων or πρὸ πάντων τῶν ποιημάτων, that is, prior to creation
(Dial. 61,1; 100,4; 129,4 et. al.). If the Apologist held
to such a basic idea that the Son is begotten at the moment
of the beginning of creation, should he not have said it?
He had numerous occasions to do so if that were the case.

There is of course the grammatical difficulty in
App. 6,3 due to the present tense of γεννώμενος. One could
attribute it to a syntactical attraction to the word συνὼν.
This suggestion seems plausible because of the presence of
the double καὶ which tends to create grammatical assimilation.
Yet, there is one more explanation for the present tense of

---

[40]*Justin der Märtyrer*, Engl. trans. 1843, Vol. II,
pp. 181 ff. Cf. J. C. T. Otto, *op. cit.*, Vol. I, p. 213,
n. 4.

[41]E. Goodenough, *op. cit.*, p. 154. See also Bosse,
op. cit., p. 39, n. 2.

[42]J. Lebreton, *op. cit.*, Vol. II, pp. 449 ff. This
is more evident in the case of Theophilus of Antioch, *Ad
Autol*. II, 10: ἔχων οὖν ὁ θεὸς τὸν ἑαυτοῦ λόγον ἐνδιάθετον
ἐν τοῖς ἰδίοις σπλάγχνοις ἐγέννησεν αὐτόν. Cf. also Athenag.
Suppl. 10: ἐξ ἀρχῆς γὰρ ὁ θεός, νοῦς ἀίδιος ὤν, εἶχεν
αὐτὸς ἐν ἑαυτῷ τὸν λόγον, ἀϊδίως λογικὸς ὤν. See more on
the subject of λόγος ἐνδιάθετος--λόγος προφορικὸς in M.
Spanneut, *Le Stoicisme des Pères de l'Eglise* (Paris, 1957),
pp. 310-16.

26

γεννώμενος. In the septuagintal text of Prov. 8,22-31,
the verb γεννᾶν is in the present tense (πρὸ δὲ πάντων
βουνῶν γεννᾷ με), whereas the other verbs concerning the
origin of wisdom are in the aorist (ἔκτισε, ἐθεμελίωσε).
We noticed already that our author is familiar with Prov.
8,25 and consequently with the form γεννᾷ με. Such an
expression in the present tense might have contributed to
the grammatical form γεννώμενος of App. 6,3.

Let us now turn to the word συνών. At first glance
the participle συνὼν seems to be superfluous in App. 6,3.
If the λόγος were "πρὸ τῶν ποιημάτων" and if it were he
"δι᾽ οὗ" (the Father) "πάντα ἔκτισε καὶ ἐκόσμησεν" then
obviously the λόγος was συνὼν τῷ πατρί. Justin could have
said simply "ὁ δὲ υἱός, ὁ λόγος πρὸ τῶν ποιημάτων δι᾽ οὗ
πάντα ἐποίησεν ὁ πατήρ." Justin is known for his lack of
literary elegance in writing and for his repetitions. So
συνὼν might well be a superfluous element in App. 6,3, a
product of rhetorical verbiage. However, one could suggest
a different explanation. The verb συνεῖναι occurs again in
Dial. 62,3 and 62,4 with reference to the pre-existing Son
and the Father.[43] There it serves the purpose of denoting
the distinctiveness of the existence of the Son and
simultaneously his togetherness with the Father. We may
safely make such an assumption on the grounds of the immediate
and larger context[44] and because of the meaning of the verb
συνεῖναι.[45]

---

[43]Dial. 62,3: ἰδοὺ ᾽Αδὰμ γέγονεν ὡς εἷς ἐξ ἡμῶν
(Gen. 3,22). οὐκοῦν εἰπὼν ὡς εἷς ἐξ ἡμῶν καὶ ἀριθμὸν
τῶν ἀλλήλοις συνόντων καὶ τὸ ἐλάχιστον δύο μεμήνυκεν;
Dial. 62,4: τοῦτο τὸ τῷ ὄντι ἀπὸ τοῦ πατρὸς προβληθὲν
γέννημα πρὸ πάντων τῶν ποιημάτων συνῆν τῷ πατρί.

[44]Dial. 62 comes at the end of a series of chapters
(viz. Dial. 56-62) where Justin, via the Old Testament
theophanies, argues for the existence of another God next
to the Father of all and subject to Him (e.g. Dial. 56,4
ὅτι ἐστὶ καὶ λέγεται θεὸς καὶ κύριος ἕτερος ὑπὸ τὸν
ποιητὴν τῶν ὅλων).

[45]Justin employs several times the verb συνεῖναι
invariably signifying by it "to be together as distinct
beings." Cf. Ap. 67,1; Dial. 6,2; 45,4; 85,4; 118,5. See
also Athenagoras *Suppl.* 11; 24; 33.

The suggestion is that in App. 6,3 we encounter the
same function of the verb συνεῖναι. The Apologist, one could
surmise, employs the term συνὼν precisely in order to stress
the supremacy and the personal existence of the Son.[46] At
the same time he utilizes the term γεννώμενος by which συνὼν
is qualified so that the absolute superiority of the Father
would remain undisputed. The study of συνεῖναι in Justin
shows that the possibility of taking it in App. 6,3 as meaning
something which is inherent or ἐνδιάθετον is slim. Συνεῖναι
does not correspond to ἐνεῖναι.

C. *The Son* δύναμις λογική

As a pivotal text for the concept of δύναμις in
relation to the pre-existing Son one could point to Dial.
61,1: ἀρχὴν πρὸ πάντων τῶν κτισμάτων ὁ θεὸς γεγέννηκε
δύναμίν τινα ἐξ ἑαυτοῦ λογικήν, ἥτις καὶ δόξα κυρίου ὑπὸ
τοῦ πνεύματος τοῦ ἁγίου καλεῖται, ποτὲ δὲ υἱός.

1. In order to understand the term δύναμις in Dial.
61,1 and the parallel texts[47] one should start by a comprehensive examination of the christological usage of δύναμις
in the Justinian works. Such an investigation would show
that the concept of δύναμις is to be found within the following basic groupings of christological passages:

a) Texts where the reference is definitely to
the pre-existing Son. A clear example is Dial. 61,1 but also
Ap. 23,2 (λόγος αὐτοῦ ὑπάρχων καὶ πρωτότοκος καὶ δύναμις),
Ap. 32, 10 (ἡ δὲ πρώτη δύναμις μετὰ τὸν πατέρα . . . καὶ
υἱὸς ὁ λόγος ἐστί), Dial. 105,1 (ἰδίως ἐξ αὐτοῦ λόγος καὶ
δύναμις γεγεννημένος), Dial. 128,4 (τὴν δύναμιν ταύτην γεγεννῆσθαι ἀπὸ τοῦ πατρός).

---

[46]J. Daniélou, *op. cit.*, pp. 323-24, assumes that
the begetting of the Son, and his co-existence (συνὼν) with
the Father, according to Justin is connected to the idea
of creation. This assumption does not seem supported by the
texts. In App. 6,3 and Dial. 62,3-4 we certainly have a
reference to creation; yet this is not in order to explain
the raison d'être of the Son but his pre-eminence over
creation and his divinity.

[47]E.g. Ap. 23,2; 32,10; 33,6; Dial. 105,1; 125,3;
128,4 etc.

b) Old Testament passages which have been used by Justin christologically or which were already established as christological texts prior to Justin. Such are Ps. 109,2 (LXX) (ῥάβδον δυνάμεως ἐξαποστελεῖ etc.),[48] Is. 8,4 (δύναμιν Δαμασκοῦ etc),[49] Is. 11,1-3 (καὶ ἀναπαύσεται ἐπ᾽ αὐτόν . . . πνεῦμα βουλῆς καὶ ἰσχύος),[50] Gen. 32,25-29 (Dial. 125, 1,3) and Josh. 5,14 (Dial. 62,5).

c) Texts where Justin discusses with Trypho some specific problems which seem to emerge from particular Jewish concepts related to δύναμις. A locus classicus of this kind is Dial. 128 where Justin tries to refute the doctrine of a δύναμις which does not exist by itself but ὁ πατὴρ ὅταν βούληται, λέγουσι, δύναμιν αὐτοῦ προπηδᾶν ποιεῖ, καὶ ὅταν βούληται πάλιν ἀναστέλλει εἰς ἑαυτόν (Dial. 128,3).

d) Passages which present a christological speculation on δύναμις based upon a quotation from a philosophical work like, e.g., Plato's *Timaeus* (Dial. 60,5 Πλάτων . . . τὴν μετὰ τὸν πρῶτον θεὸν δύναμιν κεχιάσθαι ἐν τῷ παντὶ εἶπε).

e) Passages where Christ is depicted as the one who is endowed with a formidable δύναμις which is manifested in various ways.[51]

f) A final passage, Ap. 33,1-6, where the Apologist argues that the phrase δύναμις ὑφίστου ἐπισκιάσει

---

[48]The passage is quoted and commented upon by Justin in Dial. 83,2,3,4; Dial. 45,2-5; cf. also Dial. 32,6.

[49]Cited by Justin with comments in Dial. 43,6; 66,3; 77,2-3; 78,9-10. In both Dial. 43,6 and 66,3 the specific δύναμις phrase from Is. 8,4 is found in a quotation from Is. 7,10-17 inserted between Is. 7,16 and 7,17. The combination is strange because Is. 8,4 is a reference to the son of the prophet, whereas 7,10-17 is the well-known Emmanuel prophecy.

[50]Justin discusses this passage in Dial. 87 and 88.

[51]So the δύναμις which is in Christ conquers the demons (Dial. 30,3; 49,8; 76,6; 116,1), strengthens the people (App. 10,8), is manifested in his cross (Ap. 55,1-8; Dial. 94,1-2; Cf. Ap. 35,2), and finally is given to his apostles (Ap. 45,5; Ap. 50,12; Dial. 42,1).

σοι, found in the annunciation account of Luke (Lk. 1,35), is a reference to the Logos.[52] According to Justin the Logos is the δύναμις τοῦ θεοῦ who by a miraculous way (οὐ συνουσιασ-θεῖσαν τὴν παρθένον συλλαβεῖν Ap. 33,4) impregnated the virgin Mary and through her became man.

2. a) The afore-mentioned christological passages referring to δύναμις reveal, one might contend, a functional and conceptual differentiation. Therefore, after having been exposed to the pertinent Justinian material, one would be very reluctant to accept theories which point to one specific source for the interpretation of the christological concept of δύναμις in Justin. Such is the case, for example, of C. Andresen's theory which holds that "when the word δύναμις is used by Justin with reference to Christ, then what is meant is the cosmological power which is operative everywhere in the cosmos," and that a similar meaning of δύναμις is also known by the Middle-Platonic philosophers.[53] The statement could be misleading because several δύναμις christological passages have a soteriological rather than cosmological nuance, as we have remarked, and because by implication it ascribes a priority--and a tacit exclusiveness--to the Middle-Platonic texts as possible sources for Justin.[54] Andresen is right when he quotes a passage from Atticus as presenting a δύναμις doctrine which contains some elements found also in Justin.[55] But one might simply say that those elements are

---

[52]Ap. 33,6: τὸ πνεῦμα οὖν καὶ τὴν δύναμιν τοῦ θεοῦ οὐδὲν ἄλλο νοῆσαι θέμις ἤ τὸν λόγον. Cf. Ap. 46,5: διὰ δυνάμεως τοῦ λόγου . . . διὰ παρθένου ἄνθρωπος ἀπεκυήθη. See also Dial. 54,2. The same interpretation of Lk. 1,35 is also known to Tertullian, *Adv. Prax.* 26 (quoted by Andresen, *Logos u. Nomos*, p. 320, n. 30).

[53]*Justin u. mittl. Plat.*, p. 191. Similarly Daniélou, *op. cit.*, p. 318.

[54]M. Elze, *op. cit.*, p. 71, rightly opposes such an exclusiveness, and points out the need not to overlook other possible sources, as e.g., the Hellenistic-Jewish speculations about δύναμις.

[55]The text is preserved by Eusebius (*Praep. Ev.* XV, 6,7) where Atticus claims that Plato "did ascribe (περιθείς) τῷ τοῦ παντὸς ποιητῇ δύναμιν, δι' ἧς καὶ οὐκ ὄντα πρότερον ἐποίησε τὸν κόσμον καὶ ποιήσας εἰσαεί βουλόμενός γε σῶον

of a general nature, and that they could belong to some sort
of philosophical *lingua franca* of that time.[56] One could
find passages in Atticus or Albinus or Plutarch[57] which might
come close to some Justinian expressions. This, however,
might well be a reflection of the usage of concepts currently
in circulation--and δύναμις was certainly one of them.[58]

     b) The Philonic texts offer some δύναμις-
δυνάμεις passages[59] which come closer to the Justinian ones
than the quotations from Atticus and Albinus reported by
Andresen. Let me present some examples:

     1) In *Det. Pot. Ins.* 82, Philo says τῆς μὲν οὖν
ζωτικῆς (sc. δυνάμεως) μετέχει καὶ τὰ ἄλογα, τῆς δὲ λογικῆς
(sc. δυνάμεως) οὐ μετέχει μέν, ἄρχει δὲ ὁ θεὸς ἡ τοῦ πρεσ-
βυτάτου λόγου πηγή. The text is definitely anthropological

διαφυλάξει. See Andresen, *Justin u. mittl. Plat.*, p. 191,
n. 135.

[56] The same should be said for a passage from Albinus
(*Didask.* 14, p. 170, 5 ff.) quoted by Andresen as parallel to
Justin's Ap. 55,2-8. Albinus' text is an ordinary formulation of the Platonic tenet referring to the soul of the world
as δύναμις. Justin's passage is a novel interpretation of
the might of the cross in pictorial terms.

[57] Cf. for example Plutarch, *Is. et Os.*, 67 (377F-
378A.): οὕτως ἑνὸς λόγου τοῦ ταῦτα κοσμοῦντος καὶ μιᾶς
προνοίας ἐπιτροπευούσης καὶ δυνάμεων ὑπουργῶν ἐπὶ πάντας
τεταγμένων.

[58] See more in W. Grundmann's article δύναμαι-δύναμις
in Kittel's *TWNT* (Engl. trans. vol. II, pp. 286-290, The
Concepts of Power in the Greek and Hellenistic World). Cf.
also his book, *Der Begriff der Kraft in der neutestament-
lichen Gedankenwelt*, 1932. It should be noted, however,
that these works do not present all the material available.
Cf. M. Elze, *op. cit.*, p. 71, n. 1.

[59] E. Bréhier, *Les idées Philosophiques et Religieuses
de Philon d'Alexandrie* (Paris, 1908), pp. 136 ff. discusses
extensively the problem of δυνάμεις in Philo. He seems
to prefer "le culte divin comme raison de la theorie des
puissances" instead of the theory that "les puissances
derivent . . . de la nécessité d'expliquer le rapport de
Dieu au monde" or the suggestion that they "derivent de la
conception même de Dieu; elles sont les attributs" etc. (pp.
136-137). Such a preference, however, seems to me not
justified by the texts. Cf. H. A. Wolfson, *Philo*, Vol. I
(Cambridge, Mass., 1962[3]), pp. 217-25, 233-38.

but the terminology and the notions involved (λογική δύναμις, ἄρχει ὁ θεός, ἡ τοῦ λόγου πηγή) bring it near to Dial. 61,1.

2) In Philo's *Cher*. 27 we read: κατὰ τὸν ἕνα ὄντως ὄντα θεὸν δύο τὰς ἀνωτάτω εἶναι καὶ πρώτας δυνάμεις ἀγαθότητα καὶ ἐξουσίαν . . . τρίτον δὲ συναγωγὸν ἀμφοῖν μέσον εἶναι λόγον.[60] In the same passage Philo says that through ἀγαθότης God created the world and through ἐξουσία he is ruling over it. For Justin it is the Son who plays such a role.[61]

3) In *Som*. I, 62 Philo speaks about the θεῖος λόγος ὃν ἐκπεπλήρωκεν ὅλον δι᾽ ὅλων ἀσωμάτοις δυνάμεσιν αὐτὸς ὁ θεός. The concept of the completeness of powers with which the Logos is filled emerges here clearly. Justin in Dial. 87,1-4 seems to argue for the same idea in interpreting Is. 11, 1-3, and insists that Christ is totally filled with the δυνάμεις τοῦ πνεύματος.[62]

4) Philo in *Spec. Leg.* I, 45, commenting upon the theophanic word δόξα in Ex. 33,18, places in the mouth of Moses the phrase δόξαν δὲ σὴν εἶναι νομίζω τὰς περὶ σὲ δορυφορούσας δυνάμεις. Justin also within a theophanic con- text--larger than the Philonic to be sure--makes the equation of δύναμις and δόξα. He says in our basic passage, Dial. 61,1: ὁ θεὸς γεγέννηκε δύναμίν τινα ἐξ ἑαυτοῦ λογικήν, ἥτις καὶ δόξα κυρίου ὑπὸ τοῦ πνεύματος τοῦ ἁγίου καλεῖται.

5) In *Leg. All.* II, 86 Philo makes a statement

---

[60]Cf. also Philo, *Mut. Nom.* 28-29; *Conf. Ling.* 171-172; etc.

[61]Cf. App. 6,3: δι᾽ αὐτοῦ πάντα ἔκτισε καὶ ἐκόσμησε. Note also the terminological similarities between *Cher*. 27 and Ap. 32,10 which reads: ἡ δὲ πρώτη δύναμις μετὰ τὸν πα- τέρα πάντων καὶ δεσπότην θεὸν καὶ υἱὸς ὁ λόγος ἐστίν. In both the Philonic and the Justinian passages we have the term λόγος directly connected with δύναμις and we also have the word God accompanied by strong adjectival modifiers (Philo: ἕνα ὄντως ὄντα θεόν; Justin: πατέρα πάντων καὶ δεσπότην θεόν. Cf. also the πρώτη δύναμις of Ap. 32,10 to the πρῶται δυνάμεις of *Cher*. 27.

[62]Note particularly the expressions Χριστός . . . ὅστις διὰ τῶν δυνάμεων τοῦ πνεύματος τοῦ ἁγίου . . . πληροῦται (Dial. 87,2) τὰς τοῦ πνεύματος δυνάμεις οὐχ ὡς ἐνδεοῦς αὐτοῦ τούτων ὄντος . . . (Dial. 87,3).

about the σοφία τοῦ θεοῦ that ἄκραν καὶ πρωτίστην ἔτεμεν
ἀπὸ τῶν ἑαυτοῦ δυνάμεων. Such a concept of τέμνειν might be
behind Justin's contention that the δύναμις (or σοφία) which
is Christ, γεγεννῆσθαι ἀπὸ τοῦ πατρὸς δυνάμει καὶ βουλῇ αὐτοῦ
ἀλλ' οὐ κατ' ἀποτομήν (Dial. 128,4).

c) The gnostic teachings recorded by Irenaeus
and Hippolytus are also of importance as regards the concept
of δύναμις. Here we will report on two of them:

The first occurs in Hippolytus *Ref*. VI, 14 and
belongs to Simon Magus.[63] According to this passage Simon
suggests that the phrase πρὸ πάντων τῶν αἰώνων γεννᾷ με[64]
περὶ τῆς ἑβδόμης . . . δυνάμεως λέγεται. He then goes on to
say that ἑβδόμη δὲ αὕτη δύναμις, ἥτις ἦν δύναμις ὑπάρχουσα
ἐν τῇ ἀπεράντῳ δυνάμει ἥτις γέγονε πρὸ πάντων τῶν αἰώνων
is the same as the one of which Moses speaks in Gen. 1,1
where he states "καὶ πνεῦμα θεοῦ ἐπεφέρετο ἐπάνω τοῦ ὕδατος".
Simon concludes that αὕτη ἡ δύναμις κοσμεῖ μόνη πάντα.
The fragment is significant because (a) it speaks of δύναμις
with reference to Prov. 8, (b) views its coming into
existence before creation, (c) identifies it with the spirit
of God, and (d) considers it as the agent in creation
precisely in the role of κοσμεῖν. Similar elements are
easily detectable also in Justin.[65]

The second is found in Irenaeus' *Haer*. I, 11,3
(reproduced by Hippolytus in *Ref*. VI,38). Irenaeus quotes
some gnostic teacher[66] as saying ἔστι τις πρὸ πάντων προαρχή
. . . . ἥν ἐγὼ μονότητα ἀριθμῶ· ταύτῃ τῇ μονότητι συνυπάρχει

---

[63]From some other relevant passages in Hippolytus
(*Ref*. VI,17 and VI, 18) one might safely assume that the
concept of δύναμις as a cosmological principle (with strong
theogonic overtones) plays a rather prominent role in Simon's
system. Cf. J. M. A. Salles-Dabadie, *op. cit.*, pp. 47 ff.,
142.

[64]This is apparently a variant of Prov. 8,23 πρὸ δὲ
πάντων βουνῶν γεννᾷ με, where Simon--or Hippolytus--substi-
tutes αἰώνων for βουνῶν.

[65]Cf. Dial. 61,1-3; App. 6,3; Ap. 33,6.

[66]The name is missing. Hippolytus quotes him simply
as ἄλλος δέ τις ἐπιφανὴς διδάσκαλος αὐτῶν [sc. gnostics],
without any name.

δύναμις ἦν καὶ αὐτὴν ὀνομάζω ἑνότητα. Αὕτη ἡ ἑνότης, ἥ τε μονότης τὸ ἕν οὖσαι προήκαντο . . . ἀρχὴν ἦν ὁ λόγος μονάδα καλεῖ. Ταύτῃ τῇ μονάδι συνυπάρχει δύναμις ὁμοούσιος αὐτῇ ἦν καὶ αὐτὴν ὀνομάζω τὸ ἕν . . . This passage is of considerable importance because (a) it exhibits a strong effort to preserve a monistic aspect of the deity (μονότης, ἑνότης, μονάς, τὸ ἕν) (b) it characterizes the second member of the two pairs as δύναμις and (c) it states the coexistence of the δύναμις with the ἄρρητος ἀρχὴ in terms of time (συνυπάρχειν) and of οὐσία (ὁμοούσιος). One might contend that the concept of δύναμις thus construed presents a likely kinship to the Justinian one as it appears in the passages which relate to the pre-existence of Christ. The assumption then of a relationship between the Justinian and the gnostic texts is not at all precarious.[67]

3. A plurality of elements is discernible in the background of Justin's christological concept of δύναμις. He, however, seems to have reworked them and is thus in a position, when using δύναμις for the pre-existing Son, to make some clear points.

a) One could readily observe in Justin an emphasis on the personal character of δύναμις.[68] With Plato or Atticus or Plutarch we still deal with δύναμις as with something which is impersonal, something which is a quality rather than a separate being. Philo had already taken a further step, and he shows definite traces of a hypostatization process as regards δύναμις.[69] But he never arrived at a full and unequivocal statement. When he reaches the critical point he either speaks of δυνάμεις in the sense of angels, or of δυνάμεις (or δύναμις) in the sense of attributes of God or of manifestations through which God is known or accessible to human nature. But Justin is firm and clear:

---

[67]Besides, Justin mentions various gnostic authors by name. Cf. Ap. 26,2-8; 56,1; 58,1; Dial. 35,6.

[68]Cf. Andresen, *Justin u. mitt. Plat.*, p. 191.

[69]See Daniélou, *op. cit.*, p. 322. Note that among the people influenced by Plato, apparently the "School"

δύναμις is not an impersonal force, nor a quality of God but a personal being, the Son. Justin's attitude can be seen in the fact that he never uses δύναμις without qualifications for the pre-existing Christ. He always couples it with the terms υἱός and λόγος.[70] In Dial. 61,3 the Apologist employs in addition the adjective λογική as a modifier for δύναμις. Thus the term λογικὴ δύναμις which in the Stoics[71] and in Philo[72] denotes an impersonal force appears in Justin as a hypostasis, namely, υἱὸς καὶ λόγος.[73]

b) The Son as δύναμις was born πρὸ πάντων τῶν κτισμάτων (Dial. 61,1). The begetting of the Son before the creation of the world is a central idea in Justin's christological thinking,[74] and this might account for its cropping

---

philosophers refused to take that step, which has already been taken by the "religious" philosophers.

[70]Cf. Ap. 23,2: καὶ ʹΙησοῦς Χριστὸς μόνος ἰδίως υἱὸς τῷ θεῷ γεγέννηται λόγος αὐτοῦ ὑπάρχων καὶ πρωτότοκος καὶ δύναμις; Ap. 32,10: ἡ δὲ πρώτη δύναμις μετὰ τὸν πατέρα πάντων καὶ δεσπότην θεὸν ὁ λόγος ἐστίν. Cf. also Dial. 61,1; 105,1.

[71]Sextus Emp., *Math.* VII, 307 says that some of the Stoics claim that κινεῖσθαι τὴν μὲν λογικὴν [δύναμιν] ὑπὸ τῶν νοητῶν. Cf. also ἡ λογικὴ δὲ δύναμις ἰδία οὖσα τῆς ἀνθρωπίνης ψυχῆς (apud Clement of Alex. *Strom.* II, 20 [Migne P. Gr. 8, 1056A]).

[72]Cf. Philo *Leg. All.* II, 23: πάλιν ἡ διανοητικὴ δύναμις ἰδία τοῦ νοῦ ἐστι, καὶ ἡ λογικὴ κοινὴ μὲν τάχα καὶ τῶν θειοτέρων φύσεων; cf. also *Leg. All.* II, 10; *Det. Pot. Ins.* 82; *Virt.* 13.

[73]Cf. Dial. 62,2, App. 10,1. It is noteworthy that Tatian employs the term λογικὴ δύναμις only for the Father when he calls the Son λόγος ἐκ λογικῆς δυνάμεως (*Or. Graec.* 7. Also 5). The intent of the formulation is well perceived by M. Elze (*op. cit.*, p. 72): "Aus der *hypostatischen* δύναμις λογική des Vaters ist die *selbständige* δύναμις λόγου geworden--*den Begriff des Sohnes verwendet Tatian nicht.*" (Italics mine.) The difference in "degree of hypostasis" is obvious in Tatian. Justin on the contrary does not attenuate the personal existence of the Son as δύναμις.

[74]See e.g. Dial. 48,1: προϋπάρχειν θεὸν ὄντα πρὸ αἰώνων τοῦτον τὸν Χριστόν; Dial. 62,4: πρὸ πάντων τῶν ποιημάτων συνῆν τῷ πατρί etc.

up in Dial. 61,1. C. Andresen, however, as we have seen,
contends that the concept of δύναμις is referred by Justin to
the pre-existing Christ in connection with creation, in other
words as a cosmological power.[75] Justin obviously thinks of
the Son as power in a cosmological sense and such a notion
might be implied in Dial. 61,1. One, nonetheless, may wonder
whether this is the intention of the phrase πρὸ πάντων τῶν
κτισμάτων in Dial. 61,1. The concept of creation does not
actually appear in any of the fundamental passages that
declare the pre-existing Son as δύναμις (Ap. 23,2; 32,10;
Dial. 105,1). The only text which explicitly refers to the
cosmological activity of the Son in creation does not contain
the term δύναμις (App. 6,3). What we encounter steadily in
the above passages is a reference to the incarnation and
consequently to a soteriologically oriented activity.[76]
Therefore, one should be rather hesitant about accepting in
Dial. 61,1 any indication other than that of the Son's
coming into existence before the creation.

c) Our author does not emphasize only the
personal vs. the impersonal but also the independent and
self-existing vs. that which lacks self-existence and is
ephemeral. The former pair of antitheses could refer to
philosophical tenets as we have shown, the latter pair, however, is definitely connected to some specific Jewish
modalistic speculations.[77] Justin discusses this problem
in Dial. 128. There he says that he knows of some people
who claim that in the Old Testament theophanies there

---

[75]*Justin u. mittl. Plat.*, p. 191: "Dynamis, d. h.
wirkende Kraft ist der Logos bereits von dem Zeitpunkt an,
als er für die Erschaffung der Welt aus Gott gezeugt wurde."

[76]This was already noticed by Bosse, *op. cit.*, p. 39.
Daniélou, *op. cit.*, pp. 318-24, follows Andresen's thesis
and speaks almost exclusively of the cosmological character
of dynamis in these passages. Consequently he, too, fails
to do justice to its soteriological aspects, although in
other cases talks extensively about them (e.g. pp. 153-155).
S. Agourides, *op. cit.*, pp. 53-54, is right in criticizing
Daniélou and in insisting on the necessity to do justice to
the ostensible soteriological elements, too.

[77]Cf. Andresen, *Logos u. Nomos*, p. 336. Cf. also
A. Theodorou, *op. cit.*, pp. 78-79.

appeared a δύναμις παρὰ τοῦ πατρὸς τῶν ὅλων. And that such a
δύναμις according to the same people "ἄτμητον καὶ ἀχώριστον
τοῦ πατρὸς . . . ὑπάρχειν, ὅνπερ τρόπον τὸ τοῦ ἡλίου φασὶ φῶς
ἐπὶ γῆς εἶναι ἄτμητον καὶ ἀχώριστον ὄντος τοῦ ἡλίου ἐν τῷ
οὐρανῷ· καὶ ὅταν δύσῃ συναποφέρεται τὸ φῶς· οὕτως καὶ ὁ
πατὴρ ὅταν βούληται, λέγουσι, δύναμιν αὐτοῦ προπηδᾶν ποιεῖ
καὶ ὅταν βούληται . . . ἀναστέλλει εἰς ἑαυτόν (Dial.
128,3).[78]

    A. H. Goldfahn gives some references to Talmudic
passages where one encounters a parallel doctrine.[79] The
most telling text is *Hagigah* 14a: "Samuel said to R. Hiyya
b. Rab . . . every day ministering angels are created from
the fiery stream and utter song, and cease to be for it is
said: They are new every morning, great is thy faithful-
ness."[80] A theory of that kind applied to the Son was
possibly advocated by the people alluded to by Justin in
Dial. 128,2 ἐπεὶ γινώσκω καί τινας προλέγειν ταῦτα βου-
λομένους. Goodenough misunderstands the whole passage
(i.e. Dial. 128), and surmises that Justin is actually
defending this doctrine.[81] The truth is that Justin is most
anxious to refute it and this is precisely what he is doing
in Dial. 128. He insists that in the case of δύναμις (viz.

---

[78]J. Archambault, *op. cit.*, Vol. II, p. 258, n. 3,
assumes that Philo (in *Som.* I, 72 ff.) speaks about the
Father and the Logos in a way comparable to Dial. 128,3.
He suggests, therefore, that in Dial. 128 Justin is fighting
against the pertinent Philonic teachings. I would suggest
that Archambault is not right in his assumption. Suffice it
to say that Philo in the very same passage refers the
illustration of the sun to the Logos (ἤλιον καλεῖ τὸν
θεῖον λόγον *ibid.*, 85).

[79]Justinus Martyr und die Agada, *Monatschrift für
die Geschichte und Wissenschaft des Judentums* 22 (1873),
104-105.

[80]I use here the English translation from the
edition of the *Babylonian Talmud* by Soncino Press, London.
Goldfahn's other quotations are *Baba Bathra* 25a, *Hagiga*
13b and 14a again, and *Sanhedrin* 39a. The last one is
cited because it uses the analogy of the sun with reference
to Shechinah.

[81]E. Goodenough, *op. cit.*, pp. 148 f.

the son as δύναμις) we have something which is ἀριθμῷ ἕτερον
from the Father. Hence the illustration of the sun and the
sunlight is not applicable, according to Justin, to the relation between the Father and the Son (Dial. 128,4) precisely
because the sunlight is only nominally different from the
sun ("ὀνόματι μόνον ἀριθμεῖται").

d) However, Justin's understanding of the pre-
existing Son as δύναμις personal, λογικὴ and independent is
qualified by his firm belief that the Son was begotten by the
Father and that he is subject to him. Thus he hastens to
say, in the same chapter 128 of the Dialogue, that the begetting of the δύναμις-Son took place δυνάμει καὶ βουλῇ τοῦ
πατρός . . . οὐ κατὰ ἀποτομὴν ὡς ἀπομεριζομένης τῆς τοῦ
πατρὸς οὐσίας(Dial. 128,4). Justin is strongly opposing the
terminology that (a) would imply any kind of cutting off as
a modus nascendi of the Son[83] and (b) would allow for the
possibility that something happened on the level of the deity,
without the will of the Father of all. Presumably the
Apologist is fighting here against gnostic-Marcionite speculations (cf. Ap. 26,5; 58,1). His effort might be interpreted
also as aiming at a *captatio benevolentiae* with regard to
Trypho, because of the emphasis on the unity of God and on
the absolute supremacy of the Father of all.

---

[82]H. Chadwick, Justin's Defense of Christianity,
Bull. J. Ryl. Lib. 47 (1964-5), p. 289, says characteristically that Justin "greatly prefers" the illustration of
transmitting fire from one torch to another to that of a
ray of light coming from the sun "because it brings out
better the independence (later theology would have said the
"hypostasis") of the divine Logos." Cf. A. Theodorou, *op.
cit.*, pp. 81-82; Daniélou, *op. cit.*, pp. 326-27.

[83]Note the number of terms rejected by Justin in
just two lines of Dial. 128,4: ἀποτομή, ἀπομεριζομένης,
μεριζόμενα, τεμνόμενα, τμηθῆναι. Cf. also Dial. 61,2.
Tatian (*Or. Graec.* 5) follows Justin in rejecting the
ἀποτέμνειν (or ἀποκόπτειν) terminology. He retains, nonetheless, the μερίζεσθαι vocabulary. M. Elze, *op. cit.*, pp.
76-78, argues that Tatian here uses a Platonic distinction
which pertains to the relationship between the One and the
Many. At any event, Tatian's vocabulary in this case is
more refined philosophically than Justin's.

D. *The Son* ἀπὸ τοῦ πατρὸς προβληθὲν γέννημα

There are two points to be discussed in the present section: the terms γέννημα and προβάλλεσθαι as applied by Justin to the pre-existing Son prior to creation. The fundamental passages are Dial. 62,4 (ἀλλὰ τοῦτο τὸ τῷ ὄντι ἀπὸ τοῦ πατρὸς προβληθὲν γέννημα πρὸ πάντων τῶν ποιημάτων συνῆν τῷ πατρί) and Dial. 129,4 (καὶ ὅτι γεγεννῆσθαι ὑπὸ τοῦ πατρὸς τοῦτο τὸ γέννημα πρὸ πάντων ἀπλῶς τῶν κτισμάτων).

1. The word γέννημα occurs in Justin either in singular with exclusive reference to the pre-existing Son (Ap. 21,1; Dial. 62,4; 129,4) or in plural with exclusive reference to the fruits of the earth or to that which is produced or born in general.[84] The latter usage is undoubtedly that of the Septuagint (also the New Testament: Lk. 12,18; 2 Cor. 9,10; Mt. 3,7 etc.); the former cannot be traced to the Scriptural texts.

a) We encounter in Aeschylus[85] and in Plato[86] instances where the word γέννημα has been used in order to describe the offspring of god(s). Plato in particular could be the ultimate source of the connotation of a divine-origin ascribed to the word γέννημα.[87] Justin, however, could have received this special notion of γέννημα via the Philonic

---

[84]Dial. 17,2; 81,2; 91,1; 119,2; 133,2. In all these instances the term γεννήματα (or γένημα) occurs within Old Testament passages quoted by Justin. For the form γέννημα as a variant of γένημα see the relevant entries in *A Greek-English Lexicon of the New Testament* (translated from W. Bauer's Wörterbuch by W. F. Arndt and F. W. Gingrich, Chicago, 1957).

[85]Aeschylus, *Prom.* 850-851: ἐπώνυμον δὲ τῶν Διὸς γεννημάτων τέξεις κελαινὸν "Επαφον. The words are addressed to Κάνωβος.

[86]Plato, *Tim.* 24D: [ὑμεῖς] πάσῃ τε πάντας ἀνθρώπους ὑπερβεβηκότες ἀρετῇ καθάπερ εἰκὸς γεννήματα καὶ παιδεύματα θεῶν ὄντας; *Tim.* 69C: καὶ τῶν μὲν θείων αὐτὸς γίνεται δημιουργός, τῶν δὲ θνητῶν τὴν γένεσιν τοῖς ἑαυτοῦ γεννήμασι δημιουργεῖν προσέταξεν.

[87]But note also the Platonic usage of γέννημα as a designation for the created things in *Soph.* 266B (πῦρ καὶ ὕδωρ καὶ τὰ τούτων ἀδελφὰ θεοῦ γεννήματα), 265D etc.

texts.

b) Philo employs the term γέννημα in several
instances mostly presupposing its ordinary meaning (viz.
"that which is produced or born"). In *Leg. All.* I, 31, nonetheless, when he discusses the creation of the heavenly and
the earthly man, he introduces the word γέννημα as a designation of the heavenly man in sharp opposition to the word
πλάσμα as a designation of the earthly man: τὸν μὲν οὐράνιον
(sc. ἄνθρωπον) φησιν οὐ πεπλάσθαι, κατ᾽ εἰκόνα δὲ τετυπῶσθαι
θεοῦ, τὸν δὲ γήϊνον πλάσμα ἀλλ᾽ οὐ γέννημα εἶναι τοῦ τεχνίτου.
In another passage (*Poster. C.* 63) Philo applies γέννημα in a
unique way to Israel: τὸν ᾿Ισραὴλ νεώτερον ὄντα χρόνῳ
πρωτόγονον υἱὸν ἀξιώματι καλεῖ . . . τοῦ ἀγεννήτου γέννημα
πρώτιστον.

The important elements in *Leg. All.* I, 31 are the
reference to the heavenly man and the acute contradistinction
between γέννημα and πλάσμα. A similar contradistinction can
be perceived in Justin too.[88] As for the concept of the
heavenly man, its christological connotations are obvious.
The Philonic phrase τοῦ ἀγεννήτου γέννημα πρώτιστον could be
paralleled to the Justinian τὸν λόγον πρῶτον γέννημα τοῦ
θεοῦ (Ap. 21,1). This parallelism, nonetheless, might be
a coincidental similarity, not a dependence of any sort.
Πρῶτον in Ap. 21,1 may have been used instead of the expression πρὸ πάντων τῶν ποιημάτων (or κτισμάτων) which steadily
accompanies the term γέννημα (Dial. 62,4; 129,4), and which
is missing in Ap. 21,1. This conjecture finds support in a
passage of Athenagoras who seems to use the term πρῶτον
γέννημα in the sense of before the creation of the universe.[89]

c) Justin's usage of the word γέννημα might also
have been the result of his acquaintance with the gnostic
teachings. In both the accounts of Irenaeus and Hippolytus

---

[88]In Justin instead of γέννημα vs. πλάσμα we encounter
γέννημα vs. ποιήματα (Dial. 62,4), or γέννημα vs. κτίσματα
(Dial. 129,4).

[89]Athenagoras, *Suppl.* 10. He is the only Apologist
who uses the term πρῶτον γέννημα with refernce to the pre-
existing Logos, besides Justin.

40

there are passages where the term γέννημα occurs. Irenaeus,
for instance, says in *Haer.* I.18,1 that according to a gnostic
interpretation of Gen. 1, Moses presents τὴν δευτέραν τετράδα
(i.e. ἄβυσσος, σκότος, ὕδωρ, πνεῦμα), γέννημα πρώτης
τετράδος (i.e. θεοῦ, ἀρχῆς, οὐρανοῦ, γῆς). Hippolytus in
describing the tenets of Valentinus uses the phrase ὁ δὲ Νοῦς
καὶ ἡ Ἀλήθεια ἐπεὶ εἶδον τὸν Λόγον καὶ τὴν Ζωὴν τὰ ἴδια
γεννήματα γόνιμα γεγεννημένα (*Ref.* VI, 29), and γενομένης
οὖν ἐντὸς πληρώματος ἀγνοίας κατὰ τὴν Σοφίαν καὶ ἀμορφίας
κατὰ τὸ γέννημα τῆς Σοφίας (*Ref.* VI, 31). Of particular
importance is *Ref.* VI, 29, because in it the term γέννημα
relates directly to the Logos.

     d) The suggestion is that the Justinian usage of
γέννημα for the Son has likely parallels in the gnostic and,
secondarily, in the Philonic literature. Justin, however,
places some special emphasis on particular points in his
handling of the term under discussion:

     1) With the exception of Ap. 21,1[90] in all
other three instances when γέννημα has been employed christologically it stands in clear contradistinction from κτίσματα
or ποιήματα.[91] The first impression is that the juxtaposition
γέννημα-κτίσματα simply aims at denoting priority in terms
of time. One might contend, however, that the heart of the
matter here is the absolute superiority and pre-eminence of
the Son over against the created things, a notion already
inherent in the concept of priority in terms of time.[92]

---

[90]In Ap. 21,1 the terms κτίσματα or ποιήματα do not
appear because the thrust of thought and the specific context
render the distinction between γέννημα and κτίσματα
unnecessary.

[91]Dial. 62,4a: τοῦτο τὸ γέννημα πρὸ πάντων τῶν
ποιημάτων συνῆν τῷ πατρί; Dial. 62,4b: ἀρχὴ πρὸ πάντων τῶν
ποιημάτων τοῦτ' αὐτὸ καὶ γέννημα ὑπὸ τοῦ θεοῦ ἐγεγέννητο;
Dial. 129,4: τοῦτο τὸ γέννημα πρὸ πάντων ἁπλῶς τῶν
κτισμάτων.

[92]In view of the evidence from the texts, Bosse's
assumption that Justin's Logos "ist nicht nur γέννημα sondern
auch κτίσμα Gottes, wie das durch Prov. 8,22 gefordert war"
(*op. cit.*, p. 27) is wrong. Proverbs 8,22 appears in Justin's
texts because it belongs to the passage 8,21-36 (Dial. 61,3-5)
or 8,21-25 (Dial. 129,3) which Justin quotes as a whole, as he

2) In the same passages (i.e. Dial. 62,4 and 129,4) γέννημα appears within a context which strongly underlines the distinctiveness and the self-existence of the Son (τὸ γεννώμενον τοῦ γεννῶντος ἀριθμῷ ἕτερόν ἐστι Dial. 129,4), and also his pre-eminence in being always together with the Father (πρὸ πάντων τῶν ποιημάτων συνῆν τῷ πατρὶ καὶ τούτῳ ὁ πατὴρ προσομιλεῖ, Dial. 62,4).[93]

3) Again with the exception of Ap. 21,1 which is easily explainable, the term γέννημα in Dial. 62,4 and 129, 3-4 is directly connected to the basic text Prov. 8,22-31. As we noted already, the expression πρὸ δὲ πάντων βουνῶν γεννᾷ με (Prov. 8,25) occurs in this text. One might surmise that the word γέννημα for the pre-existing Son has been employed by Justin because of the γεννᾷ με of Prov. 8,25.[94] Such a hypothesis is corroborated by Athenagoras (*Suppl.* 10) where we encounter the same connection of γέννημα to Prov. 8,22.

2. The verb προβάλλεσθαι as a term which indicates the mode-of-origin of the pre-existing Son should now attract our attention. Justin utilizes the verb προβάλλειν in general in three basic meanings.

(1) The meaning of uttering a statement, an idea, or an expression. In that case the verb is usually accompanied by Logos in a phrase like προβάλλειν λόγον.[95]

---

does with many other passages. He himself, however, never uses the verb κτίζειν or the noun κτίσμα for the Son. Cf. L. Barnard, *op. cit.*, p. 90.

[93]Justin does not go beyond the formula πρὸ πάντων τῶν κτισμάτων. He states that the Son was with the Father before (πρό) the creation, but he never explains how he understands the preposition πρό (Cf. Bosse, *op. cit.*, p. 11). Athenagoras on the contrary in his γέννημα passage (*Suppl.* 10) is very clear on this issue: πρῶτον γέννημα εἶναι τῷ πατρί, οὐχ ὡς γενόμενον ἐξ ἀρχῆς γὰρ ὁ θεὸς νοῦς ἀίδιος ὤν, εἶχεν αὐτὸς ἐν ἑαυτῷ τὸν λόγον ἀϊδίως λογικὸς ὤν.

[94]Actually in Dial. 129,3-4 Justin concludes the quotation from Prov. 8 with the verse πρὸ δὲ πάντων βουνῶν γεννᾷ με and immediately starts his comment in which the word γέννημα crops up.

[95]E.g. Dial. 67,3: εἰς ἔλεγχον νομίζετε προβάλλειν λόγων ἢ πραγμάτων; Dial. 77,1: ἀπαιτῶ σε λόγον ὃν πολλάκις προεβάλλου; cf. also Dial. 28,1; 61,2; 64,2.

42

(2) The meaning of adducing something as an argument or proof for a thesis.[96]

(3) The meaning of projecting someone in a position of prominence. The Apologist employs a few times the verb προβάλλειν in that sense, when he speaks about the demons who projected some people claiming that they were gods or attacking the true God.[97]

a) Justin uses the verb προβάλλειν christologically in two passages. In Dial. 76,1 we encounter the wording τῆς βουλῆς τοῦ προβάλλοντος αὐτόν (i.e. Χριστόν) πατρὸς τῶν ὅλων θεοῦ. The passage has to do with the incarnation and one could suggest that here we have a meaning comparable to (3) in combination with (1). The second instance, and by far more important, is the formulation τοῦτο τὸ τῷ ὄντι ἀπὸ τοῦ πατρὸς προβληθὲν γέννημα (Dial. 62,4). This is a clear reference to the mode-of-origin of the Son before creation. In what sense does the participle προβληθὲν occur here? One could propose that προβάλλειν in Dial. 62,4 is a synonym of γεννᾶν used by Justin with meaning (1) in mind. He says in the chapter immediately preceding Dial. 62,4: λόγον γάρ τινα προβάλλοντες λόγον γεννῶμεν (61,2). The phrase serves as a proof that the begetting of the Son did not cause any diminishing of the Father.[98] So προβάλλειν while expressing the meaning γεννᾶν because of its association with speech (προβάλλειν λόγον), becomes a term excluding any notion of dissection or reduction within the deity.

b) The gnostic writings might have also played

---

[96]E.g. προβάλλειν γραφήν (Dial. 65,2); προβάλλειν νόμους (App. 9,3).

[97]Ap. 26,1: προεβάλλοντο οἱ δαίμονες ἀνθρώπους τινας λέγοντας ἑαυτοὺς εἶναι θεούς; Ap. 58,1: καὶ Μαρκίωνα . . . προεβάλλοντο οἱ φαῦλοι δαίμονες, ὃς ἀρνεῖσθαι μὲν τὸν ποιητὴν τῶν οὐρανίων etc. Cf. also Ap. 54,2 ; 54,8; 56,1.

[98]Tatian (Or. Graec. 5) follows Justin in using the same example and the same argument. He, however, at the end of Or. Graec. 5, utilizes the verb προβάλλειν for the creation of the ὕλη (ἡ ὕλη . . . ὑπὸ τοῦ πάντων δημιουργοῦ προβεβλημένη). He repeats the same statement in ch. 12 (τὴν ὕλην δὲ αὐτὴν ὑπὸ τοῦ θεοῦ προβεβλημένην).

a role in Justin's selection of the participle προβληθὲν for the pre-existing Logos. It is well known that the verb προβάλλειν is a basic term for describing begetting within the deity in the various gnostic systems. Here are some examples:

1) Irenaeus states that Valentinus teaches a δυάδα ἀνονόμαστον ἧς τὸ μέν τι καλεῖσθαι "Αρρητον τὸ δὲ Σιγήν. "Επειτα ἐκ ταύτης τῆς δυάδος δευτέραν δυάδα προβεβλῆ-σθαι ἧς τὸ μέν τι Πατέρα ὀνομάζει τὸ δὲ 'Αλήθειαν (*Haer*. I.11,1). Another gnostic, Marcus, says that τόν τε λόγον αὐτοῦ ὅμοιον ὄντα τῷ προβάλλοντι καὶ μορφὴν τοῦ ἀοράτου γεγονότα (*Haer*. I.15,5).[99]

2) Hippolytus reports that according to the school of Valentinus μόνος ὑπὸ πάντων αἰώνων προβεβλημένος τῷ πατρί . . . Καρπός . . . καὶ προβέβλητο ὁ κοινὸς τοῦ πληρώματος καρπός, ὁ 'Ιησοῦς (*Ref*. VI, 32). He ascribes to the same School the teaching that προέβαλεν οὖν καὶ ἐγέννησεν αὐτὸς ὁ Πατὴρ ὥσπερ ἦν μόνος Νοῦν καὶ 'Αλήθειαν (*Ref*. VI, 29).[100]

3) The same picture emerges from the study of the *Excerpta ex Theodoto*. The verb προβάλλειν occurs many times within a theogonic context (Chs. 1, 7, 23, 29, 32, 34, 39, 53). Of specific significance is *Exc. ex.Theod*. 7 where it is affirmed that ὁ Πατὴρ προέβαλε τὸν Μονογενῆ . . . ὁ δέ ἐνταῦθα ὀφθεὶς . . . εἷς καὶ ὁ αὐτὸς ὤν ἐν μὲν τῇ κτίσει πρωτότοκός ἐστιν 'Ιησοῦς ἐν δὲ τῷ πληρώματι μονογενής . . . Καὶ οὐδέποτε τοῦ μείναντος ὁ καταβὰς μερίζεται.[101]

It is plausible to assume that Justin in Dial. 62,4 is perhaps influenced by the gnostic usage of προβάλλειν.

---

[99]See also Irenaeus *Haer*. I.1,1; I.1,2; only in these passages the verb προβάλλειν occurs more than fifteen times!

[100]Cf. Hippolytus *Ref*. VI, 31. In this passage we encounter not only the verb προβάλλειν but also the term γέννημα used separately.

[101]The last phrase comes close to the Justinian γεγεννῆσθαι ἀπὸ τοῦ πατρός . . . ὡς ἀπομεριζομένης τῆς τοῦ πατρὸς οὐσίας, ὁποῖα τὰ ἄλλα πάντα μεριζόμενα etc. (Dial. 128,4). Cf. also *Exc. ex Theod*. 36: 'Ιησοῦς τὸ ἀμέριστον μερισθῆναι . . . ἵνα ἡμεῖς . . . τῷ δι' ἡμᾶς μερισθέντι ἀνακραθῶμεν.

He, nonetheless, utilizes the verb in his own terms, in other words, as a synonym to γεννᾶν. At this juncture it would be necessary to study more specifically the terminology employed by Justin for the coming forth of the Son.

3. From what we have seen already in the previous sections as well as in the present one, it has become evident that Justin uses basically the verb γεννᾶν (Ap. 12,7; 23,2; App. 6,3; Dial. 61,1; 62,4; 129,4 etc.). The begetting "took place" simply before the creation of the world (πρὸ πάντων ἁπλῶς τῶν κτισμάτων Dial. 129,4 etc.). Justin's preference for the γεννᾶν-γεννᾶσθαι terminology could be accounted for by his frequent usage of the three Septuagint texts Prov. 8, Psalm 2 and Psalm 109 (LXX). In all of them there are crucial phrases often quoted in a christological context by Justin: Prov. 8,25: πρὸ δὲ πάντων βουνῶν γεννᾷ με; Ps. 2,7: κύριος εἶπε πρός με· υἱός μου εἶ σὺ ἐγὼ σήμερον γεγέννηκά σε; Ps. 109,3 (LXX): ἐκ γαστρὸς πρὸ ἑωσφόρου ἐγέννησά σε.

We have just encountered the verb προβάλλειν as another mode-of-origin word utilized by Justin. But here again we can see Justin's preference for the verb γεννᾶν. In the same passage Dial. 62,4, and in the same sentence to which the phrase τὸ ἀπὸ τοῦ πατρὸς προβληθὲν γέννημα belongs, Justin changes his phraseology into τοῦτ᾽ αὐτὸ καὶ γέννημα ὑπὸ τοῦ θεοῦ ἐγεγέννητο. We have also seen that in Dial. 61,2 the Apologist makes an equation between προβάλλειν and γεννᾶν: λόγον γάρ τινα προβάλλοντες λόγον γεννῶμεν. Such an equation shows that when Justin employs the verb προβάλλειν in a pre-creational christological context he understands nothing different from γεννᾶν.

Dial. 100,4 contains another verb instead of γεννᾶσθαι: the verb προέρχεσθαι. This passage reads: Καὶ υἱὸν αὐτὸν λέγοντες νενοήκαμεν ὄντα καὶ πρὸ πάντων ποιημάτων ἀπὸ τοῦ πατρὸς δυνάμει αὐτοῦ καὶ βουλῇ προελθόντα. This is the only instance in which Justin uses the verb προέρχεσθαι as a designation for the begetting of the son. The closest example of similar terminology comes from Ignatius *Mg*. 8,2: Ἰησοῦ Χριστοῦ τοῦ υἱοῦ αὐτοῦ ὅς ἐστιν αὐτοῦ λόγος ἀπὸ σιγῆς προελθών, and *Mg*. 7,2: Ἰησοῦν Χριστὸν τὸν ἀφ᾽ ἑνὸς πατρὸς προελθόντα καὶ εἰς ἕνα ὄντα καὶ χωρήσαντα. *Mg*. 8,2 might be

considered as betraying gnostic elements if we remember the
central place occupied by Σιγή in the gnostic systems.[102]
But for the Justinian passage (Dial. 100,4) it is hard to
make the same assumption only on the basis of the verb προέρχεσθαι because this verb, in the sense of procreate, occurs
rarely in the gnostic texts.[103] Another assumption could be
made. The Ignatian passages have a hymnic flavor. They might
belong to a liturgical tradition known also by Justin.
Perhaps it is not accidental that the Apologist uses the verb
προέρχεσθαι in the same participial form utilized by Ignatius.
Does Justin mean something specific when he introduces in
Dial. 100,4 the term προελθόντα? It is very doubtful. In
Dial. 128,4 he repeats verbatim the final part of Dial. 100,4
with only one change; instead of προέρχεσθαι he has γεννᾶσθαι:
γεγεννῆσθαι ἀπὸ τοῦ πατρὸς δυνάμει καὶ βουλῇ αὐτοῦ (cf. ἀπὸ
τοῦ πατρὸς δυνάμει αὐτοῦ καὶ βουλῇ προελθόντα Dial. 100,4).[104]
Evidently the verb προέρχεσθαι in a pre-creation christological sense, seems for Justin to be synonymous with
γεννᾶσθαι.[105]

Our conclusion then is that Justin uses almost
exclusively the verb γεννᾶσθαι in order to describe the begetting of the Son by the Father before the creation of the
world. The two other verbs encountered so rarely in his
texts, namely προβάλλεσθαι and προέρχεσθαι, are used in the
sense of γεννᾶσθαι or within a context that implies such a

---

[102]Cf. Irenaeus, *Haer*. I.1,1; I.1,2; I.11,1; I.13,6;
I.14,2; I.15,1; Hippolytus *Ref*. VI,22; VI,37; VI,38; VI,51;
Exc. ex Theod. 29 etc.

[103]Cf. Irenaeus, *Haer*. I.15,2. Hippolytus, *Ref*.
VI,50 actually reproduces the passage from Irenaeus.

[104]In Tatian (*Or. Graec*. 5) we encounter a clear case
where προέρχεσθαι and γεννᾶν appear together in a pre-creational christological context: ὁ λόγος προελθὼν ἐκ τῆς τοῦ
πατρὸς δυνάμεως οὐκ ἄλογον πεποίηκε τὸν γεγεννηκότα. Cf. the
pair προελθὼν γεγεννηκότα.

[105]The strong christological differentiation between
γεννᾶσθαι and προέρχεσθαι appears in the theological scene
later on. Cf. the teaching of Marcellus of Ancyra (4th cent.
A.D.) who, according to Eusebius, οὐ βούλεται . . . τὸν υἱὸν
ἐκ τοῦ πατρὸς γεγεννῆσθαι but, προελθεῖν τοῦ θεοῦ φάσκει
(Eusebius, *Contr. Marcel*. 2,8).

46

sense. The almost absolute prevalence of γεννᾶσθαι or the
absence of other terms could be accidental. I suspect it is
not. One could suggest that Justin limits himself to γεννᾶσθαι because the verb has strong biblical support and
because it does not endanger or obscure the divinity and the
self-existence of the Son.[106]

E. *Final Remarks*

1. In the four main sections of the present chapter
we have studied the vocabulary of the passages, where Justin
speaks of the Son as existing before the creation of the
world. The findings tend to suggest the following points:

a) Justin seems to share with Plato or his
"Middle-Platonic" followers such as Atticus, Albinus,
Plutarch, some of the terms which appear in the pre-creational
pre-existence passages (e.g. κοσμεῖν, γέννημα, δύναμις). One
should note that the approximation is not only terminological
but conceptual as well. This approximation, nevertheless,
and the relationship implied in it, is not of the degree and
the decisive significance ascribed to it by scholars like C.
Andresen.[107]

b) Our findings indicate that the Philonic
texts present a considerable number of similarities in

---

[106]Justin's reluctance to use mode-of-origin terms
susceptible to misinterpretation is evidenced in his handling
of the verb προπηδᾶν. He employs it only once (Dial. 128,3)
and then within a quotation of Jewish origin which presents
a doctrine refuted by him, because it endangers the self-
existence of the Son. A different attitude is followed by
Tatian who refers the verb προπηδᾶν to the mode-of-origin of
the logos (*Or. Graec.* 5). But Tatian did not want to push
the self-existence and divinity of the Son to the degree that
Justin did. Hence he uses προπηδᾶν almost in the way in
which Justin's opponents in Dial. 128,3 do.

[107]*Justin u. mittl. Plat.*, pp. 191-194. Justin's
"Platonic" terminology, which we have encountered so far, is
not the specific "School" terminology used, e.g., by Atticus,
but the more widespread Platonic language. Such language
was already employed by non-Platonic philosophers like
Panaetius, Posidonius, Cicero, Seneca and others, and, by the
time of Justin, had penetrated everywhere.

vocabulary and concepts to the Justinian passages under discussion (e.g. προϋπάρχειν, συνεῖναι, δύναμις λογική, γέννημα,
διατάσσειν etc.). For some of the terms the ultimate source
might be Plato, and so one could argue that Philo and Justin
draw from the same font. It is noteworthy, however, that the
similarities between Philo and Justin are not only terminological and conceptual, but also contextual and functional as
regards the terms involved. In that case Philo seems to be
a closer source for Justin.

c) In every section of this chapter we have
quoted gnostic texts and pointed out their terminological
resemblance to specific passages of Justin. We also added
that in this case the likeness reaches into the level of
theology, too. Especially in some particular instances (e.g.
προβάλλειν), one could safely assume a direct relationship
between Justin and the gnostic works.[108] It should be noted,
nonetheless, that the gnostic theologians, too, have been
within the scope of Platonic influence.

2. The Justinian passages which mention the existence
of the Son prior to creation have a common feature: they also
mention his incarnation. Here is a basic listing of them:

Pre-existence	*Incarnation etc.*
Ap. 21,1: λόγον πρῶτον γέννημα τοῦ θεοῦ	γεγεννῆσθαι, σταυρωθέντα, ἀπο-θανόντα, ἀναστάντα, ἀνεληλυ-θέναι εἰς τὸν οὐρανόν.
Ap. 23,1: μόνος ἰδίως υἱὸς τῷ θεῷ, λόγος, πρωτότοκος, δύναμις	τῇ βουλῇ αὐτοῦ γενόμενος ἄνθρωπος.
Ap. 32,10: ἡ δὲ πρώτη δύναμις μετὰ τὸν πατέρα καὶ υἱὸς ὁ λόγος ἐστιν	ὃς σαρκοποιηθεὶς ἄνθρωπος γέγονε
App. 6,3-5: ὁ μόνος λεγόμενος κυρίως υἱὸς ὁ λόγος πρὸ τῶν	ἄνθρωπος γέγονεν ἀποκυηθεὶς ὑπὲρ τῶν πιστευόντων ἀνθρώπων

---

[108]This could be said also for δύναμις with reservations of course, if one takes into account the central role
played by the concept of δύναμις in the system ascribed to
Simon Magus. Cf. J. M. A. Salles-Dabadie, *op. cit.*, pp.
47 ff., 142.

ποιημάτων καὶ συνῶν καὶ   καὶ ἐπὶ καταλύσει τῶν
γεννώμενος   δαιμόνων.
Dial. 48,1: προϋπάρχειν θεὸν   εἶτα καὶ γεννηθῆναι ἄνθρωπον
ὄντα πρὸ αἰώνων   γενόμενον ὑπομεῖναι.
Dial. 48,2: προϋπῆρχε θεὸς ὤν   καὶ γεγέννηται ἄνθρωπος διὰ
    τῆς παρθένου.
Dial. 48,3: ὁ Χριστὸς ὁ τοῦ   καὶ γεννηθῆναι ἄνθρωπος ὁμοιο-
θεοῦ προϋπῆρχε   παθὴς ἡμῖν σάρκα ἔχων
    ὑπέμεινε.
Dial. 87,2: θεὸν αὐτὸν προ-   καὶ σαρκοποιηθέντα διὰ τῆς
υπάρχοντα   παρθένου γεγεννῆσθαι ἄνθρωπον.
Dial. 105,1: μονογενὴς τῷ   καὶ ὕστερον ἄνθρωπος διὰ τῆς
πατρὶ ἰδίως ἐξ αὐτοῦ λόγος καὶ   παρθένου γενόμενος.
δύναμις γεγεννημένος

     There are three more passages where a pre-creational
christological statement is expressed (Dial. 61,1; 62,4;
129,4) without being accompanied with an incarnational one.
These passages, however, belong to the larger sections of
the Dialogue where Justin discusses the problem of the Old
Testament theophanies which for him are paralleled to the
incarnation as we will see (ch. 2). Thus the notion of the
incarnation is not totally absent, one might surmise, even
from Dial. 61,1; 62,4 and 129,4.

     So then the picture that emerges, primarily from the
nine passages listed above (and secondarily from the additional three just mentioned), is adequately clear: the pre-
creational existence of the Son is always coupled with his
incarnation. In one case, viz. Ap. 21,1, we do not only have
the incarnation in general, but the crucifixion and the death
of Christ as well, i.e., a humiliation terminology. Furthermore in the same passage we encounter an exaltation formula:
ἀναστάντα ἀνεληλυθέναι εἰς τὸν οὐρανόν. One could contend
then that Ap. 21,1 exhibits traces of a humiliation and
exaltation christology, where the three basic phases are
explicitly rehearsed, namely, pre-existence, humiliation,
exaltation. Are the remaining eight passages, quoted above,
of the same type of christology? If yes, how is one to
explain a) the fact that the exaltation statement is missing,
and b) that humiliation is described, if at all, in very mild
language, i.e. as incarnation?

a) The absence of the exaltation part might be
ascribed to functional reasons. If Justin transferred the
language of the liturgical-creedal formulations of the early
Church into the level of theological discussion then he
obviously used it in a free way, according to the specific
needs dictated by this discussion. In Ap. 21,1 the Apologist
needed the exaltation because of the parallelism between it
and the cases of exaltation in the pagan world (Ap. 21,3).
In the other passages under examination, the idea of exaltation would not serve any purpose, thus it is not mentioned in
the immediate context. It is stated, however, in many other
instances so that there is no doubt that Justin knows it and
presupposes it constantly. A sampling of passages will
elucidate this point:

Ap. 31,7: γεννώμενον διὰ παρθένου . . . καὶ ἀγνούμενον καὶ
   σταυρούμενον 'Ιησοῦν τὸν ἡμέτερον Χριστόν, καὶ ἀποθνήσκοντα
   καὶ ἀνεγειρόμενον καὶ εἰς οὐρανοὺς ἀνερχόμενον καὶ υἱὸν
   θεοῦ ὄντα καὶ κεκλημένον.

Ap. 42,4: 'Ιησοῦς Χριστὸς σταυρωθεὶς καὶ ἀποθανὼν ἀνέστη,
   καὶ ἐβασίλευσεν ἀνελθὼν εἰς οὐρανόν.

Ap. 46,5: διὰ παρθένου ἄνθρωπος ἀπεκυήθη καὶ 'Ιησοῦς
   ἐπωνομάσθη, καὶ σταυρωθεὶς ἀποθανὼν ἀνέστη καὶ ἀνελήλυθεν
   εἰς οὐρανόν.

Dial. 32,3: τὸν πατέρα ἀνάγοντα αὐτὸν ἀπὸ τῆς γῆς καὶ
   καθίζοντα αὐτὸν ἐν δεξιᾷ αὐτοῦ ἕως ἂν θῇ τοὺς ἐχθροὺς
   ὑποπόδιον τῶν ποδῶν αὐτοῦ. Ὅπερ γίνεται ἐξ ὅτου εἰς τὸν
   οὐρανὸν ἀνελήφθη μετὰ τὸ ἐκ νεκρῶν ἀναστῆναι ὁ ἡμέτερος
   κύριος 'Ιησοῦς Χριστός.

Dial. 34,2: ὁ γὰρ Χριστός . . . παθητὸς γενόμενος πρῶτον
   εἶτα εἰς οὐρανὸν ἀνερχόμενος.

Dial. 36,5: ὁ ἡμέτερος Χριστὸς ὅτε ἐκ νεκρῶν ἀνέστη καὶ
   ἀνέβαινεν εἰς τὸν οὐρανόν . . . ἵνα εἰσέλθῃ οὗτος ὅς ἐστι
   βασιλεὺς τῆς δόξης καὶ ἀναβὰς καθίσῃ ἐν δεξιᾷ τοῦ πατρός.

Dial. 126,1: παραγενόμενον καὶ γεννηθέντα καὶ παθόντα καὶ
   ἀναβάντα εἰς τὸν οὐρανόν.

The context of these passages and the line of argumentation requires the exaltation statement, hence Justin
includes it in his formulations. This is not the case with
the passages with which we have dealt in the present chapter.

The exaltation statement does not appear in them, because Justin could not utilize it in his argument.

b) Do the utterances of incarnation (Ap. 21,1; 23,1; 32,10; App. 6,3-5; Dial. 48,1-3; 87,2; 105,1) represent a "humiliation" language in the sense of humiliation and exaltation Christology? If we compare them to the formulations of Phil. 2,7-8, they are not. If we compare them to John 1,14 (καὶ ὁ λόγος σάρξ ἐγένετο), the answer should be in the affirmative, because they express the same concept, namely the incarnation of the pre-existing Son. The emphasis in Justin lies in the juxtaposition between the divine and the human status of the Son, and this juxtaposition is undoubtedly a feature of the humiliation and exaltation Christology.

One then could surmise that in the specific passages under discussion, Justin seems to work with a basic frame of a humiliation and exaltation Christology. The "exaltation" part is often omitted as not having any immediate bearing on the debate. The "humiliation" part is retained as incarnation, in a rather condensed form (basically ἄνθρωπος γέγονε or γεγέννηται). Finally the "pre-existence" part becomes the focus of a theological elaboration because of the immediate apologetic and kerygmatic purposes.

3. It is of fundamental significance, however, to note that in Justin the theological elaboration regarding the pre-existence of Christ is always linked to the biblical texts and founded on exegetical reasoning, not on philosophical speculation. This assumption is supported by the following observations:

a) It has been shown that in Justin the term for the description of the coming forth of the Son is γεννᾶσθαι. In the rare instances when other words have been used we always encounter some word of the γεννᾶσθαι family as a controlling factor. Now there is no question that γεννᾶσθαι is the principal term which steadily and predominantly occurs in the biblical passages so abundantly employed by Justin (Ps. 2,7; Ps. 109,3 [LXX]; Prov. 8,25). Consequently the mode of origin of the pre-existing Son is eventually described by the Apologist in biblical language.

b) Justin does not proceed to speculation about

the life within the deity before the world was created.
Athenagoras, a far cry from Justin as regards the frequency
of biblical usage, does try to answer the question by
positing the existence of the Logos "before" his begetting.[109]
Justin does not go beyond the statement that the Son was
begotten by the Father πρὸ πάντων τῶν κτισμάτων and that he
was with the Father πρὸ πάντων τῶν ποιημάτων (App. 6,3; Dial.
61,1; 62,4; 129,4). One could suggest that Justin does this,
simply because the Scriptural texts with which he works say
nothing more than that.[110] It is interesting to note that our
Apologist was even able to retain the ambivalence of the word
ἀρχή as it appears in Prov. 8,22-23.[111]

  c) Our analysis has demonstrated that Justin aims
at convincing his readers that the pre-existing Son is God and
that he is a full personal being. The Apologist time and
again comes to this subject and uses such language as to make
himself suspect of some sort of διθεΐα. His basic concept on
that level is the "numerical otherness" of the son. He speaks
about that in a manner shown in the following short passages:

Dial. 56,11: θεὸς ἕτερός ἐστι τοῦ τὰ πάντα ποιήσαντος θεοῦ,
  ἀριθμῷ λέγω.

Dial. 62,2: καὶ ἀριθμὸν τῶν ἀλλήλοις συνόντων καὶ τὸ
  ἐλάχιστον δύο μεμήνυκεν.

Dial. 128,4: . . . καὶ θεὸν καλεῖ . . . καὶ ἀριθμῷ ἕτερόν
  τι ἐστί.

---

[109]Athenagoras, *Supp.* 10: [ὁ υἱός] πρῶτον γέννημα
εἶναι τῷ πατρί, οὐχ ὡς γενόμενος (ἐξ ἀρχῆς γὰρ ὁ θεὸς νοῦς
ἀΐδιος ὢν εἶχεν αὐτὸς ἐν ἑαυτῷ τὸν λόγον ἀιδίως λογικὸς ὤν).
Cf. Tatian, *Or. Graec.* 4-5: θεὸς ὁ καθ᾽ ἡμᾶς οὐκ ἔχει
σύστασιν ἐν χρόνῳ, μόνος ἄναρχος ὢν καὶ αὐτὸς ὑπάρχων τῶν
ὅλων ἀρχή . . . "θεὸς ἦν ἐν ἀρχῇ" τὴν δὲ ἀρχὴν δύναμιν λόγου
παρειλήφαμεν.

[110]E.g. Ps. 109,3 (LXX): ἐκ γαστρὸς πρὸ ἑωσφόρου
ἐγέννησά σε; Prov. 8,22-25: κύριος ἔκτισέ με ἀρχὴν ὁδῶν
αὐτοῦ εἰς ἔργα αὐτοῦ . . . πρὸ δὲ πάντων βουνῶν γεννᾷ με;
Col. 1,15: πρωτότοκος πάσης κτίσεως etc.

[111]Note the syntactical, and semantic differences
between ἀρχὴν of v. 22 and ἐν ἀρχῇ of v. 23 in Prov. 8:
22 κύριος ἔκτισέ με ἀρχὴν ὁδῶν αὐτοῦ εἰς ἔργα αὐτοῦ
23 πρὸ τοῦ αἰῶνος ἐθεμελίωσέ με ἐν ἀρχῇ . . .
Cf. Justin, Dial. 61,1; App. 6,3.

Dial. 129,2: ὅταν λέγει . . . "ὡς εἷς ἐξ ἡμῶν" τόδε . . .
ἀριθμοῦ δηλωτικόν ἐστι.

Dial. 129,4: καὶ τὸ γεννώμενον τοῦ γεννῶντος ἀριθμῷ ἕτερόν
ἐστι.

There is no doubt that for Justin the Son is θεὸς
ἕτερος besides the Father, numerically distinctive from him.[112]

Justin, nonetheless, thinks that in defending the
ἕτερος θεὸς doctrine he does nothing more than to repeat what
the Scriptures say. So he reads Ps. 109,1 (LXX) (εἶπεν ὁ
κύριος τῷ κυρίῳ μου), Ps. 44,7-8 (LXX) (ὁ θρόνος σου ὁ θεὸς
εἰς τὸν αἰῶνα. . . διὰ τοῦτο ἔχρισέ σε ὁ θεὸς ὁ θεὸς σου),
Prov. 8,22-31, Gen. 1,26 (ποιήσωμεν ἄνθρωπον), Gen. 3,22
(Ἀδὰμ γέγονεν ὡς εἷς ἐξ ἡμῶν) etc. as irrefutable Scriptural
evidence for the existence of another God next to the Father
of all.[113]

But if the biblical texts proclaim the divinity of the
Son they also emphasize, according to Justin, that the Son is
not God the way the Father is. The Son was begotten by the
Father and so the Father is the cause not only of the
existence of the Son but of his divinity as well (Dial.
129,1). The difference in divinity is further emphasized by
Justin, as we will see, by the notion of transcendence.

It is obvious that here a very serious problem arises.
The differentiation in divinity between the Father and the
Son is so pronounced that one wonders what exactly Justin
meant when he used the term θεὸς for both of them. Did he not
realize the problem? Was it far beyond his intellectual
ability to handle it? Or perhaps there was no such problem
for Justin, simply because his understanding of the meaning
of the term God, due to his philosophical training, was dif-
fused and general rather than precise and absolute? The last
possibility might be the right one. But a definite answer
must wait until we examine all of the Justinian material
relevant to the pre-existence of the Son.

_____

[112]F. Bosse, *op. cit.*, p. 22, made the eloquent
remark that in the phrase ἕτερος θεὸς the term θεὸς is of less
importance than ἕτερος. Cf. Goodenough, *op. cit.*, p. 155.

[113]In Dial. 62 and 128-129 Justin presents a comprehensive review of the pertinent biblical evidence.

CHAPTER TWO

THE PRE-EXISTENCE OF CHRIST MANIFESTED
IN THE OLD TESTAMENT THEOPHANIES

A. *Introductory Remarks*

1.   The pre-existence of Christ manifested in the Old
Testament theophanies[1] constitutes one of the main themes of
Justin's Christology.[2]   He deals with it in two groups of
chapters in the Dialogue, namely chs. 56-62 and 125-129.[3]   He
returns to the same theme also in some other instances: Ap.
62 and 63; Dial. 37-38, 75, 86, 113 and 114.

---

[1]Justin does not use the term θεοφάνεια at all.   He
refers to a theophany by employing the word ὀπτασία found only
within a theophanic context (Dial. 56,5; 60,1, 2,4; 128,1).
Ὀπτασία is also the New Testament word for a specific type
of vision of divine things (e.g. Lk. 1,22; 24,23; Acts 26,19;
2 Cor. 12,1).   In addition Justin uses the word ἀποκάλυψις
as a synonym for theophany (Dial. 62,4) but more frequently
as a synonym for revelation (Dial. 78,2; 81,4 etc.).   Justin's
characteristic verb for the theophanic appearances is ὀρᾶν
in the passive aorist ὤφθη which is also the verb encountered
in the Septuagint theophanic texts (Dial. 56,1,2; 58,8,10;
59,2; 60,4 etc), and, in addition, the verb φαίνομαι (esp. the
participle of aorist φανείς: Dial. 59,1; 60,3; 61,1 etc.),
and the verb φανεροῦσθαι (Dial. 60,3; 75,4).   The last two
verbs occur with theophanic connotations also in the New
Testament.   Cf. Bauer-Arndt-Gingrich, *A Greek-English Lex. of
the N. Test., s.v.*

[2]For a theological analysis of Justin's christologi-
cal interpretation of the Old Testament theophanies, see B.
Kominiak, *op. cit.*, pp. 23-58.   For the Old Testament text
used in Justin's theophanic passages, see J. S. Sibinga, *The
Old Testament Text of Justin Martyr: I. The Pentateuch*
(Leiden, 1963).

[3]P. Prigent, *Justin et l'Anc. Test.*, p. 117, speaks
about a doublet in the case of chs. 56-62 and 125-129.   The
same author (*ibid.*, pp. 117-133), makes a detailed study of

The Old Testament theophanic events which Justin interprets christologically are the following:

(a) The theophany to Abraham at Mamre in connection with the theophany at Sodom (Gen. 18-19)

(b) The theophanies to Jacob at Haran (Gen. 31,10-13), at Peniel (Gen. 32,22-31), at Luz (Gen. 35,6-15), and at Bethel (Gen. 28,10-19)

(c) The theophany to Moses in the burning bush (Ex. 3)

(d) The theophany to Joshua before the conquering of Jericho (Josh. 5,13-6,5)

(e) The theophanic appearances implied in the passages Ex. 23,20-21 and Ps. 98,6-8 (LXX).[4]

Justin does not seem to be interested in the problem of the theophanies themselves.[5] If he introduces them in his writings he does so in order to prove his thesis that Scripture speaks about another God next to the Father of all: ἐπὶ τὰς γραφὰς ἐπανελθὼν πειράσομαι πεῖσαι ὑμᾶς ὅτι οὗτος ὅ τε τῷ Ἀβραὰμ καὶ τῷ Ἰακὼβ καὶ τῷ Μωυσεῖ ὤφθαι λεγόμενος καὶ γεγραμμένος θεὸς ἕτερός ἐστι τοῦ τὰ πάντα ποιήσαντος θεοῦ (Dial. 56,11). This other God is the pre-existing Christ. Thus the Old Testament theophanies become in the Justinian works evidence for, or a manifestation of, the pre-existence of Christ. What are the sources or the traditions behind such a concept? How does it function within the specific contexts? And how does it relate, if at all, to the christological schema of the humiliation and exaltation? In order to answer these questions, we have to examine carefully the pertinent chapters of the Dialogue and the First Apology. But before

---

the literary relationship between Dial. 56-62 and Dial. 125-129 (he also adds Ap. 63).

[4]It is apparent that Justin does not mention all the theophanic events which are narrated in the Old Testament. He implies, nonetheless (e.g. Dial. 127,1), that they should be interpreted in the way in which he interprets the ones quoted in Dial. 56-62 and 125-129. Cf. B. Kominiak, *op. cit.*, p. 8.

[5]In that respect Kominiak's theological understanding of the essence of the theophanic phenomenon (*op. cit.*, pp. 4-22), seems to be only indirectly connected to the Justinian problematic concerning the theophanies.

entering into the detailed exploration of the specific
passages it is necessary to discuss some general questions
which pertain to the whole body of the Justinian theophanic
texts and their possible antecedents. This approach will
provide basic clarifications and eliminate tiresome repetitions in each section.

2. The first general question that we ought to
consider is the relationship between the Justinian theophanic
texts and the New Testament. The question ultimately has to
do with the possibility of considering the New Testament as
the source for Justin's handling of the theophanies of the
Old Testament.

The study of the texts leads to the conclusion that
we encounter in the New Testament neither lengthy Old Testament passages as in Justin nor extensive comments with
reference to the Old Testament theophanies. We find in the
New Testament the following items:

a) In Mark[6] and Luke, there is a mentioning of
the incident of the burning bush. The emphasis, however, is
not on the theophany but on the fact that God is the God of
Abraham, Isaac and Jacob, which serves as evidence for the
resurrection of the dead. In the Matthean parallel (Mt. 22,
31-32) the theophanic element of the passage does not occur
at all.

b) In Acts 7,30-35, the incident of the burning
bush is included with more details in Stephen's speech. As
the context indicates, attention here is focused on Moses,
not in the theophany itself. And if there is a christological
interpretation of the passage it is centered around Moses as
the typos or forerunner of Christ.[7] An interesting element

---

[6]Mk. 12,26-27; περὶ δὲ τῶν νεκρῶν ὅτι ἐγείρονται οὐκ
ἀνέγνωτε ἐν τῇ βίβλῳ Μωυσέως ἐπὶ τῆς βάτου πῶς εἶπεν αὐτῷ ὁ
θεὸς λέγων ἐγὼ ὁ θεὸς 'Αβραὰμ καὶ ὁ θεὸς 'Ισαὰκ καὶ ὁ θεὸς
'Ιακώβ. Similarly Lk. 20,37-38. There is, of course, the
possibility that the expression ἐπὶ τῆς βάτου is simply a way
of quoting the particular passage of Exodus. Cf. E. Kloster-
mann, *Das Markus Evangelium*, Hand. zum N. Test. (Tübingen,
1950⁴), p. 126. Cf. also Strack-Billerbeck, *Kommentar zum
N. Testament*(München, 1956²), Vol. II, p. 28.

[7]The fact should not pass unnoticed that Moses'

56

contained in Acts 7,30-35 is perhaps the information that the
angel in the theophany of the burning bush accompanied Moses
and did not disappear after the event. The emphasis on the
angel is evident here as well as in v. 38 in the instance of
another theophany. We know that Justin viewed the theophanic
angel of the Old Testament and his function in pure christological terms. But then the angel occurs already in the
Septuagint text. Besides, the angels of Acts 7,35 and 38 are
within a context where the pointers to a christological
interpretation lie on other persons, not on the angels. And,
last but not least, the understanding of the theophany of the
burning bush in Acts 7,30-35 presupposes the presence of both
an angel and God. This is a fact which Justin has tried to
refute by all means since, if accepted, it would shatter his
own interpretation.

c) In John 8,56-58, Jesus concludes his debate
with the Jews with the statement, Ἀβραὰμ ὁ πατὴρ ὑμῶν ἠγαλ-
λιάσατο ἵνα ἴδῃ τὴν ἡμέραν τὴν ἐμὴν καὶ εἶδε καὶ ἐχάρη,
and ἀμὴν ἀμὴν λέγω ὑμῖν πρὶν Ἀβραὰμ γενέσθαι ἐγώ εἰμι. What
we have here is a clear reference to the pre-existing Christ
with respect to Abraham.[8] But this is still a far cry from
the lengthy and repetitive description of the appearance of
the pre-existing Christ to Abraham, which we encounter in the
writings of Justin. One cannot, however, dismiss offhand the
idea that John 8,56-58 and Justin's christological interpretation of the theophanies made to Abraham (Dial. 56) belong to
the same mode of thought. In that case traditional interpre-
tations like the one behind John 8,56-58 might perhaps be
germinal for developments of the type of Dial. 56.[9]

---

prophecy προφήτην ὑμῖν ἀναστήσει ὁ θεὸς ἐκ τῶν ἀδελφῶν ὑμῶν
ὡς ἐμὲ in Acts 7,37 is inserted between the reference to the
two theophanies on Horeb and on Sinai. Note also the repetition of the demonstrative pronoun οὗτος four times in Acts
7,35-38 with reference to Moses. Cf. E. Haenchen, *Die
Apostelgeschichte*, Meyer Komm. (Göttingen, 1968[6]), p. 234.

[8] Cf. R. Bultmann, *Das Evangelium des Johannes*,
Meyer Komm. (Göttingen, 1959[16]), p. 248f. Cf. also R. E.
Brown, *The Gospel according to John, I-XII*, The Anchor Bible
(Garden City, N. Y., 1966), pp. 360, 367-68.

[9] Cf. F. Bosse, *op. cit.*, p. 48.

57

d) In 1 Cor. 10,1-4, Paul introduces a chain of
various Old Testament events in the desert and winds up with
the statement ἡ δὲ πέτρα ἦν ὁ Χριστός. The passage goes
beyond a mere typology. The events quoted by Paul have a
theophanic nuance as they stand in Ex. 13,21-22 and Nu. 20,7-
11. Here one is allowed to speak about discernible traces of
a christological interpretation of the Old Testament
theophanies.

Justin himself could have known the above tradition
which is pre-Pauline as far as the enumeration of the biblical
events is concerned.[10] In Dial. 131 for example he mentions
many of the events that Paul quotes in 1 Cor. 10,1-10. Yet
because of the common traditional provenance of the events
one cannot establish a dependence of Justin on 1 Cor. 10,1-10.

The most significant component in 1 Cor. 10,1-4, with
regard to the question of theophanies, is the final statement
ἡ δὲ πέτρα ἦν ὁ Χριστός. Justin utilizes the word πέτρα as a
designation for Christ.[11] Could we posit the Pauline passage
behind Justin's designation? And if yes, is it possible to
consider the alleged dependence as a basic factor in Justin's
christological handling of the theophanies in the Old Testament? An examination of the instances where Justin employs
πέτρα as a designation for Christ leads to the following
observations:

1) In Dial. 70,1,2, Justin relates the term
πέτρα to Dan. 2,34 and secondarily to Is. 33,16, and connects
it with the incarnation of Christ.[12]

---

[10]R. Horsley, *Paul and the Pneumatikoi: First Cor-
inthians investigated in terms of the Conflict between two
different religious mentalities* (Unpublished Ph.D. thesis,
Harvard University, 1970), pp. 226-250, has shown that behind
1 Cor. 10,1-4 lies a large and variegated set of traditions
of Exodus motifs. Cf. H. Conzelmann, *Der erste Brief an die
Korinther,*Meyer Komm. (Göttingen, 1969), pp. 194-197. See
also J. Jeremias' article Μωυσῆς in Kittel's *Theol. Dict. of
the N. Test.*, E.T., Vol. IV, pp. 869-70.

[11]Dial. 113,6: λίθος καὶ πέτρα ἐν παραβολαῖς ὁ
Χριστὸς διὰ τῶν προφητῶν ἐκηρύσσετο. Cf. also Dial. 70,1,2.

[12]Cf. Dial. 76: καὶ τὸ λίθον τοῦτον [sc. Christ]
εἰπεῖν ἄνευ χειρῶν τμηθέντα [Dan. 2,34] . . . οὐκ ἔστιν
ἀνθρώπινον ἔργον, ἀλλὰ τῆς βουλῆς τοῦ προβάλλοντος αὐτὸν
πατρὸς τῶν ὅλων θεοῦ.

2) In Dial. 113,6, Jesus Christ is called λίθος καὶ πέτρα because of the spiritual circumcision that he effects upon his followers as his typos Joshua did (5,2-5).[13]

3) Dial. 114,4 is the only text where πέτρα as a characterization of Christ is derived from the same biblical event which also 1 Cor. 10,4 presupposes. Here, however, the relevant phrase from Dan. 2,34 shows up again, in a case where the context did not necessitate it.

The conclusion is that whereas the designation of πέτρα-Χριστὸς in 1 Cor. 10,4 hinges basically upon Ex. 17,6 (and its parallels Nu. 20,7-11 etc.), the same designation in Justin builds primarily upon Dan. 2,34 and Josh. 5,2.[14] Under these circumstances one cannot conclusively defend the idea of a direct connection between Justin's λίθος-πέτρα-Χριστὸς terminology and 1 Cor. 10,1-4.

3. The examination of the Apostolic Fathers as possible sources for Justin's christological interpretation of the theophanies yields in general no positive answers. Neither do we find in them a christological interpretation, nor do we encounter even the reference of the basic Old Testament theophanies with which Justin is preoccupied. It is interesting to note that *The Epistle of Barnabas* which abounds with examples of a typological christological interpretation of scriptural events, names, and the like,[15] does not exhibit

---

[13]Cf. Josh. 5,2: ποίησον σεαυτῷ μαχαίρας πετρίνας ἐκ πέτρας ἀκροτόμου καὶ καθίσας περίτεμε τοὺς υἱοὺς Ἰσραὴλ *to* Dial. 113,6 ἐκεῖνος [sc. Joshua] λέγεται . . . περιτομὴν μαχαίραις πετρίναις τὸν λαὸν περιτετμηκέναι, ὅπερ κήρυγμα ἦν τῆς περιτομῆς ταύτης ἧς περιέτεμεν ἡμᾶς αὐτὸς Ἰησοῦς . . . ὅτι γὰρ λίθος καὶ πέτρα ἐν παραβολαῖς ὁ Χριστὸς ἐκηρύσσετο.

[14]R. Horsley's examination of the exegetical traditions of the "accompanying rock-well" motif which appears in 1 Cor. 10,4 points to traditions which cannot be proven as known by Justin (*op. cit.*, pp. 237-244).

[15]E.g., *Barnabas* VII, 6-11; XII, 1-7 etc. It is worth noticing that Barnabas, although he often mentions that God spoke to Moses (IV, 7-8; XII,2; XV,1), does not make any attempt to interpret christologically the event. W. Shotwell (*op. cit.*, p. 70), is right when he says that "even Barnabas, if known and used by Justin, could have contributed little to his exegesis."

any trace of a christological understanding of the Old
Testament theophanies. The other Apologists of the second
century do not furnish any positive information either.

In the known texts then of the first and second
centuries, there is no christological interpretation of the
Old Testament theophanies except in Justin's works. B.
Kominiak is right when he states that Justin's writings are
the earliest Christian documents that we know of on such a
subject.[16]

4. Recently P. Prigent has tried to show, on the
basis of the biblical texts used by Justin, that our author
is likely to have utilized in both the Dialogue and the
First Apology a writing which, in all probability, he himself
had composed previously, and which could very well be the
lost Σύνταγμα κατὰ πασῶν τῶν γεγενημένων αἱρέσεων."[17]
Prigent has devoted a whole chapter of his monograph to the
study of the Justinian texts pertaining to the Old Testament
theophanies, arguing that his hypothesis may well be verified
in this specific area.[18] One might have serious objections
to the proposition that behind the scriptural argumentation
of the Dialogue is the text of the specific Σύνταγμα κατὰ
πασῶν τῶν γεγενημένων αἱρέσεων. Furthermore, even if one
could have established such a hypothesis, the problem of the
sources of Justin in his dealing with the Old Testament
theophanies would have been transposed, not solved.

5. One more point should be added to the present
preliminary considerations. Quotations from Philo are going
to appear frequently in the pages that follow. In anticipation of my conclusions, I should like to say that Philo offers
a number of parallels which come close to the Justinian
texts devoted to the theophanies. The degree of closeness
and the possibility of influence--its kind and extent--shall

---

[16]B. Kominiak, *op. cit.*, p. 4.

[17]Prigent, *Justin et l'Anc. Test.*, pp. 11-13. The
lost writing is mentioned by Justin in Ap. 28,8.

[18]*Ibid.*, pp. 117-133. Cf. H. Chadwick, *op. cit.*,
p. 281.

60

be discussed in each particular case.

B. *The Theophanies at Mamre and at Sodom*

1. Justin discusses the theophany at Mamre in conjunction with the theophany at Sodom in Dial. 56. Again he discusses the theophany at Mamre, in an abbreviated fashion, in Dial. 126. At the beginning of Dial. 56, Justin repeats that his basic purpose in presenting the theophanies at Mamre and at Sodom is to prove that Scripture speaks about another God next to the One who abides in absolute transcendence in heaven.[19] Then the Apologist proceeds to his christological interpretation of the two theophanies which runs as follows:

Gen. 18,1ff. tells about a visit of God to Abraham. The text speaks about God and at the same time about three men. Actually two of them were angels whereas the third was God himself. We know it because one of the three, who had been in the tent and who also said, "in due season I will return unto thee and Sarah shall have a son" (Gen. 18,14), appears to have come again. This happened when Sarah had a son, and the word of the prophet in that instance indicates that he is God (Gen. 21,9-12). This in turn signifies that he truly was God when he had conversed earlier with Abraham. God, having spoken with Abraham, went off while the two angels left for Sodom. God himself afterwards visited Lot, saved him from catastrophe and rained on Sodom and Gomorrah brimstone and fire from the Lord as Scripture says: καὶ κύριος ἔβρεξεν ἐπὶ Σόδομα καὶ Γόμορρα πῦρ καὶ θεῖον παρὰ κυρίου ἐκ τοῦ οὐρανοῦ (Gen. 19,24).

In both events then at Mamre and at Sodom we have the appearance not only of angels but of God himself. This God is not the Father of all but another God, his Son. He is also called ἄγγελος because he announces the messages of God the maker of all.[20]

---

[19]Dial. 56,1: Μωυσῆς . . . μηνύων ὅτι ὁ ὀφθεὶς τῷ Ἀβραὰμ πρὸς τῇ δρυὶ τῇ Μαμβρῆ θεός . . . ὑπὸ ἄλλου τοῦ ἐν τοῖς ὑπερουρανίοις ἀεὶ μένοντος καὶ οὐδενὶ ὀφθέντος ἢ ὁμιλήσαντος δι᾽ ἑαυτοῦ ποτε . . .

[20]Dial. 56,10: καὶ θεός ἐστι καὶ ἄγγελος καλεῖται ἐκ τοῦ ἀγγέλλειν, ὡς προέφην, οἷσπερ βούλεται τὰ παρ᾽ αὐτοῦ ὁ

2. The closest parallel to Justin's dealing with the theophanies at Mamre and at Sodom is found in Philo. There are several points of contact between the two authors:

a) As we have seen, Justin introduces the theophany at Mamre by saying that ὁ ὀφθεὶς τῷ 'Αβραὰμ πρὸς τῇ δρυὶ τῇ Μαμβρῇ θεός . . . [πεμφθεὶς] ὑπὸ ἄλλου τοῦ ἐν τοῖς ὑπερουρανίοις ἀεὶ μένοντος καὶ οὐδενὶ ὀφθέντος ἢ ὁμιλήσαντος δι' ἑαυτοῦ ποτε, ὃν ποιητὴν τῶν ὅλων . . . νοοῦμεν (Dial. 56,1). Philo was the first to make a similar statement in *Mut. Nom.* 15: τὸ τῶν ὄντων πρεσβύτατον ἄρρητον . . . καὶ ὁ λόγος αὐτοῦ κυρίῳ ὀνόματι οὐ ρητὸς ἡμῖν . . . ὥστε τὸ ὤφθη κύριος τῷ 'Αβραὰμ λέγεσθαι ὑπονοητέον οὐχ ὡς . . . ἐπιφαινομένου τοῦ παντὸς αἰτίου . . . ἀλλ' ὡς μιᾶς τῶν περὶ αὐτὸ δυνάμεων τῆς βασιλικῆς προφαινομένης.[21]

b) Philo insists on a substantial differentiation between the three angels-visitors at Mamre. He uses the phrase ὁ θεὸς δορυφορούμενος ὑπὸ δυοῖν τῶν ἀνωτάτω δυνάμεων ἀρχῆς τε αὖ καὶ ἀγαθότητος."[22] Philo in another instance tells us that the three are actually one, the three being a result of φαντασία but such a statement does not negate the notion of substantial differentiation.[23] Here Justin could

---

τῶν ὅλων ποιητῆς θεός. It is apparent that Justin identifies the angel of the Lord (Malh'ak Yahve) with God--and finally with Christ--whereas in the biblical texts the identification of the angel of Yahve with God is problematic. See more in B. Kominiak, *op . cit* ., pp. 9-22. For the problem of the angel of Yahve see J. M. Lagrange, L'Ange de Iahve, *Revue Biblique* 12 (1903), pp. 212-225. For a comprehensive study of the title ἄγγελος used for Christ see W. Michaelis, *Zur Engelchristologie im Urchristentum* (Basel, 1942). Cf. also J. Barbel, *Christos Angelos* (Bonn, 1941) (*n.v.*).

[21]It is true that in this same passage Philo includes a phrase which points to the human weakness as a factor of the inaccessibility of the real God, but the other side of the inaccessibility viz. the transcendence of God is constantly presupposed in the Philonic texts.

[22]*Sacr. AC.* 59. Cf. also *Abr.* 121: πατὴρ μὲν τῶν ὅλων ὁ μέσος, ὃς ἐν ταῖς ἱεραῖς γραφαῖς κυρίω ὀνόματι καλεῖται ὁ ὤν, αἱ δὲ παρ' ἑκάτερα αἱ πρεσβύταται καὶ ἐγγυτάτω τοῦ ὄντος δυνάμεις, ἡ μὲν ποιητική ἡ δ' αὖ βασιλική.

[23]Philo himself after speaking of φαντασία and one person in *Abr.* 119,122,131-132, comes again in *Abr.* 142-145 into a sharp statement of differentiation between the three: τῶν τριῶν ὡς ἀνδρῶν ἐπιφανέντων τῷ σοφῷ δύο μόνους εἰς τὴν

62

find an exegesis of Gen. 18,1ff. by which he would be able
to bypass the current rabbinical exegesis which spoke of
three angels.[24]

    c) Furthermore Philo made the identification of
God who appeared at Mamre and Sodom with Logos in more than
one instance.[25] It is worth noting that in *Leg. All.* III,
217-19 Philo introduces the λόγος promising to Sarah the
begetting of a son, as it becomes evident from the answer of
Sarah "οὔπω μοι γέγονεν τὸ εὐδαιμονεῖν ἕως τοῦ νῦν· ὁ δὲ
κύριός μου θεῖος λόγος πρεσβύτερός ἐστι . . . ᾧ πιστεύειν
καλὸν ὑπισχνουμένῳ."[26] The Philonic passage is of significance when we remember that the main weight of Justin's
argument in Dial. 56 rests on the connection of the theophany
at Mamre with the promise to Sarah that she shall have a son.

    It should be noted also that in the theophany at
Sodom, Philo ascribes the catastrophe of the town to the
λόγος. Philo does not include in his quotation of Gen. 19,
24 the phrase "παρὰ κυρίου" which both the Hebrew text and
the Septuagint have. Instead he reads Gen. 19,23a together

ἀφανισθεῖσαν χώραν [i. e. Sodom] τὰ λόγιά φησιν ἐλθεῖν . . .
τοῦ τρίτου μὴ δικαιώσαντος ἥκειν ὅς γε κατὰ τὴν ἐμὴν ἔννοιαν
ἦν ὁ πρὸς ἀλήθειαν ὤν.

[24]For a list of the pertinent rabbinical passages
see A. H. Goldfahn, *op. cit.*, pp. 111-112. Cf. also G.
Archambault, *op. cit.*, Vol. I, pp. 244-47 (n. 1), and A. L.
Williams, *op. cit.*, p. 111, n. 4. Archambault is wrong when
he states that here Justin "ne paraît en aucune manière se
souvenir de Philon" (*ibid.*, p. 245). Archambault overlooks
the fact that Philo departs from the traditional idea of the
three visitors as being three angels and introduces instead
a sharp diffentiation between them. This is the precise
point which could be used by Justin. Cf. also W. Shotwell,
op. cit., pp. 96-97.

[25]E.g. *Som.* I, 85; *Leg. All.* III, 217-219; *Migr. Abr.*
173-4. J. Daniélou, *op. cit.*, p. 151, by limiting himself
only to Philo's *Abr.* 13 and by not considering as a unity
the narratives of the theophanies at Mamre and at Sodom,
fails here to recognize the connection between Philo and
Justin.

[26]The term θεῖος λόγος is here employed by Philo
quite deliberately--it does not belong to the cited biblical
text--in order to switch the reference from Abraham to
logos.

with Gen. 19,24 and makes the sun of v. 23a the cause of the burning of Sodom and Gomorrah. At the same time the sun is for him the λόγος.[27] Justin of course did not need the allegory of sun-λόγος since the expression κύριος παρὰ κυρίου of the text itself (Gen. 19,24) was sufficient for him.

　　d) In Dial. 56,4 and 10 Justin gives an explanation of the name ἄγγελος by which the second God is designated in the theophanies at Mamre and at Sodom: ὃς καὶ ἄγγελος καλεῖται, διὰ τὸ ἀγγέλλειν τοῖς ἀνθρώποις ὅσαπερ βούλεται αὐτοῖς ἀγγεῖλαι ὁ τῶν ὅλων ποιητής. Justin returns to that explanation in Dial. 60,3, Ap. 63,5 and elsewhere. Philo had already offered such an interpretation of ἄγγελος within a theophanic context in *Vit. Mos.* I, 66: καλείσθω δὲ ἄγγελος, ὅτι σχεδὸν τὰ μέλλοντα γενήσεσθαι διήγγελλε. The similarity might be coincidental. But there is a verbatim agreement between the Philonic passage and the Justinian one in Dial. 60,3 which can hardly be accidental.[28] We shall return to this point in the section pertaining to the theophany in the burning bush.

　　The conclusion is that the Philonic and the Justinian texts which pertain to the theophanies at Mamre and at Sodom offer evidence that there are points of resemblance between the two authors. Is Philo then the source behind Dial. 56?

　　J. Lebreton, who discussed the problem of relationship between Philo and Justin in the issue of the theophanies, concluded that we should not insist upon a strong Philonic influence on Justin. B. Kominiak repeated virtually Lebreton's thesis without going into the same detailed discussion.[29] E. Goodenough on the other hand, after discussing briefly the theophany at Mamre says that "Justin is

---

[27]*Som.* I, 85: ἥλιον καλεῖ τὸν θεῖον λόγον τὸ τοῦ κατ᾿ οὐρανοῦ περιπολοῦντος . . . παράδειγμα, ἐφ᾿ οὗ λέγεται ὁ ἥλιος ἐξῆλθεν ἐπὶ τὴν γῆν . . . etc. (Gen. 19,24-25).

[28]Cf. Per Beskow, *Rex Gloriae: The Kingship of Christ in the Early Church* (Stockholm, 1962), p. 112. Beskow rightly suggests that ἄγγελος in Justin means primarily "messenger" not "angel" (*ibid.*, 112).

[29]Cf. J. Lebreton, *op. cit.*, Vol. II, p. 677; B. Kominiak, *op. cit.*, pp. 13-14.

unmistakably echoing the Philonic interpretation though he
rejects or misunderstands or had never heard the more elaborate theories of Philo's doctrine of the godhead."[30]

Comparative study of the Philonic and the Justinian
theophanic passages on Gen. 18-19 immediately reveals the
difference between them.[31] However, as we have shown, there
are points of similarity between the two authors, and these
points are not secondary. To my knowledge we do not have any
other writings prior to Justin's which could explain his
dealing with the theophany at Mamre. To think that our author
contrived the christological interpretation of the divine
apparitions at Mamre and at Sodom, and that his interpretation, by mere coincidence, approximates in its essentials the
Philonic one, seems to me highly unlikely. It is, therefore,
plausible to surmise that Justin had an acquaintance with the
Philonic interpretation pertaining to Gen. 18-19.[32]

3. The Philonic interpretation, nonetheless, cannot
account for all the substantial elements of the Justinian
handling of the theophanies at Mamre and at Sodom. For
instance, a crucial exegetical argument used in Dial. 56
derives from Psalms 44 (LXX) and 109 (LXX). Not a single
verse from these two Psalms has been ever quoted or commented
upon in the extant writings of Philo.

Justin's dialectic in Dial. 56 aims eventually at
leading the discussion to Gen. 19,24: καὶ κύριος ἔβρεξεν
ἐπὶ Σόδομα καὶ Γόμορρα θεῖον καὶ πῦρ παρὰ κυρίου ἐκ τοῦ
οὐρανοῦ.[33] The reason is obvious: the passage is taken by

---

[30]*Op. cit.*, pp. 114-115.

[31]Cf. the relevant discussion in Lebreton's *op. cit.*,
pp. 669-675 and Kominiak's *op. cit.*, pp. 13-14.

[32]The fact that Philo speaks in many instances about
the theophany at Mamre and Sodom would increase the possi-
bility of a reader being acquainted with his exegesis. Cf.
Philo, *Abr.* 118, 119-124, 131-132, 142-145; *Sacr. AC.* 59;
Migr. Abr. 173-4; *Som.* I, 85-86; *Quest. and Answ. in Gen.*
IV, 9,12,29,30 etc.

[33]*Dial.* 56,12. This is the first time that the
passage of Gen. 19,24 turns up in the Dialogue. But the
introductory sentence implies that Justin had already mentioned Gen. 19,24 before. Apparently the passage was quoted

Justin as clear evidence for the existence of a second Lord-God next to the One who is in heaven. This Lord who destroyed Sodom is the same Lord who appeared and talked with Abraham in Gen. 18, who is called Lord and God, and who finally is identified with the pre-existing Christ.[34]

The importance of Gen. 19,24 within Dial. 56 is all too conspicuous. A careful reading of the whole theophanic section makes clear that Gen. 19,24 has an even greater importance for Justin. It should be classified among his basic christological passages. It occurs six times in the Dialogue.[35] The context, although theophanic, is diversified in each case. This might be an indication of Justin's familiarity with Gen. 19,24 which enabled him to employ the passage in variegated combinations.

It is significant that Gen. 19,24 is introduced in Dial. 56,12 independently, without the narrative of which it is part.[36] Then Justin, even before going into the narrative, cites two passages, one from Ps. 109,1 (LXX) (λέγει ὁ κύριος τῷ κυρίῳ μου· κάθου ἐκ δεξιῶν μου etc.) and another from Ps.

---

in Dial. 56,2 within the omitted text Gen. 18,3-19,26. F. Bosse, *op. cit.*, p. 21, has rightly emphasized the exegetical significance of Gen. 19,24 for Justin. Nonetheless, he has made the remark that Gen. 19,24 should be viewed on a par with Ps. 109,1 (LXX) and 44,7 (LXX), as far as exegetical importance is concerned.

[34]Justin's argument runs from Dial. 56,17 to 56,21. In 56,22 he concludes it with a summary which ends once more with the crucial verse from Gen. 19,24: κύριος ἔβρεξε . . . πῦρ παρὰ κυρίου. Archambault, *op. cit.*, Vol. I, p. 263, n. 23, says that Justin's interpretation of Gen. 19,24 follows a Philonic (also Midrashic) exegetical rule. Shotwell, *op. cit.*, pp. 34-38 has shown that this rule is the analogy, employed extensively by Justin throughout his interpretation of the theophanies.

[35]Dial. 56,12,21,22; 60,5; 127,5; 129,1.

[36]The narrative begins only in Dial. 56,17 and finishes in 56,21 with Gen. 19,24. In the next verse 56,22 Justin quotes for the third time Gen. 19,24 with which he concludes ch. 56.

66

44,7-8 (LXX) (ὁ θρόνος σου ὁ θεὸς εἰς τὸν αἰῶνα τοῦ αἰῶνος . .
. . διὰ τοῦτο ἔχρισέ σε ὁ θεὸς ὁ θεός σου ἔλαιον etc.). The
connection between Ps. 109,1 (LXX), Ps. 44,7-8 (LXX), and Gen.
19,24 is the double κύριος and the double θεὸς which for
Justin is irrefutable evidence for the existence of a second
God.

Here a new possibility opens up for the understanding
of Justin's handling of the theophany to Abraham. Both Ps.
109,1 (LXX) and Ps. 44,7-8 (LXX) are christological texts
which must have become commonplace by the time of Justin.[37]
It is likely that these Psalms together with some other Old
Testament texts susceptible of christological interpretation
could circulate in small collections of scriptural quotations.[38] The text Gen. 19,24 might have been a link in a
chain of such quotations to which also Ps. 109,1 (LXX) and Ps.
44,7-8 (LXX) belonged, and might have reached Justin in that
form.[39] Hence it appears together with them in Dial. 56 and
becomes the focal point within this chapter.

4. The suggestion is that Justin's interpreation of
the theophanies at Mamre and at Sodom implies a certain
degree of acquaintance with two sources: the Philonic
exegesis of Genesis 18-19 and a collection of Old Testament
passages of the type of Testimonia. Like Philo, Justin

---

[37]Ps. 109,1 (LXX) occurs several times already in the
New Testament (e.g. Mt. 22,44 and paral., Acts 2,34, Hebr.
1,3 etc.). Ps. 44,7-8 (LXX) is quoted in Hebr. 1,8-9.

[38]One cannot be sure about the extent of these collections, the so-called testimonia, but one cannot deny their
existence in the early Church. Cf. the concise introduction
to the problem of testimonia in P. Prigent, *L'Epître de
Barnabé I-XVI et ses sources* (Paris, 1961), pp. 16-28. See
also the informative discussion on the same problem in P.
Beskow, *op. cit.*, pp. 74-122.

[39]W. Bousset, *Jüdisch-Christlicher Schulbetrieb in
Alexandria und Rom* (Göttingen, 1915), p. 308 (cf. also pp.
304-307), has argued that not only the specific passages
quoted above, but the frame of the whole biblical apparatus
of Justin's writings belongs to traditional collections that
circulated widely through the so-called διδασκαλεῖα of the
early christian teachers. Bousset's opinion could be verified, but only in part. It suffers, one might contend, from
an oversimplifying tendency, which does not do justice to
the complexity of the Justinian texts.

insists that God, the Father of all, should be excluded as an
agent from the theophanies made to Abraham and to Lot. Also
like Philo, our Apologist places Logos in the center of the
theophanic appearance. Unlike Philo, however, Justin does
not view the theophany from the angle of the inaccessibility
of the transcendent God or from the standpoint of man's long-
ing for union with Him. Instead he views the theophanic
event from the standpoint of the intent of Testimonia i.e.,
as evidence for the belief that the Son is God and Lord.
In this case the concept of the pre-existence of Christ
functions as an exegetical guide. At the same time it becomes
the object and the purpose of the exegesis of the theophanic
texts because of theological and apologetic reasons.

In the christological handling of Dial. 56 we
encounter two phenomena worth mentioning:

a) By identifying the pre-existent Christ with
the divine agent of the theophanies at Mamre and at Sodom,
Justin appropriates for the Son all the appellations used in
the corresponding passages of Gen. 18-19: θεός, κύριος,
ἄγγελος, ἀνήρ. We shall see that Justin will increase the
number of appellations as he proceeds in the discussion of the
theophanies. This direct association of the pre-existing Son
with the names or titles of the agent(s) who appeared in the
theophanic narratives of the Old Testament becomes in Justin
a fundamental exegetical method used by him in order to establish his christological interpretation of the theophanies.[40]

b) In Dial. 56,10 the Apologist makes the statement τοῦτον [i.e. the Son] φαινόμενον τῷ Ἀβραάμ, τὸν καὶ πρὸ
ποιήσεως κόσμου ὄντα θεόν. This formulation indicates that
when Justin speaks about the Son as an agent in the theophanic appearances to Abraham and to Lot, he has in mind that
this Son is pre-existing in a status of God before the
creation of the world. It is interesting to note that at the
end of the section which deals with the theophany to Abraham,
and before the section which expounds the theophanies to
Jacob, Justin inserts a question asked by Trypho: πῶς οὗτος
ὁ τῷ Ἀβραὰμ ὀφθεὶς θεός . . . διὰ τῆς παρθένου γεννηθεὶς

---

[40]Cf. P. Prigent, *Justin et l'A.T.*, pp. 121, 124-126.

ἄνθρωπος ὁμοιοπαθὴς πᾶσιν, ὡς προέφης, γέγονεν (Dial. 57,3). In connection with the statement in Dial. 56,10 this passage, which is not required by the context, shows, one might contend, that Justin works with a schema in which pre-existence is coupled with incarnation. We have already encountered this pattern in the previous chapter of this dissertation and we have made the plausible assumption that this might be a form of the humiliation and exaltation pattern.

C. *Theophanic Appearances to Jacob*

1. Justin presents the theophanies made to Jacob in Dial. 58 in an extensive form. He mentions one of them again briefly in Dial. 125,3,5 and 126,3. In Dial. 58 he speaks about four instances of a theophanic appearance to Jacob:

(a) at Haran, Gen. 31,10-13 (Dial. 58,4-5)

(b) at Peniel, Gen. 32,22-31 (Dial. 58,6-7)

(c) at Luz, Gen. 35,6-15 (Dial. 58,8-9)

(d) at Bethel, Gen. 28,10-19 (Dial. 58,11-13)

Justin's approach to the theophanies made to Jacob is different from that which he uses for the theophanies made to Abraham. Here he arranges one after the other the four theophanic narratives from Gen. 31,32,35 and 28 almost without comment. The dialectic as well as the exegesis are uncomplicated.

The key phrase is, I think, Dial. 58,3: ὑπὸ Μωυσέως . . . γέγραπται . . . ὅτι οὗτος ὁ ὀφθεὶς τοῖς πατριάρχαις λεγόμενος θεὸς καὶ ἄγγελος καὶ κύριος λέγεται. After this introduction Justin proceeds to quote the four theophanic narratives in which Jacob is involved. In them Justin sees that God who appeared to Jacob is called by different names: ἄγγελος (Gen. 31,11-13), ἄνθρωπος (Gen. 32,15-31), θεὸς (Gen. 35,9-12), κύριος (Gen. 28,13-19).

The array of the biblical passages is interrupted only once in Dial. 58,10. Here Justin inserts a sentence which virtually is a different formulation of his introductory phrase in 58,3: οὗτος καὶ ἄγγελος καὶ θεὸς καὶ κύριος καὶ ἐν ἰδέᾳ ἀνδρὸς τῷ Ἀβραὰμ φανεὶς καὶ ἐν ἰδέᾳ ἀνθρώπου αὐτῷ τῷ Ἰακὼβ παλαίσας. Dial. 58,10 differs from 58,3 essentially in its addition of ἄνθρωπος as one of the forms under which

God appeared to Abraham and to Jacob. But the addition does not substantially change the course of thought.

The thesis advanced by Justin in Dial. 58 is then easy to grasp: in the theophanies made to Jacob God is called angel, lord, god, man. But these are also the names by which the second God is called in the theophanies made to Abraham too. Consequently in the case of Jacob we have a further evidence for the existence of another God who is none other than the pre-existing Christ.

2. The relative simplicity of the exposition in Dial. 58, and the fact that the whole argument leans heavily on the interpretation of the theophany to Abraham, makes Dial. 58 appear as an appendix to Dial. 56. One would not have serious difficulties in contending that Justin, once having thought out the christological interpretation of the Abrahamic theophanies, easily enlarges the circle and includes those made to Jacob as well.[41] Even the phrase ὁ θεὸς 'Αβραὰμ καὶ ὁ θεὸς 'Ισαὰκ καὶ ὁ θεὸς 'Ιακὼβ which Justin employs very often[42] could have contributed to such a development. Yet, a solution of this kind seems to oversimplify the issue. Behind Dial. 58 one might detect other factors involved.

Philo in his *De Somniis* I speaks several times[43] about the theophanies which Justin mentions in Dial. 58. He leaves out only the theophany at Luz (Gen. 35,6-10), but then this text of Genesis reports the theophany at Bethel and only in one or two verses makes a reference to the theophany at Luz without describing it. Philo's handling of the divine appearances to Jacob contains some fundamental elements which occur in one form or another in Justin too:

a) According to Philo, the one who appeared to

---

[41]Bosse, *op. cit.*, p. 47 actually suggests that the whole theophanic section in Justin's writings has developed out of the Abrahamic theophanies. Such a contention, however, cannot account for the multi-faceted Justinian texts.

[42]E.g. Dial. 59,2,3; 60,2; 80,4; 85,3; 126,2 etc.

[43]Philo, *Som.* I, 61-68,70,115-121,127-130,184-188,227-230,238-241. See also *Migr. Abr.* 5-6; *Mut. Nom.* 85-87.

Jacob was the λόγος: δεόντως οὖν εἰς αἴσθησιν ἐλθών [sc.
Jacob in Gen. 28,11] οὐκέτι θεῷ, λόγῳ δ' ὑπαντᾷ θεοῦ καθὰ καὶ
ὁ πάππος αὐτοῦ τῆς σοφίας 'Αβραάμ.[44] Philo does not refrain
from making time and again the same identification.[45]

b) In the same theophanic events related to
Jacob, Philo makes another important identification: the
ἄγγελος is the λόγος. In Mut. Nom. 87 we read: διὰ τοῦτο τὸν
μὲν 'Αβραάμ, ἐπειδὴ μένειν ἔμελλεν ἐν ὁμοίῳ, μετωνόμασεν ὁ
ἄτρεπτος θεός [Gen. 17,5] . . . τὸν δὲ 'Ιακώβ [in Gen. 32,28]
ἄγγελος ὑπηρέτης τοῦ θεοῦ λόγος.[46] Philo of course makes
the same identification in other instances where the context
is not a specific theophany to Jacob[47] but this fact supports,
does not weaken, our position.

c) A third identification, to which Philo proceeds, is even more important. Commenting on the theophany
made to Jacob at Haran (Gen. 31,10-13), Philo, in Som. I,
228-230, equates λόγος with θεός. Though I have quoted the
passage in the previous chapter, it is necessary to repeat it
here because of its significance: ἐξέτασον εἰ τῷ ὄντι δύο
εἰσὶ θεοί· λέγεται γὰρ ὅτι ἐγὼ εἰμὶ ὁ θεὸς ὁ ὀφθείς σοι οὐκ
ἐν τόπῳ ἐμῷ ἀλλ' ἐν τόπῳ θεοῦ ὡς ἂν ἑτέρου. Τί οὖν χρὴ
λέγειν; ὁ μὲν ἀληθείᾳ θεὸς εἷς ἐστιν, οἱ δ' ἐν καταχρήσει
λεγόμενοι πλείους. Διὸ καὶ ὁ ἱερὸς λόγος ἐν τῷ παρόντι τὸν
μὲν ἀληθείᾳ διὰ τοῦ ἄρθρου μεμήνυκεν . . . τὸν δ' ἐν καταχρήσει χωρὶς ἄρθρου . . . καλεῖ δὲ θεὸν τὸν πρεσβύτατον αὐτοῦ
λόγον. There is no doubt that here the term θεὸς for λόγος
is severely restricted. Nonetheless, the term θεός is applied

---

[44]Philo, Som. I,70. Note the reference to Abraham in
the same passage.

[45]Cf. Som. I,129: ὁ δέ [θεῖος λόγος] δέχεται τὸν
ἀθλητήν [sc. Jacob in Gen. 32,22-30] καὶ διερειδόμενος
παλαίειν ἀναγκάζει . . . καὶ καλέσας αὐτὸν μεταχαραχθέντα
καινὸν τύπον 'Ισραήλ; Migr. Abr. 5-6: ὁ ἀσκητής [sc. Jacob
in Gen. 28] ὁμολογεῖ ὅτι οὐκ ἔστι τοῦτο ἀλλ' ἡ οἶκος θεοῦ . .
. . ὁ λόγος.

[46]Cf. also Som. I, 238-239: ὅταν φῇ ἐγὼ εἰμὶ ὁ θεὸς
ὁ ὀφθείς σοι ἐν τόπῳ θεοῦ [Gen. 31,13] τότε νόησον ὅτι τὸν
ἀγγέλου τόπον ἐπέσχε . . . τὴν τοῦ θεοῦ εἰκόνα, τὸν ἄγγελον
αὐτοῦ λόγον.

[47]E.g. Leg. All. III,117; Fug. 5; Cher. 3 etc.

to λόγος however many reservations accompany it.

The conclusion is that in the Philonic corpus there are numerous references to the theophanies made to Jacob, and that in those references the agent is the Logos, identified with ἄγγελος and θεός. The suggestion then that in Justin's Dial. 58 one might detect elements of Philonic provenance is well founded.

3. A particular element that shows up in Dial. 57 and 58 will strengthen the above suggestion. Justin in Dial. 57,3 puts in the mouth of Trypho the expression οὗτος ὁ τῷ 'Αβραὰμ ὀφθεὶς θεὸς καὶ ὑπηρέτης ὢν τοῦ ποιητοῦ τῶν ὅλων θεοῦ . . . . The expression is repeated with a certain modification in Dial. 58,3, οὗτος ὁ ὀφθεὶς τοῖς πατριάρχαις λεγόμενος θεὸς . . . ἵνα καὶ ἐκ τούτων ἐπιγνῶτε αὐτὸν ὑπηρετοῦντα τῷ τῶν ὅλων πατρί, immediately before the first theophanic narrative related to Jacob. Attention should be drawn here to the phrases ὑπηρέτης τοῦ ποιητοῦ τῶν ὅλων θεοῦ (57,3), and ὑπηρετεῖν τῷ τῶν ὅλων πατρί (58,3). The word ὑπηρέτης for the second God or Son is used only in Dial. 57,3 and this is the only instance for such a usage not only in Justin but in the New Testament, the Apostolic Fathers, and the Apologists as well.[48] The Septuagint should be excluded as a source of ὑπηρέτης in Dial. 57,3. Philo, however, did make the combination of ὑπηρέτης with λόγος: δίδωσι δὲ [ὁ θεός] λόγῳ χρώμενος ὑπηρέτῃ δωρεῶν ᾧ καὶ τὸν κόσμον εἰργάζετο.[49] But, more importantly, Philo repeated once more the combination. And this time within the context of the theophany made to Jacob at Peniel (Gen. 32,22-31), and by bringing together not only ὑπηρέτης and λόγος but ἄγγελος too: τὸν δὲ 'Ιακὼβ [μετω-

_____

[48]There is one passage in the *Epistle to Diognetus* (VII,2) where the word ὑπηρέτης is mentioned together with ἄγγελος and ἄρχων simply in order to be rejected as a christo-logical term: [ὁ παντοκράτωρ θεός] οὐκ . . . ἀνθρώποις ὑπηρέτην τινὰ πέμψας ἢ ἄγγελον ἢ ἄρχοντα ἢ τινα τῶν διεπόντων τὰ ἐπίγεια . . . ἀλλ' αὐτὸν τὸν τεχνίτην καὶ δημιουργὸν τῶν ὅλων.

[49]Philo, *Deus Imm.*, 57. Cf. also A. L. Williams, *op. cit.*, p. 120, n. 2. G. Archambault, *op. cit.*, Vol. I, p. 268, n. 3.

νόμασεν] ἄγγελος ὑπηρέτης τοῦ θεοῦ λόγος."[50] It seems that the Philonic passage and usage of ὑπηρέτης for λόγος is the best explanation for the ὑπηρέτης of Dial. 57,3.

Justin puts the expression ὑπηρέτης ὢν τοῦ ποιητοῦ τῶν ὅλων θεοῦ in the mouth of Trypho. Justin himself never employs the word with reference to the pre-existing Christ. Instead he utilizes either the infinitive or the participle in the present tense of the verb ὑπηρετεῖν.[51] He does it many times and in almost all of them within the chapters where he deals with the theophanies.[52] The difference between ὑπηρέτης and ὑπηρετεῖν (or ὑπηρετῶν) is pronounced. The noun indicates a status inferior, whereas the verb a function which does not necessarily connote the same degree and type of lowliness. One could suggest that Justin is conscious of the difference and that he consistently prefers the verb to the noun because of his christological presuppositions. Nonetheless the ultimate source of both the verb and the noun seems to be Philo.

4. From the Justinian account of the theophanies made to Jacob two sets of christological formulations emerge: a) The pre-existent Christ is called θεὸς ὑπηρετῶν τῷ τῶν ὅλων πατρί. As I have noted before the expression occurs time and again in Justin's theophanic sections. Our author uses it because it connotes a difference between the Father of all and the Son which Justin deliberately maintains. At the same time the formulation implies a unity. The way in which it is employed in Dial. 58,3 suggests that Justin aims at presenting the theophanic activity of the pre-existing Son as an expression of his "serving" (ὑπηρετεῖν)

---

[50] *Mut. Nom.* 87. "τοῦ θεοῦ" here corresponds to the Justinian τοῦ τῶν ὅλων θεοῦ [or πατρός] because Philo in the passage under discussion calls him ἄτρεπτος and κατὰ τὰ αὐτὰ καὶ ὡσαύτως ἔχων.

[51] The verbal form is coupled with expressions like τῷ ὑπὲρ κόσμον θεῷ (Dial. 60,5) or τῷ πατρικῷ βουλήματι (Dial. 61,1) or τῇ τοῦ πατρὸς βουλῇ (Dial. 125,3) etc.

[52] E.g. Dial. 56,22; 58,3; 60,2,5; 61,1; 125,3; 126,5; 127,4.

the Father of all.[53] (In other instances Justin would say
ὑπηρετεῖν τῷ πατρικῷ βουλήματι [Dial. 61,1] or θελήσει or
βουλῇ [Dial. 60,2].)

b) The second set of formulations has as a
common denominator the usage of various appellations for the
pre-existent Christ: θεὸς καὶ ἄγγελος καὶ κύριος λέγεται
(Dial. 58,3; also 58,10). This set of formulations with
reference to the pre-existent Son has been utilized by Justin
frequently. It has enabled him to increase infinitely the
cases where he could find the pre-existing Christ behind a
designation like ἄγγελος κύριος, θεὸς within the scriptural
theophanic passages.

D. *The Theophany of the Burning Bush*

1. Justin's exposition of the theophany of the
burning bush (Ex. 3,1-4,17) covers chapters 59 and 60 of the
Dialogue, and in addition it is sporadically mentioned in
Dial. 126 and 127. It is the only theophany discussed by
Justin in his First Apology (chs. 62 and 63).

The argument in Dial. 59-60[54] develops initially on
the premise that the identity of names used for God who
appeared to Abraham, Jacob, and Moses involves the same God
in all cases, namely the Son. Trypho, however, insists that
in the theophany of the burning bush there were two persons:
an angel and God.[55] Justin replies that even if we grant

---

[53]In Dial. 125,3 where Justin speaks again about the
theophany made to Jacob at Peniel (Gen. 32,22-31), he
explicitly defines the theophanic appearance of Christ as an
act of obedient service to the will and decision of the Father:
φαινομένου μέν [Χριστοῦ] ἐκ τοῦ τῇ τοῦ πατρὸς βουλῇ
ὑπηρετεῖν.

[54]The scriptural text in Dial. 59 is apparently not
quoted in its full extent by the copyist (cf. B. Kominiak,
op. cit., p. 49). In all probability the copyist is also
responsible for the reading 'Αβραὰμ καὶ 'Ισαὰκ instead of the
correct 'Αβραὰμ καὶ 'Ιακώβ (see A. L. Williams, *op. cit.*,
p. 123, n. 2).

[55]For a rabbinical interpretation similar to Trypho's
(in Dial. 60,1) see A. H. Goldfahn, *op. cit.*, p. 114. Cf.
W. Shotwell, *op. cit.*, p. 75.

74

Trypho's interpretation, God in the burning bush was not the
Father of all who is transcendent, but the One τῇ τοῦ ποιητοῦ
τῶν ὅλων θελήσει ὑπηρετῶν (Dial. 60,2). He then proceeds to
show that actually in the burning bush there was only one
agent, namely the Son, who is called both θεός and ἄγγελος in
Ex. 3,1-4,17, exactly as he is called in some of the theophanies made to Jacob.

The presentation of the theophany of the burning bush
in Ap. 62-63 is entirely different. Justin takes for granted
and simply states that God who appeared to Moses was Christ,[56]
Son of God and Logos and God himself, and who is called also
angel and apostle because he announces the things that should
be known and because he is sent in order to make the announce-
ments.[57] The presentation is interspersed with accusations
against the Jews, who maintain that in the burning bush it
was the Father of all, who appeared, and who by their
insistence prove themselves to be ignorant not only of the
Son of God but of the Father of all, as well.[58] Evidently
Justin in both accounts of the theophany to Moses exhibits
the same eagerness to establish as a fact the appearance of
only one divine agent and to identify him with the Logos or
Son or Christ.

2. The Philonic writings provide an eloquent parallel.
In *Vit. Mos.* I, 66 Philo, describing the theophany of the
burning bush, says that κατὰ δὲ μέσην τὴν φλόγα μορφή τις ἦν
περικαλλεστάτη, τῶν ὁρατῶν ἐμφερὴς οὐδενί, θεοειδέστατον
ἄγαλμα, φῶς αὐγοειδέστατον τοῦ πυρὸς ἀπαστράπτουσα, ἥν ἄν τις
ὑπετόπησεν εἰκόνα τοῦ ὄντος εἶναι· καλείσθω δὲ ἄγγελος ὅτι
τὰ μέλλοντα γενήσεσθαι διήγγελλε. The terminology used here
does not leave any doubt that the agent of the theophany is
the Logos. Philo in more than one passage has shown that by

----

[56]Ap. 62,3: ἐν ἰδέᾳ πυρὸς ἐκ βάτου προσωμίλησεν αὐτῷ
[Μωυσεῖ] ὁ ἡμέτερος Χριστός.

[57]Ap. 63,4-5: ὁ λόγος δὲ τοῦ θεοῦ ἐστιν ὁ υἱὸς
αὐτοῦ ὡς προέφημεν. Καὶ ἄγγελος δὲ καλεῖται καὶ ἀπόστολος.
Αὐτὸς γὰρ ἀπαγγέλλει ὅσα δεῖ γνωσθῆναι, καὶ στέλλεται μηνύσων
ὅσα ἀγγέλλεται.

[58]Cf. Ap. 63,1,11,14-15.

εἰκὼν τοῦ ὄντος he means the Logos.[59] Philo commenting upon the theophany to Jacob at Haran (Gen. 31,13), characteristically couples the expression εἰκὼν τοῦ θεοῦ (variant of εἰκὼν τοῦ ὄντος) with the designation ἄγγελος but this time he adds also λόγος: τὴν τοῦ θεοῦ εἰκόνα τὸν ἄγγελον αὐτοῦ λόγον."[60]
In Pseudo-Ezekiel's *Exagoge* cited by Philo[61] there is the interesting verse [Μωυσῆ] ὁ δ᾽ ἐκ βάτου σοι θεῖος ἐκλάμπει λόγος. If the quotation is genuinely Philonic we have here an added indication of Philo's understanding of the theophany of the burning bush. One then is allowed to speak of Philonic traces in Justin's Ap. 62-63, and Dial. 59-60.[62]

There is perhaps additional evidence for such an assumption. It pertains to another substantial ingredient of Justin's demonstration, namely his concept of the transcendence of God in the interpretation of the theophanies in general, and in the incident of the burning bush in particular. When Justin in Dial. 60,2 makes the concession to Trypho--temporarily to be sure--that in the theophany of the burning bush there might have been two agents, viz. God and an angel, he insists that God the Father of all should be definitely excluded as an agent. Because οὐ τὸν ποιητὴν τῶν ὅλων καὶ πατέρα καταλιπόντα τὰ ὑπὲρ οὐρανὸν ἅπαντα ἐν ὀλίγῳ γῆς μορίῳ

---

[59]E.g. *Spec. Leg.* I, 81: κατὰ τὴν εἰκόνα τοῦ ὄντος· λόγος δ᾽ ἐστὶν εἰκὼν θεοῦ. *Conf. Ling.* 97: ἐφίεσθαι μὲν τοῦτο τὸ ὂν ἰδεῖν εἰ δὲ μὴ δύναιντο, τὴν γοῦν εἰκόνα αὐτοῦ, τὸν ἱερώτατον λόγον.

[60]Philo, *Som.* I, 238-9.

[61]It is Eusebius (*Praep. Ev.* IX, 30) who quotes Philo. We cannot be sure whether or not the quotation is genuinely Philonic. Goodenough, *op. cit.*, p. 144, who cites the passage, apparently takes it as authentic.

[62]One could even notice similarities in vocabulary as the following comparisons show:

Philo *Vit. Mos.* I, 68	Justin *Dial. 60,3*
καλείσθω δὲ	ὃς καὶ ἄγγελος
ἄγγελος	καλεῖται
ὅτι . . . διήγγελλε	ἐκ τοῦ διαγγέλλειν
Vit. Mos. I, 68	Ap. *63,16*
κατὰ δὲ μέσην τὴν φλόγα	διὰ τῆς τοῦ πυρὸς
μορφή τις ἦν	μορφῆς
. . . εἰκόνα	καὶ εἰκόνος
τοῦ ὄντος	ἀσωμάτου

πεφάνθαι πᾶς ὁστισοῦν, κἄν μικρὸν νοῦν ἔχων τολμήσει εἰπεῖν.
Justin's argument interprets transcendence in terms of space
and movement. Philo too has presented a similar interpretation in dealing with the theophany on Mt. Sinai. He says:
"What is the meaning of the words," and "the glory of God come
down upon Mt. Sinai? (Scripture) clearly puts to shame those
who whether through impiety or through foolishness believe
that there are movements of place or of change in the
Deity."[63] One could detect some further points of contact
between the Philonic passage just quoted and Dial. 60,2. One
could suggest, for example, that the Justinian τολμήσει εἰπεῖν
echoes the "impiety" (or ἀσέβεια) and the μικρὸν νοῦν ἔχων
reflects the "foolishness" (or ἠλιθιότης) referred to in the
above Philonic passage. In another passage Philo returns to
the same notion of God's transcendence but this time the λόγος
is also brought into the picture: "and holy and divine is
this place alone in which He [i.e. God] is said to appear,
for he himself does not go away or change his position but
he sends the powers which are indicative of his essence. And
if it is right (to say so, we may) say that this place is that
of his Logos, since he [i.e. God] has never given a suspicion
of movement but of always standing etc."[64] Certainly Philo's
understanding of transcendence is centered around the concept
of the unchangeable nature of God,[65] but in his exposition he
does not refrain from utilizing language rich in spatial

---

[63]Philo, *Questions and Answers on Exodus*, trans. from
the ancient Armenian version of the original Greek by R.
Marcus, Suppl. II in Loeb edition of Philo, Book II, No. 45
(p. 89). R. Marcus (*ibid.*) quotes also the Greek fragment
from the Catenae which reads: ἐναργέστατα δυσωπεῖ τοὺς ἐγγὺς
ὑπὸ ἀσεβείας εἴτε ἠλιθιότητος οἰομένους τοπικὰς καὶ μεταβατικὰς κινήσεις εἶναι περὶ τὸ θεῖον.

[64]Philo, *Quest. and Answ. on Exodus*, Book II, No. 37
(p. 78 f.).

[65]Philo, *Quest. and Answ. on Exodus*, Book,II, No. 37
(p. 79): "Now he has represented the unchanged and immutable
nature of God. . . ."

categories.[66]

3. One cannot refute easily the assumption that there are Philonic traces discernible in Dial. 59-60, and Ap. 62-63. On the other hand Ap. 63 shows that some concepts of a different origin and nature are at work in the Justinian texts under discussion.[67] Justin, after presenting briefly the theophany of the burning bush (Ap. 63,7-9), says (v. 10), that all those things have been written in order to be evidence that υἱὸς τοῦ θεοῦ καὶ ἀπόστολος ᾿Ιησοῦς ὁ Χριστός ἐστι, πρότερον λόγος ὤν, καὶ ἐν ἰδέᾳ πυρὸς ποτὲ φανείς, ποτὲ δὲ καὶ ἐν εἰκόνι ἀσωμάτῳ· νῦν δὲ ὑπὲρ τοῦ ἀνθρωπείου γένους ἄνθρωπος γενόμενος ὑπέμεινε καὶ παθεῖν.

The emphasis seems to be shifting from pre-existence to incarnation. The two phases are marked by the pair of adverbs πρότερον-νῦν. The introduction of the incarnation is not accidental. A few lines later (Ap. 63,15-16) Justin makes again the same combination of pre-existence and incarnation on the occasion of the burning bush incident.[68] This time the statements are more elaborate and the ending soteriologically oriented.[69]

The introduction of the developed christological statements in Ap. 63,10 and 63,15-16 does not seem abrupt, and the incarnational part of them comes in natural sequence

---

[66]For example in the Philonic passages just cited we encounter the expressions τοπικὰς καὶ μεταβατικὰς κινήσεις εἶναι περὶ τὸ θεῖον or "He [i.e. God] does not go away or change His position," etc.

[67]But note in the opening sentence of Ap. 63 ᾿Ιουδαῖοι . . . διδάσκουσι τὸν ἀνωνόμαστον θεὸν λελαληκέναι τῷ Μωυσεῖ, the term ἀνωνόμαστος. Daniélou, *op. cit.*, p. 300, reports that this term was applied to God for the first time by Philo.

[68]Dial. 63,15: ὃς [υἱός] καὶ λόγος πρωτότοκος ὤν τοῦ θεοῦ καὶ θεὸς ὑπάρχει. Καὶ πρότερονδιὰ τῆς τοῦ πυρὸς μορφῆς καὶ εἰκόνος ἀσωμάτου τῷ Μωυσεῖ καὶ τοῖς ἑτέροις προφήταις ἐφάνη· νῦν δέ . . . διὰ παρθένου ἄνθρωπος γενόμενος κατὰ τὴν τοῦ πατρὸς βουλὴν ὑπὲρ σωτηρίας τῶν πιστευόντων αὐτῷ καὶ ἐξουθενηθῆναι καὶ παθεῖν ὑπέμεινε ἵνα ἀποθανὼν καὶ ἀναστὰς νικήσῃ τὸν θάνατον.

[69]Cf. K. Bayer, *Justin Philosoph und Märtyrer die erste Apologie* (München, 1966), pp. 136-37.

to the pre-existential one. A closer examination of the two
passages renders plausible the hypothesis that here Justin inserted or added the phrases relevant to the theophany made to
Moses into a christological creedal formulation which he
already knew.[70] As a matter of fact, we encounter in Justin
several passages where the christological formulation resembles
those of Ap. 63,10 and 63,15-16, but where the theophanic
element is missing.[71]

Is the christological model used in Ap. 63,10 and 63,
15-16 related to the humiliation and exaltation Christology?
One might answer in the affirmative, if one takes into account
the fact that Ap. 63,10 and 63,15-16 exhibit a clear-cut pre-
existence and incarnation schema which, as we have seen, could
be a part of the humiliation and exaltation pattern. In Ap.
63,10 and 63,15-16, however, we have more than plain incarnation statements. Here incarnation is directly connected to
suffering and even death (Ap. 63,10: ἄνθρωπος γενόμενος
ὑπέμεινε καὶ παθεῖν; Ap. 63,16: ἄνθρωπος γενόμενος . . . καὶ
ἐξουθενηθῆναι καὶ παθεῖν ὑπέμεινε, ἵνα ἀποθανών . . .). The
terminology has an undeniable nuance of humiliation. Furthermore Ap. 63,16 ends up with an affirmation of resurrection and
victory over death (ἵνα ἀποθανὼν καὶ ἀναστάς [i.e. Christ]
νικήσῃ τὸν θάνατον) which could be viewed as an expression of
exaltation.[72] One then might contend that in Ap. 63,15-16

---

[70]As an example I could cite Ap. 63,10. There the
passage could be ʾΙησοῦς Χριστὸς πρότερον λόγος ὤν [. . .]
νῦν δὲ διὰ θελήματος θεοῦ ὑπὲρ τοῦ ἀνθρωπείου γένους
ἄνθρωπος γενόμενος. The text which I omitted (between the
brackets) might be the special addition on the occasion of the
theophany: καὶ ἐν ἰδέᾳ πυρὸς ποτὲ φανεὶς ποτὲ δὲ καὶ ἐν
εἰκόνι ἀσωμάτῳ.

[71]E.g. Dial. 48,1; 63,1; 100,2. We shall deal with
the whole group of those passages in another section of the
present dissertation.

[72]A corroboration of this assumption is furnished by
Dial. 85,2 which is a statement similar to Ap. 63,16, and
which ends with an explicit exaltation formula: κατὰ γὰρ τοῦ
ὀνόματος αὐτοῦ τούτου τοῦ υἱοῦ τοῦ θεοῦ καὶ πρωτοτόκου πάσης
κτίσεως καὶ διὰ παρθένου γεννηθέντος καὶ παθητοῦ γενομένου
ἀνθρώπου, καὶ σταυρωθέντος . . . καὶ ἀποθανόντος καὶ ἀναστάντος
ἐκ νεκρῶν καὶ ἀναβάντος εἰς τὸν οὐρανόν, πᾶν δαιμόνιον
ἐξορκιζόμενον νικᾶται καὶ ὑποτάσσεται. Cf. also Ap. 31,7;
Ap. 42,4; Ap. 46,5.

Justin works with a humiliation and exaltation christological pattern. One, however, could immediately see how flexible this pattern becomes in Justin's hands and how freely it is used by him in his theological argumentation. In both Ap. 63,10 and Ap. 63,15-16, for instance, Justin includes a soteriological statement by which he makes clear the salvific purpose of incarnation to his pagan readers (Ap. 63,10: ὑπὲρ τοῦ ἀνθρωπείου γένους; Ap. 63,16: ὑπὲρ σωτηρίας τῶν πιστευόντων αὐτῷ). But most importantly, he quotes the theophanic appearance at the burning bush as if it were a part of a creedal statement.

Attention should be drawn to the fact that the theophanic statement of Ap. 63,15-16 is separated from the one which refers to the pre-existence in general. Justin after stating that Christ λόγος πρωτότοκος ὢν τοῦ θεοῦ καὶ θεὸς ὑπάρχει, introduces the theophanic part with the adverb πρότερον followed by the incarnational segment which is introduced by the adverbial νῦν δέ. The structure of the passage implies that the theophanic appearance is paralleled to the incarnation.[73] Thus the theophanic element seems to be related to the pre-existence and to the incarnation of Christ as well. The case of Ap. 63,15-16 (also 63,10) might be indicative of how the language and the concepts of the liturgical-creedal formulations of the humiliation and exaltation passages in the New Testament are transferred into the realm of theological discussion.

4. Before closing the present section we should add that Dial. 59-60 exhibits the same sets of christological formulations which we have met also in Dial. 57-58. The ὑπηρετεῖν formulations occur three more times (Dial. 60,2 twice; 60,5). The formulations containing appellations run repeatedly through Dial. 59-60 (Dial. 59,1; 60,3; 60,4; 60,5), thus constituting a steadily resounding motif. Viewed from

---

[73]As further indication for such a parallelism in Justin one could mention the usage of the verb φαίνεσθαι (in various tenses and modes))for both the Old Testament theophanic appearances of Christ and his incarnation (e.g. Ap. 31,8; 32,9; 63,10; 63,16; App. 10,1; Dial. 49,1; 69,6; 76,1; 113,4; 128,1).

the angle of the two sets of christological formulations Dial.
59-60 is a further addition to Dial. 57-58 utilizing similar
christological terminology.

E. *The Theophany to Joshua*

1. Justin concludes the lengthy section of his
christological exposition of theophanic appearances in the Old
Testament with the theophany to Joshua. He gives the scriptural text of the theophany at the end of Dial. 62 whereas his
own comment and understanding of the event is to be found in
the beginning of the previous chapter which reads: ποτὲ δὲ
ἀρχιστράτηγον ἑαυτὸν λέγει [the Son] ἐν ἀνθρώπου μορφῇ
φανέντα τῷ τοῦ ʾΙησοῦ τοῦ Ναυή."[74]

The biblical text is Josh. 5,13-6,2 which is reproduced almost verbatim in its Septuagint version. Our author
reads 6,1 as an immediate continuation of 5,13 and not as the
inception of a new section. Thus he assumes that ἄνθρωπος
(5,13), ἀρχιστράτηγος (5,14), and κύριος (6,2) are appellations
of one and the same person, who is the second God. The implicit reasoning apparently suggested by the context of Dial.
61,1[75] is the one we already know: ἄνθρωπος-ἀρχιστράτηγος
is equated to κύριος of the theophany to Joshua, a fact which
approximates this theophany to the others where the designations ἄνθρωπος and κύριος have been used. Consequently, God
appearing to Joshua according to Josh. 5,13-6,2 must be the
same God who revealed himself to Abraham, Jacob, Moses and
others, according to the theophanic appearances mentioned
previously. The inclusion of the theophany to Joshua into the
group of theophanic texts by Justin might be the result of his
intention to strengthen his whole argument by one additional
event connected with a great figure of Israelite history, and

---

[74]Dial. 61,1. Between the comment of Dial. 61,1
and the text of the theophany in Dial. 62,5 Justin inserts the
wisdom hymn of Prov. 8,21-36 and the passages Gen. 1,26-28
and 3,22 as witnesses of the eternal pre-existence of the Son
before the creation of the universe.

[75]Also Dial. 34,2 follows a similar pattern.

to increase the biblical designations for Christ by
ἀρχιστράτηγος.[76]

2. In the case of the theophany to Joshua Philo ought
to be excluded either as a stimulus or as a source for
Justin.[77] Philo does not mention it at all. His interpreta-
tions are restricted to the Pentateuch (at least as far as
they are preserved).

Prior to Justin, the *Epistle of Barnabas*[78] by combining
the Septuagint texts Nu. 13,16-17 and Ex. 17,14-16 and by
changing them--or by using a particular version which we do
not know[79]--presented the first elaborate christological interpretation, on a typological basis, of the figure of Joshua.[80]
The passage from Barnabas is significant from another point of
view. It concludes with a quotation of the christological
Ps. 109,1 (LXX) εἶπεν ὁ κύριος τῷ κυρίῳ μου, and it is preceded by an enumeration of events from the history of Israel
in the desert, in which the cross of Christ is typologically

---

[76]For the christological usage of the term ἀρχιστράτηγος within the early Christian tradition, see P. Beskow, *op.
cit.*, pp. 265-66.

[77]Apart from the theophany made to Joshua there is
perhaps an element of Philonic origin in Dial. 62. Justin
says in Dial. 62,3 that the human body was created by angels,
according to the Jewish teachers. W. Shotwell (*op. cit.*, p.
75), who quotes the passage reports that "Philo is the only
Jewish writer whose works are preserved who seems to hold to
the idea that the angels aided in the creation of man (*Fug.* 13;
Op. Mund. 24). Cf. also A. L. Williams, *op. cit.*, p. 129,
n. 4.

[78]*Barn.* XII, 8-10: τὶ λέγει πάλιν Μωυσῆς 'Ιησοῦ υἱῷ
Ναυή, ἐπιθεὶς αὐτῷ τοῦτο τὸ ὄνομα . . . ἵνα μόνον ἀκούσῃ πᾶς
ὁ λαὸς ὅτι ὁ πατὴρ πάντα φανεροῖ περὶ τοῦ υἱοῦ 'Ιησοῦ; . . .
῎Ιδε πάλιν 'Ιησοῦς, οὐχὶ υἱὸς ἀνθρώπου ἀλλὰ υἱὸς τοῦ θεοῦ,
τύπῳ δὲ ἐν σαρκὶ φανερωθείς.

[79]Note, e.g., the insertion of the phrase ὁ υἱὸς τοῦ
θεοῦ after the word 'Αμαλήκ. The whole christological interpretation of the passage depends absolutely upon the inserted
words.

[80]Philo had already paved the way for an allegorical
or typological interpretation of Joshua's changing of name.
Mut. Nom. 121 reads: ἀλλὰ καὶ τὸν 'Ωσηὲ μετονομάζει Μωυσῆς
εἰς τὸν 'Ιησοῦν [Nu. 13,16] . . . 'Ωσηὲ μὲν ἑρμηνεύεται ποιὸς
οὗτος, 'Ιησοῦς δὲ σωτηρία κυρίου.

82

prefigured. It is likely that Justin knew Barnabas' text or the tradition to which it belongs.[81] This possibility is strengthened by traces of resemblance between Dial. 91,3-4 and Barnabas XII 2-3, 5-7, 8-10 where three biblical events are combined in a chain of typological christological exegesis. Besides, the name of Joshua and some incidents of his life susceptible to christological typological interpretation could have attracted the attention of Justin, as it becomes conspicuous in passages like Dial. 90,4 or 131,4-5.

An example of how Justin could utilize christologically the name or the person of Joshua is encountered in Dial. 75,1-2 where he argues that the angel of Exod. 23,20 is Joshua, because he led the Israelites into the promised land, and that finally the person intended by the passage is Jesus.[82] Justin's interpretation is unusual because, as we know, the initial phrase of Ex. 23,20 ἰδοὺ ἐγὼ ἀποστέλλω τὸν ἄγγελόν μου πρὸ προσώπου σου is a standard reference for John the Baptist by the synoptic tradition.[83] Justin, although having a knowledge of the synoptic tradition and speaking extensively about John as forerunner of Christ (Dial. 59-61), paradoxically never uses the passage Ex. 23,20 for John. He employs it exclusively for Joshua. Philo could be responsible for Justin's interpretation, because in two instances where he mentions Ex. 23,20, he understands by ἄγγελος the λόγος: προστησάμενος τὸν ὀρθὸν αὐτοῦ λόγον καὶ πρωτόγονον υἱόν . . . καὶ γὰρ εἴρηταί που ἰδοὺ ἐγώ . . . ."[84] Justin could have an acquaintance with this kind of interpretation, since he prefers it to the standard one (i.e. ἄγγελος = John the Baptist).

---

[81]According to P. Prigent this was a christian midrashic tradition, a suggestion which is not unfounded (P. Prigent, *L'Epître de Barnabé*, pp. 122-23, 126).

[82]Dial. 75,1: ʼΕν δὲ τῷ βιβλίῳ τῆς ʼΕξόδου, ὅτι αὐτοῦ τὸ ὄνομα τοῦ θεοῦ ʼΙησοῦς ἦν . . . διὰ Μωυσέως ἐν μυστηρίῳ ὁμοίως ἐξηγγέλθη.

[83]Cf. Mt. 11,10; Mk. 1,2; Lk. 7,27.

[84]Philo, *Agric* 51. Cf. *Migr. Abr.* 174: ἡγεμόνι θείῳ λόγῳ· χρησμὸς γάρ ἐστιν· ἰδοὺ ἀποστέλλω τὸν ἄγγελόν μου πρὸ προσώπου σου.

One might, however, raise the objection that in commenting on
Ex. 23,20 Philo speaks about λόγος whereas Justin speaks
about Joshua. The truth is that Justin in Dial. 75,1-2
through Joshua clearly points to Christ the Logos. Nonetheless, the introduction of the person of Joshua into the interpretation of Ex. 23,20 seems to be Justin's own contribution.

This example, as well as the frequent mentioning of
Joshua by Justin within various christological contexts (e.g.
Dial. 49,6; 89,1; 90,4; 91,3; 111,4; 113,2; 115,4,5; 131,5),
shows that our author is acquainted with a variety of exegetical traditions related to Joshua. This acquaintance could
also account for his christological understanding of the
theophany to Joshua.

3. The christological formulation, in which the
theophany to Joshua is mentioned, contains a new component:
the begetting of the Son by the Father. Otherwise Justin's
statement in Dial. 61,1 follows the pattern which we know
from Dial. 56,4; 58,3; 59,1 et al., namely the name-designation
type.

The formulations referring to the begetting of the Son
are due to the fact that in Dial. 61 Justin quotes the whole
wisdom hymn from Proverbs 8,21-36. The cropping up of Prov.
8,21-36 and of some other non-theophanic texts in Dial. 61,3
through 62,4 is a problem which we shall study shortly.
Attention should presently be drawn to Justin's assumption
encountered in Dial. 61,1 that the appellations for the Son
derive from both his ministering to the Father's purposeful
will and his having been born of the Father: "ἔχει γὰρ πάντα
προσονομάζεσθαι ἔκ τε τοῦ ὑπηρετεῖν τῷ πατρικῷ βουλήματι καὶ
τοῦ ἀπὸ τοῦ πατρὸς θελήσει γεγεννῆσθαι." The whole formulation in Dial. 61,1 balances the emphasized distance between
the Father and the Son by connecting the pre-existing Son's
attribute of having been begotten by the Father with his function of ministering to the Father. The distance has been
stressed because in Dial. 56-60 pre-existence is mostly understood in terms of theophanic function of the Son over against
the absolute transcendence of the Father. Now Dial. 61,1
emphasizes the pre-existence in terms of ontology, and thus
the distance is reduced.

The fact should not pass unnoticed that immediately after the end of the biblical narration of the theophany to Joshua, Justin introduces a christological statement of the humiliation and exaltation type: οὗτος [i.e. the pre-existing Son] διὰ τῆς παρθένου ἄνθρωπος γεννηθῆναι . . . καὶ σταυρωθῆναι καὶ ἀποθανεῖν· δῆλον δὲ καὶ ὅτι μετὰ ταῦτα ἀναστὰς ἀνελήλυθεν εἰς τὸν οὐρανόν (Dial. 63,1). The statement is introduced by Trypho, but actually expresses Justin's belief.

One could argue that Dial. 63,1 serves as point of connection and/or transition between the theophanic section (Dial. 56-62) and what follows. What follows in Dial. 63, nonetheless, does not require the fully developed christological formulation of Dial. 63,1. The presence of such a formulation could better be explained through the assumption that Justin thinks basically within the frame of a humiliation and exaltation pattern, and that he does not lose sight of this pattern even when he is dealing with particular christological aspects.

F. *Final Remarks*

1. From the analysis presented in the preceding pages it is evident that in Dial. 56-62, 125-29 and Ap. 62-63 Justin works with diversified material which could be classified into four categories:

(a) Old Testament theophanic narratives (basically Gen. 18-19; Gen. 28,31,32,35; Ex. 3; Josh. 5,13-6,5) in elaborate form (Dial. 56-62) or in brief selected citations (Dial. 125-29 and Ap. 62-63).

(b) Special psalmic verses of the type Ps. 109,1 (LXX) or Ps. 44,7-8 (LXX), and special passages like Prov. 8,21-36 or Gen. 1,26-28 and 3,22 (Dial. 56,14; 61,3-62,3 and D. 129,2), already established as christological proof texts.

(c) Texts where the appellation type is the key christological feature (Dial. 61,1; 126,1).

(d) Christological formulae of a creedal nature (Ap. 63,10,16; also Dial. 38,1).

Not only the material but also the interpretative ideas and the concepts used in the Justinian theophanic texts are as well differentiated, particularly as far as their

origin is concerned. We have had the opportunity to indicate
the precise points where the source of a concept or of an
interpretation might be Philo. We have seen, on the other
hand, how scriptural texts connected with the humiliation and
exaltation Christology (e.g. Ps. 109,1 [LXX]; Ps. 44,7-8 [LXX]
etc.) might have been instrumental in Justin's christological
understanding of the Old Testament theophanies.

Nevertheless, in spite of the diversity of the
material both in form and content, the picture that emerges
from Dial. 56-62,125-129 and Ap. 62-63 is a picture of a
coherent christological interpretation of the theophanies.
That interpretation seems to be Justin's own achievement.

2. Justin's center of interest in his dealing with
the Old Testament theophanies is different from Philo's. The
Apologist does not try to understand and explain the theophanic
events in themselves. When he introduces the patriarchal
theophanies in his dispute with Trypho his purpose is to bring
scriptural evidence for the existence of another God besides
the Father and Maker of all. Hence he adduces as complementary
evidence passages parallel to them like Ps. 109,1 (LXX), Prov.
8,21-36 or Gen. 1,26-28 and 3,22.[85] The common denominator of
all those texts is the explicit or implicit mentioning of a
second divine person. A few decades later, Irenaeus in his
Adv. Haer. III, 6,1, where he follows Justin's theophanic
section very closely,[86] quotes and comments in a series the
passages Ps. 109,1 (LXX), Gen. 19,24 and Ps. 44,7-8 (LXX),
as if they belong to one and the same category. Obviously
Irenaeus understood correctly Justin's intentions in Dial.
56-62.

---

[85]It is worth mentioning that Philo, in interpreting
Gen. 1,26 and 3,22, suggests a plurality of subjects behind
the verb ποιήσωμεν and the expression ὡς εἲς ἡμῶν (*Conf. Ling.*
168-69). He further explains that these are God and his
powers. Cf. G. Archambault, *op. cit.*, Vol. II, pp. 260-61.
W. Shotwell, *op. cit.*, pp. 94-95, quotes some additional
passages from Philo.

[86]For the dependence of Irenaeus' *Adv. Haer.* III, 6,1
on Justin's Dial. 56-62 see P. Prigent, *Justin et l'Ancien
Testament*, pp. 127-133. Cf. also P. Beskow, *op. cit.*, p. 85.

3. In his effort to demonstrate that in the theophanies Scripture speaks of the Son as God besides God the Father, Justin abides firmly by a fundamental presupposition: the absolute transcendence of the Father. Dialogue 60,2 shows that Justin would not make any compromise on that subject. The paramount importance ascribed by the Apologist to the principle of the transcendence of God is constantly revealed in Dial. 56-62 and 125-129.[87] In Dial. 127 Justin presents a rather elaborate statement of that same tenet. The statement runs through verses 2 to 4. One could perhaps find parallels for the various parts of Dial. 127,2-4,[88] but not for the whole passage which is clearly composite[89] and is almost totally geared to biblical texts. What transpires in Dial. 127 is a concept of transcendence formulated to exclude anthropomorphic notions[90] and suggestions of spatial movement; in addition, transcendence in Dial. 127 is also viewed from the angle of human weakness to withstand the appearance of God, but the concept is couched in language of biblical events not of abstract philosophical tenets. Generally the text Dial. 127 is biblically oriented.[91]

---

[87]Cf. Dial. 56,1; 60,2,3; 127,1-5; Ap. 63,14 etc.

[88]Cf. Dial. 127,2 καὶ πάντα ἐφορᾷ καὶ πάντα γινώσκει καὶ οὐδεὶς ἡμῶν λέληθεν αὐτό to Philo, Jos. 265 ὃς ἐφορᾷ πάντα καὶ πάντων ἐπακούει . . . τὸν ἀεὶ βλέποντα καὶ τὰ ἐν μυχοῖς τῆς διανοίας. The first part of the Philonic passage comes from Homer's Od. A 109, M323.

[89]A. L. Williams, op. cit., p. 263, says that "the commentators refer to Origen Contra Celsum IV, 5 for a fuller statement of the argument." The comment could be misleading. Origen's statement is parallel to Justin's in only one point and even there the terminology is different.

[90]Cf. Dial. 114,3 where anti-anthropomorphism is in the form of a reductio ad absurdum: . . . οἰόμενοι χεῖρας καὶ πόδας καὶ δακτύλους καὶ ψυχὴν ἔχειν ὡς σύνθετον ζῷον τὸν πατέρα τῶν ὅλων καὶ ἀγέννητον θεόν, οἵτινες καὶ διὰ τοῦτο ὦφθαι τῷ Ἀβραὰμ καὶ τῷ Ἰακὼβ αὐτὸν τὸν πατέρα διδάσκουσι.

[91]Cf. Dial. 127,5 ἐὰν μὴ οὕτω νοήσωμεν τὰς γραφὰς etc. Cf. also Dial. 55,3: προσέχετε τοιγαροῦν οἷσπερ μέλλω ἀναμιμνήσκειν ἀπὸ τῶν ἁγίων γραφῶν, οὐδὲ ἐξηγηθῆναι δεομένων ἀλλὰ μόνον ἀκουσθῆναι; Dial. 58,1: γραφὰς ὑμῖν ἀνιστορεῖν μέλλω, οὐ κατασκευὴν λόγων ἐν μόνῃ τέχνῃ ἐπιδεικνυσθαι σπεύδω· οὐδὲ γὰρ δύναμις ἐμοὶ τοιαύτη τις ἐστιν, ἀλλὰ χάρις παρὰ θεοῦ μόνη εἰς τὸ συνιέναι τὰς γραφὰς αὐτοῦ ἐδόθη μοι.

The concept of the transcendence of the Father of all, consistently maintained by Justin, creates an impasse for any interpretation of the appearances of God in Old Testament other than christological.[92]

Christ is confessed as God, but he is God ὑπηρετῶν τῷ ὑπὲρ κόσμον θεῷ (Dial. 60,5), and ἀπὸ τοῦ πατρὸς θελήσει γεγεννῆσθαι (Dial. 61,1). The Son does not have the transcendence which the Father has, hence he is in a position to appear and converse in visible forms during the various Old Testament theophanies. But then how can he be God unreservedly? The dilemma is inescapable: either the Son is God like the Father, equally transcendent, and thus he should also be excluded as an agent of the theophanies; or if he is the agent who appeared in the theophanies he cannot be God like the Father. However Justin apparently does not face that dilemma.[93] He retains the contradictory formulations and he is not tired of constantly repeating them.[94]

An explanation of such an attitude could be that Justin views transcendence as a particular attribute of God as Father, not merely as God. In that case absolute transcendence would be on a par with the ἄρρητον, ἀγέννητον and the like of the Father of all, and the Son could be God without necessarily having the absolute transcendence as he neither has the ἀγεννησία.

Nonetheless the problem is there even in a latent way. Already Irenaeus detected it as we could gather from his

---

[92]Cf. Dial. 127,1-4: ὅταν μου ὁ θεὸς λέγει· ἀνέβη ὁ θεὸς ἀπὸ ᾿Αβραὰμ ἤ ἐλάλησε κύριος πρὸς Μωυσῆν καὶ κατέβη κύριος τὸν πύργον ἰδεῖν ὃν ᾠκοδόμησαν οἱ υἱοὶ τῶν ἀνθρώπων ἤ ὅτε ἔκλεισεν ὁ θεὸς τὴν κιβωτὸν Νῶε ἔξωθεν μὴ ἡγεῖσθε αὐτὸν τὸν ἀγέννητον θεὸν καταβεβηκέναι ἤ ἀναβεβηκέναι ποθέν . . . ἀλλ᾿ ἐκεῖνον τὸν κατὰ τὴν βουλὴν τὴν ἐκείνου καὶ θεὸν ὄντα, υἱὸν αὐτοῦ.

[93]Cf. a similar attitude a few years later in Theophilus of Antioch. In his *Autol.* II, 22 when commenting on Gen. 3,8 he says: Σὺ φῂς τὸν θεὸν ἐν τόπῳ μὴ δεῖν χωρεῖσθαι καὶ πῶς νῦν λέγεις αὐτὸν ἐν τῷ παραδείσῳ περιπατεῖν; . . . ῾Ο μὲν θεὸς καὶ πατὴρ τῶν ὅλων ἀχώρητος ἐστὶν καὶ ἐν τόπῳ οὐχ εὑρίσκεται . . . ὁ δὲ λόγος αὐτοῦ οὗτος παρεγίνετο εἰς τὸν παράδεισον ἐν προσώπῳ τοῦ θεοῦ καὶ ὡμίλει τῷ ᾿Αδάμ.

[94]Cf. Dial. 56,1,4,10,11; 57,3; 60,2,3,5; 127,1-5; 129,1-4.

Demonstration of the Apostolic Preaching, ch. 47. In that text, which belongs to a cluster of chapters (43-49) heavily influenced by Justin's theophanic sections,[95] Irenaeus says: "So then the Father is Lord and the Son is Lord, and the Father is God and the Son is God; for that which is begotten of God is God. And so in the substance and power of His being there is shown forth one God; but there is also according to the economy of our redemption both Son and Father. Because to created things the Father of all is invisible and unapproachable, therefore those who are to draw near to God must have their access to the Father through the Son."[96] One might assume that here Irenaeus modifies the Justinian statements in an attempt to eliminate the contradiction inherent in them or, at least, make it less pronounced. For example the transcendence of the Father is retained but it is not presented with reference to the Son. It is rather related to human weakness and to soteriology. On the other hand the distance between the Father and the Son is drastically reduced by the emphasis on the oneness of God. Note, for instance, the phrase "he is . . . both Son and Father."

4. During the exploration into the theophanic passages of the Dialogue and the First Apology we have found instances in which the formulation could belong to a humiliation and exaltation Christology:

Dial. 57,3: . . . πῶς οὗτος ὁ τῷ ᾿Αβραὰμ ὀφθεὶς θεός . . . διὰ τῆς παρθένου γεννηθείς, ἄνθρωπος ὁμοιοπαθὴς πᾶσιν . . . γέγονεν.

---

[95] For details pertaining to the textual relationship between Irenaeus' *Demonstration* 43-50 and Justin's Dialogue 56-62 and 125-129 see P. Prigent, *Justin et l'Ancient Testament*, pp. 127-33. For further relationship between Justin and Irenaeus see W. Bousset, *Jüdisch-Christlicher Schulbetrieb*, pp. 304-07; N. Brox, Zum literarischen Verhältniss zwischen Justin und Irenäus, *ZNW* 58 (1957), 121-28.

[96] St. Irenaeus, *The Demonstration of the Apostolic Preaching*, translated from the Armenian by J. A. Robinson (London, 1920), p. 112. I have checked the accuracy of the English translation with the help of the French one done by L. M. Froidevaux (Sources Chrétiennes, Paris, 1959).

Dial. 63,1: οὗτος [ὃς πρὸ πάντων τῶν ποιημάτων συνῆν τῷ πατρί: Dial. 62,4] διὰ τῆς παρθένου ἄνθρωπος γεννηθῆναι . . . καὶ σταυρωθῆναι καὶ ἀποθανεῖν· δῆλον δὲ καὶ ὅτι μετὰ ταῦτα ἀναστὰς ἀνελήλυθεν εἰς τὸν οὐρανόν.

Ap. 63,10: υἱὸς θεοῦ καὶ ἀπόστολος 'Ιησοῦς ὁ Χριστός ἐστι, πρότερον λόγος ὤν, καὶ ἐν ἰδέᾳ πυρὸς ποτὲ φανείς . . . νῦν δέ . . . ἄνθρωπος γενόμενος ὑπέμεινε καὶ παθεῖν.

Ap. 63,15-16: ὃς καὶ λόγος πρωτότοκος ὤν τοῦ θεοῦ καὶ θεὸς ὑπάρχει. Καὶ πρότερον διὰ τῆς τοῦ πυρὸς μορφῆς καὶ εἰκόνος ἀσωμάτου τῷ Μωυσεῖ . . . ἐφάνη· νῦν δέ . . . διὰ παρθένου ἄνθρωπος γενόμενος . . . ὑπὲρ σωτηρίας τῶν πιστευόντων αὐτῷ καὶ ἐξουθενηθῆναι καὶ παθεῖν ὑπέμεινε, ἵνα ἀποθανὼν καὶ ἀναστὰς νικήσῃ τὸν θάνατον.[97]

At this juncture it is fitting to report the instructive case of Dial. 36,5-38,1. Justin in Dial. 36,3-6 rehearses Ps. 23,1-10 (LXX) in connection with Ps. 109,1 (LXX) in order to show that Scripture foretells in detail the exaltation (ascension and enthronement) of Chirst. In Dial. 37,1-4 Justin adds one more Psalm, which contains the exaltation phrase ἀνέβη ὁ θεὸς ἐν ἀλαλαγμῷ (Ps. 46,6-10 [LXX]), and interprets it christologically. Then he quotes Ps. 98.1-9 (LXX) and applies all of its expressions of kingship and lordship to Christ again. This Psalm has a theophanic reference: Μωυσῆς καὶ 'Ααρὼν ἐν τοῖς ἱερεῦσιν αὐτοῦ . . . ἐν στύλῳ νεφέλης ἐλάλει πρὸς αὐτούς (vv. 6-7). Trypho, struck by the implied christological interpretation of the theophanic reference, immediately registers his objection: βλάσφημα γὰρ πολλὰ λέγεις, τὸν σταυρωθέντα τοῦτον ἀξιῶν πείθειν ἡμᾶς γεγεννῆσθαι μετὰ Μωυσέως καὶ 'Ααρὼν καὶ λελαληκέναι αὐτοῖς ἐν στύλῳ νεφέλης, εἶτα ἄνθρωπον γενόμενον σταυρωθῆναι καὶ ἀναβεβηκέναι εἰς τὸν οὐρανόν . . . .[98]

Here the pre-existence of Christ, manifested in a theophanic event, is quoted (1) within a larger context (Dial. 36,2-38,1) of exaltation passages,[99] and (2) as part of a

---

[97]Cf. also Dial. 113,4; 127,4.

[98]Needless to say that Trypho's objection formulates exactly what Justin believes.

[99]P. Beskow, *op. cit.*, pp. 101, 103-06, 129, has

90

formulation which is presumably of the humiliation and
exaltation type.

The passage Dial. 38,1 as well as those cited before
(Dial. 57,3; 63,1; Ap. 63,10; 63,15-16) offer, one could
suggest, enough evidence that in his christological interpretation of the Old Testament theophanies Justin has a humiliation
and exaltation schema in mind. This schema, although in some
cases appearing in its full form, i.e. including a statement
of exaltation, in most instances occurs in a bipartite pattern,
namely as pre-existence and incarnation.

It is this pattern, one might contend, that enables
Justin in his handling of the theophanies, strongly to insist
on his christological interpretation, because through that
pattern Justin ultimately effects a conceptual approximation
of pre-existence (manifested in Old Testament theophanies) and
incarnation.[100] The following cases exemplify such a
suggestion:

(a) In Dial. 127,4 Justin makes the statement with
reference to Christ ὃν καὶ ἄνθρωπον γεννηθῆναι διὰ τῆς
παρθένου βεβούληται [ὁ πατήρ], ὃς καὶ πῦρ ποτε γέγονε τῇ πρὸς
Μωυσέα ὁμιλίᾳ τῇ ἀπὸ τῆς βάτου. There is no doubt that incarnation and theophanic appearance in the burning bush are here
contemplated as belonging to a similar category.

(b) In Apol. 63,16 incarnation and theophanic
appearance are presented as a pair joined by the adverbs
πρότερον-νῦν δέ: Christ πρότερον διὰ τῆς τοῦ πυρὸς μορφῆς καὶ
εἰκόνος ἀσωμάτου τῷ Μωυσεῖ καὶ τοῖς ἑτέροις προφήταις ἐφάνη·
νῦν δέ . . . ἄνθρωπος γενόμενος. The approximation of the
two events is conspicuous.

(c) In Dial. 113,4 we encounter again a simultaneous
contemplation of theophanic appearance and incarnation:

---

demonstrated that Ps. 23,1-10 (LXX), Ps. 46,6-10 (LXX), and
Ps. 109,1 (LXX) are christological exaltation texts, used
frequently by early Christian authors. Ps. 46,6-10 (LXX) in
particular seems to be extensively used for the first time
by Justin (*ibid.*, p. 103).

[100]Cf. H. Chadwick, *op. cit.*, p. 290; J. Danielou, *op.
cit.*, p. 151; C. I. K. Story, *The Nature of Truth in "The
Gospel of Truth" and in the Writings of Justin Martyr*
(Leiden, 1970) pp. 86-87.

Ἰησοῦς ἦν ὁ τῷ Μωυσεῖ καὶ τῷ Ἀβραὰμ καὶ τοῖς ἄλλοις ἁπλῶς
πατριάρχαις φανεὶς καὶ ὁμιλήσας . . . ὃς καὶ ἄνθρωπος γεννηθῆναι διὰ τῆς παρθένου Μαρίας ἦλθε.

(d) Dial. 75,4 offers an example in a reverse way:
εἰ οὖν ἐν τοσαύταις μορφαῖς οἴδαμεν πεφανερῶσθαι τὸν θεὸν
ἐκεῖνον τῷ Ἀβραὰμ καὶ τῷ Ἰακὼβ καὶ τῷ Μωυσεῖ πῶς ἀποροῦμεν
καὶ ἀπιστοῦμεν κατὰ τὴν τοῦ πατρὸς τῶν ὅλων βουλὴν καὶ
ἄνθρωπον αὐτὸν διὰ παρθένου γεννηθῆναι μὴ δεδυνῆσθαι. Here
the theophanies are being used as evidence for the possibility
of the incarnation. Justin, however, could not have conceived
of such an argument had he not moved in the opposite direction
and arrived at the point of considering the Old Testament
theophanies as manifestations comparable to incarnation.

We find an astonishingly clear reworking of Justin's
idea in Tertullian's *Against Praxeas*. Chapters 5 through 16
of that work presuppose a full acquaintance with Justin's
theophanic sections.[101] In chapter 16 Tertullian sums up:
"Filius itaque est qui ab initio judicavit, turrim superbis-
simam elidens, linguasque dispertiens, orbem totum aquarum
violentia puniens, pluens super Sodomam et Gomorrham ignem et
sulphurem Dominus a Domino (Gen. 19,24). Ipse enim et ad
humana semper colloquia descendit, ab Adam usque ad Patriar-
chas et Prophetas, in visione, in somnio, in speculo, in
aenigmate, ordinem suum praestruens ab initio semper, quem
erat persecuturur in finem. Ita semper ediscebat . . . ut
nobis fidem sterneret, ut facilius crederemus Filium Dei
descendisse in saeculum, si et retro tale quid gestum cog-
nosceremus." Tertullian interprets Justin correctly: the
pre-existent Son descends, speaks and acts in Old Testament
theophanies and history in general in a manner similar to his
descending in incarnation ("et retro tale quid gestum").

Through Justin's interpretation of the theophanies,
the pre-existence of Christ embraces the whole realm of Old
Testament history. Christ is not only foretold or typologically prefigured in the Old Testament but he is actually the
God who acts in Old Testament history. He acts in a way which
is considered as an anticipation of his incarnation. Such a

---

[101]For details see P. Prigent, *Justin et l'Ancien
Testament*, pp. 127-32.

concept of the pre-existence of Christ fully manifested in
the theophanies of the Old Testament produces a unifying
effect: there is one and the same God who appears in both the
Old and the New Testament and this is Christ. Justin, on the
basis of his interpretation of the theophanies, does not
hesitate to call Abraham and Isaac and Jacob not "men of God"
but "men of Christ": τὸ δὲ εἰρημένον ἐκ βάτου τῷ Μωυσεῖ,
ἐγὼ εἰμὶ ὁ ὤν, ὁ θεὸς Ἀβραὰμ καὶ ὁ θεὸς Ἰσαὰκ καὶ ὁ θεὸς
Ἰακὼβ καὶ ὁ θεὸς τῶν πατέρων σου, σημαντικὸν τοῦ καὶ
ἀποθανόντας ἐκείνους μένειν καὶ εἶναι αὐτοῦ τοῦ Χριστοῦ
ἀνθρώπους. (Ap. 63,17).

CHAPTER THREE

THE PRE-EXISTING CHRIST AND THE PAGAN WORLD

A. *Introductory Remarks*

1. Justin is the first Christian author to express in
elaborate statements the belief that the pre-existing Christ
had been at work within the pagan world. This pre-incarnation-
al activity of Christ is primarily understood in terms of
illumination in discovering and acquiring the truth concerning
God, and of help in leading a moral and virtuous life. Most
of the pertinent statements occur, as it should be expected,
in the First and the Second Apology. The Justinian passages,
where a reference to the relationship between the pre-existent
Christ and the heathen world is made, could be classified into
four categories:

(a) Texts where there is an explicit connection--if
not an identification--of the pre-existing Christ with the
Λόγος who spoke through or illumined the ancient Greek
philosophers and the pagan people in general: Ap. 5,4 and
46,2-4; App. 8,1-3; 10,1-8; 13,1-6.

(b) Texts where terms like ὀρθὸς λόγος--as a
universal principle--or expressions like ἀλόγως βιοῦν occur
in a context which might suggest a latent reference to the
pre-existing Λόγος in his connection with the heathen; App.
7,7; 9,4; Dial. 141,1. Ap. 12,5; 57,1; 58,2 et al.

(c) Texts in which Justin expounds his theory about
the Greek philosophers borrowing various truths from the
prophets through whom the pre-existing Λόγος spoke: Ap. 44,
9-10; 59,1-5; 60,1-10 et al.

(d) Texts where the demons are the protagonists in
disseminating distorted truth (given by or referring to the
Λόγος) and thus in keeping the pagan people in a condition of

error and sin, and finally in a status of separation from
Λόγος: Ap. 54,1,2,4; App. 9,4; Dial. 69,1ff. et al.

2. Several scholars have argued that the main concept
by means of which Justin was able to bring the pre-existent
Christ within the pagan world is the concept of λόγος and
more specifically, σπερματικὸς λόγος. This concept has been
the object of an intensive exploration. Most of the research-
ers have tried to detect its philosophical background and have
come up with various hypotheses.[1] According to I. M.
Pfaettisch[2] there are only Platonic postulates behind the
σπερματικὸς λόγος theory of Justin, although in the final
stage of formulation one can detect Stoic models at work. For
H. Meyer,[3] on the other hand, the Stoic doctrine of λόγος
σπερματικὸς is the sole and adequate background for Justin's
theory with only the reservation that our author reshaped the
Stoic tenets according to his own intentions. M. Pohlenz[4]
modified Meyer's hypothesis and suggested that Justin did not
work with the general Stoic conception of σπερματικὸς λόγος
but with the specific version of it which identifies λόγος
σπερματικὸς with the concept of *semina virtutum* viz. the moral
disposition of the human soul. On the basis of Pohlenz's
suggestion, C. Andresen was able to take a significant step
forward and propose the thesis that the logos spermatikos as
semina virtutum came to Justin via the Middle-Platonic
philosophers who remodelled the concept and gave to it a

---

[1]For a presentation and critical evaluation of the
various hypotheses up to 1958 see R. Holte, *op. cit.*, pp.
112-16. For additional information as recently as 1964 see
J. H. Waszink, "Bemerkungen zu Justins Lehre vom Logos
spermatikos," in *Mullus* (Festschr. Th. Klausner), (Münster,
1964), pp. 380-90. Cf. also Hyldahl, *op. cit.*, pp. 70-85.

[2]*Der Einfluss Platos auf die Theologie Justins des
Martyrers* (Paderborn, 1910), p. 104.

[3]*Geschichte der Lehre von den Heimkräften von der
Stoa bis zum Ausgang der Patristik* (Bonn, 1914), p. 88. See
also M. Spanneut, *Le Stoicisme des Pères de l'Eglise* (Paris,
1957), pp. 316-20.

[4]*Die Stoa, Geschichte einer geistigen Bewegung,*
Vol. I (Göttingen, 1948), p. 412; Vol. II (Göttingen, 1949),
p. 199.

religious nuance.[5] After Andresen it was R. Holte who advanced the research with his paper on the subject.[6] Holte offers a deeper analysis of the concept of σπερματικὸς λόγος in Justin. He also furnishes a plausible explanation for the co-existence of Justin's theory of σπερματικὸς λόγος with two other theories,[7] viz. the so-called loan-theory (Plato and other philosophers "borrowing" from Moses many truths) and demon-theory (the demons taking from the prophets and presenting in a distorted fashion various prophecies).[8]

3. However, the scholarly work on λόγος σπερματικὸς cannot exhaustively answer the question of how Justin understands the relationship between the pre-existent Christ and the pagan world. From the four categories of passages listed at the beginning of this introduction one could readily see that other important elements are involved, besides the concept of logos spermatikos.

One might point out two such elements which seem to play a decisive role in Justin's development of the ideas relating to the connection between the pre-existing Christ and the heathen:

a) The demonological element. Justin has a strong sense of the existence of the demonic powers. It is noteworthy that in almost all the passages which refer to the

---

[5]C. Andresen, "Justin und der mittlere Platonismus," *ZNW* 44 (1952-53), pp. 157 ff.

[6]"Logos Spermatikos," *Stud. Theol.* 12 (1958), pp. 109-68.

[7]Cf. Ap. 54,2; Ap. 59,1. The relationship between the theory of spermatikos logos and the loan- and demon-theories in Justin has been an important problem. See A. Harnack, *Lehrbuch der Dogmengeschichte*, Vol. I (Tübingen, 1909[4]), p. 511; H. Meyer, *op. cit.*, p. 92; R. Holte, *op. cit.*, pp. 159-65.

[8]After R. Holte the only paper that deals specifically with the theory of Logos spermatikos, as far as I know, is J. H. Waszink's "Bemerkungen zu Justins Lehre vom Logos spermatikos," in *Mullus* (Festschr. Th. Klauser), (Münster, 1964), pp. 380-90. Waszink works along the lines of Andresen and Holte and further elaborates on them. Cf. also *idem*. "Bemerkungen zum Einfluss des Platonismus im frühen Christentum," *Vigiliae Christianae* 19 (1965), pp. 129-62.

relationship between the pre-existing Christ and the pagans
there are continuous references to the demons too. The demons
are a constant element. This fact cannot be accidental and
should be explored in conjunction with the connection between
the pre-existing Christ and the heathen.

　　　　　b) The eschatological element. What is
involved here is the idea of the inescapable judgment of all
people by Christ in his παρουσία. Such an idea is strongly
operative in the configuration of Justin's concepts which
refer to the relationship between the Logos and the pagan
people.

Because of the importance of the demonological and
the eschatological-judgmental element, we shall deal with them
immediately. Then we will proceed to the examination of the
basic passages in which Justin expounds his ideas concerning
the pre-existing Christ and the heathen. Our ultimate
objective is, as in the two preceding chapters, the exploration of the concept of the pre-existence of Christ--its
sources, function, and relationship to the humiliation and
exaltation Christology.

　　　　　B.　*The Demonological Element*

　　　　　1.　Demonology seems to be an active and permanent
issue in the Justinian texts.[9] This is demonstrable even
statistically: the word δαίμονες occurs more than fifty
times and the terms διάβολος, δαιμόνια and σατανᾶς almost
forty. Demonology also plays a role in Justin's dealing with
the problem of the relationship between the pre-existing Λόγος
and the pagan world. It is from this specific angle that I am
viewing the demonological element here.

One might discern in Justin's demonology the
convergence of two lines of tradition. The first is connected

---

[9]For an informative introduction to this issue see J.
Daniélou, "Démon" in *Dictionnaire de Spiritualité*, Tome III
(Paris, 1957), cols. 152-89; *idem.*, *Message évangélique et
culture hellénistique* (Tournai, 1961), pp. 391-97. Cf. also
E. Goodenough, *op. cit.*, pp. 189-205; F. Andrès, *Die Engel-
lehre der griechischen Apologeten des zweiten Jahrhunderts und
ihr Verhältnis zur griechisch-römischen Dämonologie* (Paderborn, 1914).

directly either with the New[10] or with the Old[11] Testament.
The terms used within this tradition are predominantly--but
not exclusively--διάβολος, σατανᾶς and δαιμόνια,[12] found
mostly in the Dialogue. The second line of Justin's demonological concepts derives, I assume, from traditions similar
to those encountered in the intertestamental literature. The
terms mostly used are δαίμονες or δαίμονες φαῦλοι[13] and they
occur almost exclusively in the two Apologies. To this line
of tradition belongs Justin's speculation about the origin of
the demons, who were angels assigned by God to keep a protect-
ing eye on the world, but who παραβάντες τήνδε τὴν τάξιν
γυναικῶν μίξεσιν ἡττήθησαν.[14]

Philo and Josephus know this concept,[15] connected
exegetically with Gen. 6,2, but it is the *Book of Enoch* that
elaborates it.[16] There is an additional element in the

---

[10]E.g. Dial. 103,6: Καὶ γὰρ οὗτος ὁ διάβολος ἅμα τῷ
ἀναβῆναι αὐτόν ['Ιησοῦν] ἀπὸ τοῦ ποταμοῦ 'Ιορδάνου . . . ἐν
τοῖς ἀπομνημονεύμασι τῶν ἀποστόλων γέγραπται προσελθὼν αὐτῷ
καὶ πειράζων . . .

[11]E.g., Dial. 79,4; ἀλλὰ καὶ Ζαχαρίας φησίν . . . ὅτι
ὁ διάβολος εἰστήκει ἐκ δεξιῶν 'Ιησοῦ τοῦ ἱερέως . . . καὶ
πάλιν ἐν τῷ 'Ιὼβ γέγραπται . . . ὅτι οἱ ἄγγελοι ἦλθον στῆναι
ἔμπροσθεν κυρίου καὶ ὁ διάβολος ἅμα αὐτοῖς ἐληλύθει.

[12]Cf. Dial. 49,8; 76,5; 79,4; 103,5-6; 115,2; 121,3;
125,4; 131,5.

[13]Cf. Ap. 5,2,4; 9,1; 12,5 etc.

[14]App. 5,2-3. Cf. Ap. 5,2. Athenagoras (*Suppl.* 24)
expresses a similar idea in more elaborate form. Interesting
is Athenagoras' theory that a special angel was assigned by
God περὶ τὴν ὕλην and that this angel turned against God;
he is called ἄρχων τῆς ὕλης καὶ τῶν ἐν αὐτῇ εἰδῶν (*ibid.*, 24
and 25). A dualistic tendency of Platonizing origin is discernible here. Tatian (*Or. Graec.* 15) would make the connection between demons and ὕλη stronger by stating that the
demons τῆς ὕλης καὶ πονηρίας εἰσὶν ἀπαυγάσματα. He, however,
would give an ascetic twist to the dualism: τούτους δὲ
νικᾶν ἄν τις θελήσῃ τὴν ὕλην παραιτησάσθω (*ibid.*, 16). See
more on Tatian's demonology in M. Elze, *op. cit.*, pp. 100-03.

[15]Cf. Philo, *Gig.* 6ff.; Josephus, *Ant.* I,73: πολλοὶ
γὰρ ἄγγελοι θεοῦ γυναιξὶ συνιόντες . . . .

[16]*Enoch*, VI, 2. Cf. also *Enoch*, VII, 1-2; XV, 3,8;
XIX, 1 etc. I am using the English translation by R. H.
Charles, in his *The Apocrypha and Pseudepigrapha of the Old
Testament*, Vol. II, pp. 163-281.

98

demonology of *Enoch* and this is the idea of calling the giants
of Gen. 6,2 "evil spirits."[17] This is the only passage which
could explain Justin's paradoxical substitution in App. 5,3
of the biblical giants by the demons: οἱ δ' ἄγγελοι . . .
γυναικῶν μίξεσιν ἡττήθησαν καὶ παῖδας ἐτέκνωσαν οἵ εἰσιν οἱ
λεγόμενοι δαίμονες.[18]

There are further points of connection between Justin
and intertestamental literature, particularly the *Book of
Enoch* and the *Book of Jubilees*. They pertain to the harmful
activity of the demons. We find of course in Tannaitic
Judaism references to such demonic activity. But in this
literature it is mainly limited "to doing harm to life and
limb." Furthermore "the Rabbis do not connect the demons with
Satan."[19] Things are different with *Enoch* and *Jubilees*. In
these two works the demonic activity is strong and multi-
faceted and the demons are constantly in touch with the chiefs
of the evil hosts called by various names. They are sent by
them "to do all manner of wrong and sin, and all manner of
transgression, to corrupt and destroy and to shed blood upon
earth,"[20] "to lead astray the children of the sons of Noah,
and to make to err and destroy them,"[21] to "afflict, oppress,
destroy, attack, do battle, and work destruction on the earth
and cause trouble,"[22] to "defile mankind and lead them astray

---

[17]*Enoch*, XV, 8-9 "and now the giants who are produced
from the spirits and flesh shall be called evil spirits upon
the earth." Cf. *Jubilees*, X, 1-5. The Jubilees quotations
have been taken also from R. H. Charles' translation (*op.
cit.*, pp. 1-82).

[18]Cf. also Athenagoras *Suppl.* 25. In view of *Enoch*,
XV, 8-9 one could hardly defend E. Goodenough's opinion (*op.
cit.*, p. 199) that Justin is the first to substitute demons
for giants.

[19]For details and passages see the article δαίμων by
Foerster in Kittel's *Theol. Diction. of the New Testament*,
Engl. trans. Vol. II, pp. 12-14 and "Exkurs 21, zur Alt-
jüdischen Daemonologie," in H. Strack-P. Billerbeck, *Kommentar
zum neuen Testament*, Vol. IV, pp. 501-35.

[20]Cf. *Jubilees*, XI, 5.

[21]Cf. *Jubilees*, X, 1.

[22]Cf. *Enoch*, XV, 11.

into sacrificing to demons [as gods]."[23]

We find demonological passages in Justin which approximate significantly the statements of *Enoch* and *Jubilees*. He says, for instance, that the demons "εἰς ἀνθρώπους φόνους, πολέμους, μοιχείας, ἀκολασίας καὶ πᾶσαν κακίαν ἔσπειραν," "τὸ ἀνθρώπειον γένος ἑαυτοῖς ἐδούλωσαν (App. 5,4), and that they try ἀπάγειν τοὺς ἀνθρώπους ἀπὸ τοῦ ποιήσαντος θεοῦ (Ap. 58,3). He further states that the idols have ἐκείνων τῶν φανέντων κακῶν δαιμόνων καὶ ὀνόματα καὶ σχήματα,[24] and, like *Enoch* and *Jubilees*, he connects the demons with their chief, saying that παρ' ἡμῖν μὲν γὰρ ὁ ἀρχηγέτης τῶν κακῶν δαιμόνων ὄφις καλεῖται καὶ σατανᾶς καὶ διάβολος (Ap. 28,1). Justin, however, despite his emphasis on the demons, never pushes his demonology to the level of the radical dualism which we encounter in the gnostic systems. In this respect he is again in agreement with the intertestamental books mentioned above.

2. Justin connects demonology to Christology not only when he makes the assertion that the demons try ἀπάγειν τοὺς ἀνθρώπους ἀπὸ τοῦ ποιήσαντος θεοῦ καὶ τοῦ πρωτογόνου αὐτοῦ Χριστοῦ (Ap. 58,3) but even more so when he affirms that the demons tried to imitate and distort the main events of Christ's life already before his incarnation.[25] By such an assumption he brings Greek mythology under the complete control of the demonic powers: οἱ δὲ παραδιδόντες τὰ μυθοποιηθέντα ὑπὸ τῶν ποιητῶν . . . εἰρῆσθαι ἀποδείκνυμεν κατ' ἐνέργειαν τῶν

---

[23]*Enoch*, XIX, 1. Cf. Abraham's prayer in *Jubilees*, 12,20: "Deliver me from the hands of evil spirits who have dominion over the thoughts of men's hearts and let them not lead me astray from thee my God."

[24]Ap. 9,1. Cf. Ap. 5,2. Tatian in a lengthy demonological section of his *Or. Graec.* (chs. 7-20) gives full development to this idea with detailed references to Greek mythology. (Cf. M. Elze, *op. cit.*, p. 102.) Athenagoras does the same thing but to a more limited degree (*Suppl.* 26). Cf. Daniélou, *Démon*, cols. 155-58.

[25]See Ap. 54,1-10; Dial. 69,1 etc. Neither Athenagoras nor Tatian, in spite of their lengthy demonological passages, elaborate on that idea.

100

φαύλων δαιμόνων.[26] At the same time Justin places the various
forms of pagan worship under the spell of the demons by
characterizing it as the demonically perverted version of the
Christian worship.[27] Justin uses another basic demonological
concept, namely the murderous disposition and activity of the
demons and applies it christologically. Thus Christ's passion
and death was brought about at the instigation of demons:
[Χριστός] ὑπέμεινε παθεῖν ὅσα αὐτὸν ἐνήργησαν οἱ δαίμονες δια-
τεθῆναι ὑπὸ τῶν ἀνοήτων ᾿Ιουδαίων (Ap. 63,10). The persecution and killing of the Christians is also inspired by the
demonic powers and carried out by judges who are demon-
possessed (App. 1,2; Ap. 5,1). Thus, according to Justin
there is a full-fledged demonic activity directed against
Christ which is manifested:

     (a) as an unceasing effort on the part of the demons
to lead people astray from God and Christ (Ap. 58,3 et al.),

     (b) as a successful attempt to pervert the truth con-
cerning Christ through Greek mythology (Ap. 23,3; 54,1 et al.),

     (c) as an equally successful attempt to use pagan
worship as a weapon against God and Christ (Ap. 62,1; 66,4
et al.),

     (d) as a masterfully organized execution of Christ
through the Jews (Ap. 63,10), and

     (e) as a moving power behind the persecution and the
killing of Christians by the Roman authorities (Ap. 1,2;
5,1 et al.).

     3. Strong elements of this demonic activity, however,
especially as described in sections (a), (b), (c), and (e)
above, are mainly operative in the pagan world prior to the

[26]Ap. 54,1. Cf. also Ap. 23,3.

[27]Ap. 62,1; 66,4 etc. It is noteworthy that Athenagoras and Tatian do not present pagan worship as the perversion
of the Christian one. On the other hand both authors portray
the demons as involved even materially with the worship of the
idols. Athenagoras for instance says οἱ περὶ τὴν ὕλην
δαίμονες λίχνοι περὶ τὰς κνίσας καὶ τὸ τῶν ἱερείων αἷμα
Suppl. 27. Also 26). Tatian (Or. Graec. 9) is more advanced:
τὰ γὰρ ἐπὶ τῆς γῆς ἑρπετά . . . καὶ νηκτὰ καὶ τετράποδα μεθ᾿
ὧν ἐποιοῦντο τὴν δίαιταν ἔκβλητοι τῆς ἐν οὐρανῷ διαίτης [οἱ
δαίμονες] ταῦτα τῆς ἐπουρανίου τιμῆς ἠξίωσαν (cf. M. Elze,
op. cit., p. 100. Cf. Daniélou, Démon, cols. 158-59.

incarnation of Λόγος. Yet in this same world one could readily
discern cases of an opposing activity which did antagonize the
demonic one. Since the demonic action is "anti-Christ" its
opposition must be "pro-Christ," in other words positively
connected with Christ the Λόγος. This is precisely the dialectic by which Justin, via demonology, brings about the connection of the Λόγος with the pagan world.

Chapter 5 of the First Apology provides an enlighten-
ing example of that type of christological dialectic. In Ap.
5,2 we have a description of the demonic activity which is
followed in Ap. 5,3 by the statement ὅτε δὲ Σωκράτης λόγῳ
ἀληθεῖ καὶ ἐξεταστικῶς ταῦτα εἰς φανερὸν ἐπειρᾶτο φέρειν καὶ
ἀπάγειν τῶν δαιμόνων τούς ἀνθρώπους, καὶ αὐτοὶ οἱ δαίμονες
διὰ τῶν χαιρόντων τῇ κακίᾳ ἀνθρώπων ἐνήργησαν ὡς ἄθεον καὶ
ἀσεβῆ ἀποκτεῖναι. What Socrates did, according to this statement, was not to teach the truth in general nor to utter some
philosophical aphorisms but to expose the demons. He spoke
in order to show that the gods in whom the people believed
were in fact demons, and in order to deliver the people from
them. In that respect Socrates' activity is automatically
paralleled to Christ's (Ap. 5,4) precisely because it is anti-
demonic. And then Socrates' persecution is paralleled to the
persecution of the Christians because both are incited by the
demons (Ap. 5,3 οἱ δαίμονες . . . ἐνήργησαν ὡς ἄθεον καὶ
ἀσεβῆ ἀποκτεῖναι [Σωκράτην] . . . καὶ ὁμοίως ἐφ' ἡμῖν τὸ αὐτὸ
ἐνεργοῦσιν. The conclusion of Ap. 5,4 emerges quite naturally:
οὐ γὰρ μόνον ῞Ελλησι διὰ Σωκράτους ὑπὸ λόγου ἠλέγχθη ταῦτα
ἀλλὰ καὶ ἐν βαρβάροις ὑπ' αὐτοῦ τοῦ λόγου μορφωθέντος καὶ
ἀνθρώπου γενομένου καὶ ᾿Ιησοῦ Χριστοῦ κληθέντος. The Λόγος
ἐλέγχων the demons is Jesus Christ who acted also through
Socrates against them. In view of the preceding analysis one
might argue that the relationship between the pre-existing
Λόγος and Socrates (as a representative of the pagan world),
expressed in the statement διὰ Σωκράτους ὑπὸ λόγου ἠλέγχθη
ταῦτα is defined and conditioned by Justin's demonological
considerations.

One could arrive at comparable conclusions by citing
another basic passage as an example, namely App. 8.1-5. Here
Justin presents Heraclitus and Musonius and some of the Stoics
as persons who lived according to the λόγος (κατὰ λόγον βιοῦν

σπουδάζοντας καὶ κακίαν φεύγειν Ap. 8,2) and therefore were
hated. This brings them close to the Christians who also are
hated because of their adherence to the Logos. It is apparent
that here Justin's primary objective, because of his apologetic
purposes, is to parallel the persecution of the Christians to
the persecution of the noble pagans of old. This parallelism
is effected by considering both events as obvious cases where
the demonic rage bursts forth against the people connected
with the Logos. One might see in App. 8.1-5 how the demonological considerations of Justin[28] contribute to his understanding of the connection between the pre-existing Christ-
Logos and pagans.

We will return to Ap. 5 and App. 8 for a more specific
study. We mentioned them here in order to illustrate in
advance the importance of the demonological element in the
problem under discussion.

C. *The Eschatological-Judgmental Element*

1. Our purpose here is to focus on a specific
eschatological point which has a direct bearing on Justin's
understanding of the relationship between the pre-existing
Christ and the pagan people. This point constitutes a constant which recurs invariably within the multi-faceted and
often contradictory[29] eschatological material handled by
Justin. To what we are referring is the idea of the inevitable
judgment which awaits all men at the "second coming"[30] of

---

[28]Athenagoras too makes a reference to the persecution
of Socrates, Heraclitus and others. He, however, ascribes it
to the general principle κατά . . . θεῖον νόμον καὶ λόγον
παρηκολούθηκε προσπολεμεῖν τὴν κακίαν τῇ ἀρετῇ (*Suppl.* 31).
Justin's approach is markedly different, due to his demonological presuppositions.

[29]E. Goodenough is not far from the truth when he
speaks about "contradictory descriptions" (*op. cit.*, p. 286),
"retaining of distinct traditions" (*op. cit.*, p. 288) or "too
many inconsistencies in Justin's eschatology" (*op. cit.*,
p. 289).

[30]Δευτέρα παρουσία is the eschatological term used by
Justin in order to designate what the New Testament calls
παρουσία. Cf. Ap. 52,3; Dial. 32,2; 49,2 etc.

Christ. Justin might be vague or contradictory in other
eschatological points which he touches upon. He is resolutely
clear and firm in his belief in the last judgment.

Our author might express the idea of judgment in
various ways. In App. 1,2 for instance he is using philosophically tinged language: τοὺς ἀδίκους καὶ ἀκολάστους ἐν
αἰωνίῳ πυρὶ κολασθήσεσθαι, τοὺς δ' ἐναρέτους καὶ ὁμοίως Χριστῷ
βιώσαντας ἐν ἀπαθείᾳ συγγενέσθαι τῷ θεῷ.[31]

In Ap. 52,3, to cite an example of different kind,
we are close to the Pauline language: ὅτε καὶ τὰ σώματα
ἀνεγερεῖ πάντων τῶν γενομένων ἀνθρώπων καὶ τῶν μὲν ἀξίων
ἐνδύσει ἀφθαρσίαν, τῶν δ' ἀδίκων ἐν αἰσθήσει αἰωνίᾳ εἰς τὸ
αἰώνιον πῦρ πέμψει.[32] In Ap. 57,1 and App. 2,3 Justin
utilizes even the Stoic concept of ἐκπύρωσις and transforms
it from a cosmological term into an eschatological-judgmental
designation. Justin goes so far as to employ the concept of
eschatological judgment in order overtly to threaten the Roman
authorities: προλέγομεν γὰρ ὑμῖν ὅτι οὐκ ἐκφεύξεσθε τὴν
ἐσομένην τοῦ θεοῦ κρίσιν ἐὰν ἐπιμένητε τῇ ἀδικίᾳ.[33]

The idea of the last judgment is almost always coupled
with the anthropological concept of the freedom of choice or
the possibility of choice between good and evil. Justin
firmly believes that men are given the ability to recognize
good and evil and to act accordingly. He says in App. 7,5:
ὅτι αὐτεξούσιον τό τε τῶν ἀγγέλων γένος καὶ τῶν ἀνθρώπων τὴν
ἀρχὴν ἐποίησεν ὁ θεὸς δικαίως ὑπὲρ ὧν ἂν πλημμελήσωσι τὴν
τιμωρίαν ἐν αἰωνίῳ πυρὶ κομίσονται.[34] From the remark in
Ap. 44,8 ὥστε καὶ Πλάτων εἰπὼν αἰτία ἑλομένου θεὸς δ'

---

[31]Note in the Justinian passage the amalgamation of
the Platonic θεῷ συγγενέσθαι with the Stoic ἐν ἀπαθείᾳ.

[32]Cf. 1 Cor. 15,53: δεῖ γὰρ τὸ φθαρτὸν τοῦτο
ἐνδύσασθαι ἀφθαρσίαν.

[33]Ap. 68,2. The admonition is not a rhetorical finale
of the First Apology. Justin had already uttered a similar
warning in Ap. 18,1-2.

[34]Cf. Ap. 28,3: καὶ τὴν ἀρχὴν νοερὸν καὶ δυνάμενον
αἱρεῖσθαι τἀληθῆ καὶ εὖ πράττειν τὸ γένος τὸ ἀνθρώπινον
πεποίηκεν ὥστ' ἀναπολόγητον εἶναι τοῖς πᾶσιν ἀνθρώποις τῷ
θεῷ. See also Ap. 43,2-8. Cf. H. Chadwick, op. cit., p. 284.

104

ἀναίτιος[35] we could gather that Justin is aware of the support
given by philosophy to the belief in the freedom of choice.
His belief nevertheless seems to depend more on biblical than
on philosophical traditions.[36]

2. Justin knew, however, that there were serious
objections to his assertions concerning the final judgment.
A first objection pertains to the human ability to know the
truth, or, more precisely, to know what is good and what is
evil. Justin never raises the question directly but he
obliquely answers it in various cases.[37] A second major
objection is prompted by the widespread belief in εἱμαρμένη
which actually negates, or at least drastically diminishes, the
freedom of acting within the sphere of ethics.[38] There is a
third acute criticism against the idea of judgment, and this
is the relativity of the notions of good and evil.[39] Justin
sharpens the criticism when he adds that even the demons have
appointed laws conformable to their onw wickedness, in which
men who are like them delight (App. 9,4).

Our author firmly abides by the idea of eschatological
judgment,[40] thus he tries to refute the objections levelled
against it. In his argument we find that Justin works mainly
with four basic concepts:

a) The concept of φύσις.[41] Justin contends

---

[35]Plato, *Resp.* X, 617E.

[36]Cf. for example the relevant series of passages from
the Old Testament presented in Ap. 44, 1-7.

[37]Cf. Ap. 28,3; App. 14,2 etc.

[38]Cf. Ap. 43,1-8; App. 7,3-9 etc.

[39]How could the people be judged when, according to
App. 9,3, παρ' οἷς μὲν ἀνθρώποις τάδε καλὰ τὰ δὲ αἰσχρὰ
νενόμισται, παρ' ἄλλοις δὲ τὰ παρ' ἐκείνοις αἰσχρὰ καλὰ καὶ
τὰ καλὰ αἰσχρὰ νομίζεται.

[40]Justin would counter that if this talk about
inescapable judgment is just empty words and threats and not
the truth then οὔτε ἔστι θεὸς ἤ, εἰ ἔστιν, οὐ μέλλει αὐτῷ
τῶν ἀνθρώπων, καὶ οὐδέν ἐστιν ἀρετὴ οὐδὲ κακία . . .
(App. 9,1).

[41]On the term φύσις see the informative article by
H. Koester in Kittel's *Theologisches Wörterbuch zum Neuen*

that ἐν τῇ φύσει τῶν ἀνθρώπων εἶναι τὸ γνωριστικὸν καλοῦ καὶ
αἰσχροῦ (App. 14,2).[42] It is so because [ὁ θεός] τὴν ἀρχὴν
νοερόν . . . τὸ γένος τὸ ἀνθρώπινον πεποίηκεν . . . λογικοὶ
γὰρ καὶ θεωρητικοὶ γεγένηνται [οἱ πάντες ἄνθρωποι] (Ap. 28,3).
The terminology here sounds Stoic[43] (but compare the phrase
ὥστ' ἀναπολόγητον εἶναι in Ap. 28,3 to Rom. 1,20). The word
θεωρητικὸς in particular which occurs only here in Justin with
a specific reference to moral judgment corresponds perfectly
to the Stoic usage. Within such terminology the adjective
λογικὸς acquires a distinctive nuance: it tends to denote
that which pertains to the λόγος rather than that which is
reasonable. This assumption is corroborated by the Justinian
texts. Our author uses the adjective λογικὸς six times. In
three of them the reference is to Christ the Λόγος (App. 10,1;
Dial. 61,1; 62,2). The other three pertain to man (Ap. 10,4;
28,3; Dial. 93,3). With the exception of Dial. 93,3 which
contains the ordinary expression λογικὸν ζῷον for man, the
remaining five betray an obvious congeniality.[44] But if there
is any doubt it cannot be sustained in view of App. 10,1 διὰ
τοῦ τὸ λογικὸν τὸ ὅλον τὸν φανέντα δι' ἡμᾶς Χριστὸν γεγονέναι.[45] We shall return to this passage.

Testament, Vol. IX (1970-71), pp. 246-71. See also *idem.*,
"Νόμος Φύσεως": The Concept of Natural Law in Greek Thought,
in *Religions in Antiquity* (Essays in Memory of E. R. Goodenough) (Leiden, 1968), pp. 521-41.

[42]Justin uses φύσις in a special type of formulation
but with the same reference to morality and ethical responsibility in Dial. 45,4 τὰ καθόλου καὶ φύσει καὶ αἰώνια καλά,
and Dial. 45,3 ἐν τῷ Μωυσέως νόμῳ τὰ φύσει καλὰ . . .
νενομοθέτηται.

[43]Cf. το πᾶν . . . λογικόν τε καὶ νοερόν (Zeno, quoted
by Sextus, *Math.* IX, 104 in Arnim's, *Stoicorum Vet. Fragm.*
I, p. 32). Οἱ Στωϊκοὶ νοερὸν θεὸν ἀποφαίνονται (Arnim, *op.
cit.*, II, p. 306). Τὸν γὰρ ἐνάρετον θεωρητικόν τε εἶναι καὶ
πρακτικὸν τῶν ποιητέων (*ibid.*, III, p. 72), etc.

[44]Cf. for example the expression λογικῶν δυνάμεων
of Ap. 10,4 to δύναμιν λογικὴν of Dial. 61,1.

[45]We meet in Athenagoras (*Suppl.* 10) a similar usage
of λογικὸς with reference to God and to Λόγος: ἐξ ἀρχῆς γὰρ
ὁ θεός, νοῦς ἀίδιος ὢν εἶχεν αὐτὸς ἐν ἑαυτῷ τὸν λόγον, ἀϊδίως
λογικὸς ὤν. Cf. also Tatian, *Or. Graec.* 5 and 7. But more
relevant to this point is Philo, *Op. Mund.* 77, τῆς αὐτοῦ συγ-
γενείας μεταδοὺς ὁ θεὸς ἀνθρώπῳ τῆς λογικῆς.

b) The concept of ὀρθὸς λόγος. Justin directs it against the allegation that ethics is relative. For our author ὀρθὸς λόγος is a universal ethical criterion: καὶ ὀρθὸς λόγος παρελθὼν οὐ πάσας δόξας οὐδὲ πάντα δόγματα καλὰ ἀποδείκνυσι ἀλλὰ τὰ μὲν φαῦλα τὰ δὲ ἀγαθά (App. 9,4).[46] It is not difficult to discern the Stoic background of Justin's affirmation. Chrysippus spoke about νόμος ὁ κοινὸς ὅσπερ ἐστὶν ὁ ὀρθὸς λόγος διὰ πάντων ἐρχόμενος, ὁ αὐτὸς ὢν τῷ Διί.[47] But as we will see, it is rather the Philonic tradition which is behind the Justinian ὀρθὸς λόγος.

c) The concept of λόγος in the special expression κατὰ λόγον ζῆν or μετὰ λόγου ζῆν (oppos. ἄνευ λόγου ζῆν).[48] The expression is used by Justin as if it were an objective criterion easily acceptable and recognizable and consequently normative in matters of morality. This concept is also of Stoic origin (κατὰ λόγον ζῆν is a variant of the stoic ὁμολογουμένως ζῆν) as it can be seen, e.g., in a passage from Chrysippus' Περὶ τελῶν: τοῦ δὲ λόγου τοῖς λογικοῖς κατὰ τελειοτέραν προστασίαν δεδομένου τὸ κατὰ λόγον ζῆν ὀρθῶς γίνεται [τούτοις] κατὰ φύσιν.[49]

d) The concept of φυσικαὶ ἔννοιαι. Justin utilizes this concept in a passage where he affirms that all people know what is morally right or wrong and therefore they are responsible except for those who ὑπὸ ἀκαθάρτου πνεύματος ἐμπεφορημένοι καὶ ἀνατροφῆς καὶ ἐθῶν φαύλων καὶ νόμων πονηρῶν διαφθαρέντες τὰς φυσικὰς ἐννοίας ἀπώλεσαν, μᾶλλον δὲ ἔσβεσαν ἢ ἐπεσχημένας ἔχουσιν (Dial. 93,1). The corrective tendency implicit in μᾶλλον δὲ betrays Justin's belief that even in a grave case of seemingly amoral status the φυσικαὶ ἔννοιαι are

---

[46] Cf. App. 7,7; Dial. 141,1.

[47] Quoted by Diogenes Laertius VII, 88. Cf. also H. Koester, *Physis*, p. 259.

[48] Ap. 46,3,4; App. 8,2.

[49] Quoted by Diogenes Laertius, VII, 86.

still there.[50] Now it is known that κοιναὶ φυσικαὶ ἔννοιαι
(otherwise called φυσικαὶ ἔννοιαι or κοιναὶ ἔννοιαι) is a
fundamental Stoic concept which as early as in Chrysippus was
considered a criterion for the truth.[51] By the time of Justin
the term was more and more used within ethical contexts not
only by Stoics but also by Platonic thinkers.[52]

The four concepts here presented viz. φύσις, ὀρθὸς
λόγος, κατὰ λόγον ζῆν, φυσικαὶ [κοιναὶ] ἔννοιαι as I have
already hinted, seem to have their ultimate point of reference
to the Logos. It is this reference, one would suggest that
explains why and how Justin connects the pre-existing Logos-
Christ to pagan people in matters of ethics and moral
responsibility (Ap. 46,1-4 etc.). One might further suggest
that this reference has been decisively advanced by Philo.

3. Philo employs the four concepts many times and in
situations comparable to the Justinian ones. More importantly,
he makes always a basic association of the four concepts to
the same point of reference, namely the ὀρθὸς λόγος. He often
speaks for example about the φύσεως ὀρθὸς λόγος[53] or about
living κατὰ νόμον τὸν ὀρθὸν φύσεως λόγον.[54] He compares the
ὀρθὸς λόγος to a man because he implants the seed of virtues
into the soul as a semen. In the same passage he changes
the expression "seed of virtues" into sowing ἐννοίας

---

[50]The statement that follows in Dial. 93,2 verifies
our point. Origen who possibly knew Dial. 93,1-2 is more
emphatic on this point. In *Contra Celsum*, VIII, 52 and
within a judgmental context he says οὐδὲ γὰρ τὰς κοινὰς
ἐννοίας περὶ καλῶν καὶ δικαίων καὶ αἰσχρῶν καὶ ἀδίκων εὕροι
τις ἂν πάντως ἀπολωλεκότας.

[51] . . διὰ τῶν κοινῶν ἐννοιῶν, μάλιστα δὲ κριτήρια
τῆς ἀληθείας φησὶν ἡμᾶς παρὰ τῆς φύσεως λαβεῖν ταύτας
(quoted by Alexander Aphrod. in "de Mixtione," 216,14, apud
von Arnim's *Stoic. Vet. Fragm.* Vol. II, p. 154).

[52]See R. Holte, *op. cit.*, p. 137.

[53]Philo, *Op. Mund.* 143; *Spec. Leg.* I, 46; *Spec. Leg.*
II, 29 etc. See more in H. Koester, *Nomos Physeos*,
pp. 532-35.

[54]Philo, *Omn. Prob. Lib.* 62.

ἀρίστας.[55] 'Ορθὸς λόγος is understood by Philo as a criterion
(*Agric.* 130: τὰς περὶ θεοῦ δόξας κανόνι ὀρθοῦ λόγου διακεκρίσ-
θαι); it is eternal (*Ebr.* 142: τὸ πρὸς ἀλήθειαν νόμιμον
εὐθὺς ἐστιν αἰώνιον ἐπεὶ καὶ ὁ ὀρθὸς λόγος ὅς δὴ νόμος ἐστιν
οὐ φθαρτός); it is not something external and perishable
ἀλλ' ὑπ' ἀθανάτου φύσεως ἄφθαρτος ἐν ἀθανάτῳ διανοίᾳ τυπωθείς
(*Omn. Prob. Lib.*, 46). Philo would call it νόμος θεῖος (*Op.
Mund.* 142), and even use it as a designation for the word of
Scripture (*Poster. C.* 142: φησὶν ὁ ὀρθὸς λόγος; *Migr. Abr.*
60: ἧς ὁ ὀρθὸς λόγος ἀφηγεῖται), and, finally for the Logos:
[ὁ θεός] προστησάμενος τὸν ὀρθὸν αὐτοῦ λόγον καὶ πρωτόγονον
υἱόν (*Agric.* 51).

Apparently in the Philonic texts we encounter the
convergence of the basic concepts--used also by Justin--to
one point, namely the ὀρθὸς λόγος and finally to λόγος καὶ
πρωτόγονος υἱὸς τοῦ θεοῦ.[56] In Justin this point is Christ the
Λόγος.

One can see how the emphasis on the inescapable judgment and moral responsibility, and the need to uphold them,
lead Justin to an extensive usage of concepts which already
in Philo had acquired a status of absolute ethical norms and
universal criteria. These in turn imply the presence of the
Λόγος. Thus the relationship between the Λόγος and the pagan
people on a judgmental basis becomes a self-evident reality.
Within such a context Justin can easily say, for example,
that τὸν Χριστὸν πρωτότοκον τοῦ θεοῦ εἶναι ἐδιδάχθημεν καὶ
προεμηνύσαμεν λόγον ὄντα, οὗ πᾶν γένος ἀνθρώπων μετέσχεν
(Ap. 46,2). This statement is not a formulation of a

---

[55]Philo, *Spec. Leg.* II, 29-30: ὁ αὐτὸς λόγος οὗτος
. . . σπείρων ἀνδρὸς τρόπον ἐννοίας ἀρίστας (another term for
κοιναὶ or φυσικαὶ ἔννοιαι).

[56]H. Koester, *"Nomos Physeos"*, pp. 530-40, has shown
that Philo was able to create a synthesis in which the Greek
concept of φύσις has fused together with the belief in a
divine legislator and with the doctrine of the most perfect
law (Torah). Such a synthesis (called by Philo νόμος φύσεως,
φύσεως ὀρθὸς λόγος, θεῖος νόμος or νόμος καὶ θεσμὸς ἄγραφος)
could easily be viewed as an absolute norm or moral criterion
of universal validity. The Philonic synthesis is particularly
important because in it the term ὀρθὸς λόγος and ultimately
λόγος, occupies a prominent position.

relationship understood in abstract terms. It is directly
related to the problem of moral responsibility and eschatological judgment ἵνα μή τινες . . . ἐπικαλῶσιν ὡς ἀνευθύνων πάντων
τῶν προγεγενημένων ἀνθρώπων (Ap. 46,2), and therefore
deliberately restricted and specifically formulated. In the
following sections we will frequently return to this point.

D. *Justin, Apology 5,1-4*

Ap. 5,4: οὐ γὰρ μόνον "Ελλησι διὰ Σωκράτους ὑπὸ
λόγου ἠλέγχθη ταῦτα ἀλλὰ καὶ ἐν βαρβάροις ὑπ' αὐτοῦ
τοῦ λόγου μορφωθέντος καὶ ἀνθρώπου γενομένου καὶ ᾽Ιησοῦ
Χριστοῦ κληθέντος.

The passage, as I have already explained, belongs to
a demonologically tinged context. The Christians are accused
as ἄθεοι (Ap. 6,1). But according to Justin they are ἄθεοι
only in the sense that they do not believe in the false gods
who actually are demons in disguise (Ap. 5,2; 6,1). This,
however, was the case with Socrates too. He was accused as
ἄθεος καὶ ἀσεβής and was executed for that reason under the
impulse of the demons precisely because he tried to liberate
the people from the demons (Ap. 5,3) as Christ and the
Christians do the same (Ap. 5,4). The example of Socrates is
cited because of the nature of the accusation and the reason
for his execution.[57] The purpose of the quotation is clearly
apologetic.

1. In exploring the passage Ap. 5,4, one should start
with the term Logos which occurs twice. It is used two more
times in the same chapter and in the same broader passage to
which Ap. 5,4 belongs. A fifth time might also be included
when a derivative of λόγος is utilized, namely,the adjective
ἄλογος (Ap. 5,1). Through Ap. 5 Justin employs the word λόγος
with gradually increasing christological connotations.

---

[57]On Socrates and Christ see A. Harnack, *Sokrates und
die alte Kirche* (Berlin, 1900); I. M. Pfaettisch, "Christus
und Sokrates bei Justin," *Theolog. Quartalschrift* 90 (Tübingen, 1908), pp. 503-23; E. Benz, "Christus und Sokrates in der
alten Kirche," *ZNW* 43 (1950-51), pp. 195-224. As W. Jaeger
has remarked "Die Parallele Zwischen Sokrates und Christus
geht durch das ganze Werk" [i.e. the two Apologies by Justin]
(cited by J. H. Waszink, *Bemerkungen zu Justins Lehre*, p. 382).

a) Our author begins with the expression
ἀλόγῳ πάθει in Ap. 5,1. He accuses the Roman authorities that
in the case of Christians they do not examine the charges but
they ἀλόγῳ πάθει καὶ μάστιγι δαιμόνων φαύλων ἐξελαυνόμενοι
κολάζουν. The adjective ἄλογος appears frequently in the
Justinian texts. In four instances,[58] when connected with the
word ζῷα it simply means irrational. In two other cases the
context and the immediate association of the term implies
again the same meaning i.e., irrational, absurd.[59] In the
remaining ten passages the word ἄλογος (or its adverbial form
ἀλόγως) connotes something more than irrational in the sense
of unreasonable or absurd. It is used as a modifier with nouns
like ὁρμὴ and πάθος (Ap. 2,3; 5,1) or verbs like βιοῦν and
πράττειν (Ap. 12,5; 57,1; App. 1,1) or it might stand free.[60]
But in all those cases the term ἄλογος is connected with a
deeply sinful life (e.g. Ap. 57,1 ἐμπαθῶς ἐν ἔθεσι φαύλοις
τεθραμμένους) a subjection to the demons (e.g. Ap. 5,1 ἀλόγῳ
πάθει καὶ μάστιγι δαιμόνων φαύλων ἐξελαυνόμενοι),[61] or a worship of the idols.[62] We certainly encounter in the Stoics[63]
terminological similarities as regards the usage of ἄλογος
in Justin, but Philo is undoubtedly much closer to this usage
than anybody else. We find in the Philonic texts a large
number of passages (more than two hundred) where the terms
ἄλογος and ἀλόγως occur, and particularly in combinations

---

[58]Cf. Ap. 24,1; 55,4; App. 12,5;;Dial. 107,1-4.

[59]Cf. Ap. 3,1 ἄλογον φωνὴν and App. 11,6 σκληρὰ καὶ
ἄλογα. Cf. Acts 25,27 ἄλογον γάρ μοι δοκεῖ.

[60]See for instance Ap. 9,3; 58,2; App. 2,15; Dial.
30,1.

[61]Cf. Ap. 12,5 δαιμόνων φαύλων οἳ καὶ τῶν ἀλόγως
βιούντων αἰτοῦσι θύματα καὶ θεραπείας.

[62]Ap. 9,2: καὶ ἐξ ἀτίμων πολλάκις σκευῶν διὰ τέχνης
τὸ σχῆμα μόνον ἀλλάξαντες καὶ μορφοποιήσαντες θεοὺς ἐπονο-
μάζουν. Ὅπερ οὐ μόνον ἄλογον ἡγούμεθα ἀλλὰ καὶ ἐφ' ὕβρει
τοῦ θεοῦ γίνεσθαι. Cf. also Tatian, *Or. Graec.* 9.

[63]For instance, we encounter the expressions ἄλογον
πάθος or ἄλογος ὁρμὴ or ἀλόγως ζῆν. Cf. Von Arnim, *Stoic.
Vet. Fragmenta*,Vol. III, pp. 43, 94, 130 etc.

which also appear in the Justinian texts.[64] But even more
important is the fact that in some of the Philonic passages
the term ἄλογος is related directly to λόγος and/or to God or
the divine truth. In *Leg. All.* III, 229, for instance, Philo
says, ἀληθὲς μέν ἐστι δόγμα τὸ πιστεύειν θεῷ, ψεῦδος δὲ τὸ
πιστεύειν τοῖς κενοῖς λογισμοῖς. ῞Αλογος δὲ ὁρμὴ ἐξέρχεται
καὶ φοιτᾷ ἐφ᾽ ἑκατέρων τῶν τε λογισμῶν καὶ τοῦ νοῦ τοῦ
διαφθείροντος τὴν ἀλήθειαν.[65] More clear still is the
passage in *De Poster. Cai.* 68-69: ὅταν γὰρ ὁ προστάτης ἢ
ἐπίτροπος ἢ πατήρ . . . ὁ ὀρθὸς λόγος οἴχηται καταλιπὼν τὸ ἐν
ἡμῖν ποίμνιον, ἀτημέλητον ἐαθὲν διόλλυται μὲν αὐτό . . .
᾽Επεὶ γὰρ τὸ ποίμνιον ἄλογον, ὁ δὲ θεὸς πηγὴ λόγου, ἀνάγκη τὸν
ἀλόγως βιοῦντα τῆς τοῦ θεοῦ ζωῆς ἀπεσχοινίσθαι.

One could assume that Justin[66] shares the Philonic
understanding of ἄλογος as reflected in the above passages
and, when employing the word ἄλογος makes in the end a latent
association to the Logos (the Logos understood in all its
meanings).

b) In the next verse (Ap. 5,2) Justin uses
the term λόγος in the expression λόγῳ κρίνειν which is placed
over against the expression δέει συναρπάζεσθαι. Here Logos
means sound reasoning. Immediately afterwards (Ap. 5,4)
Justin introduces again the term λόγος. This time he associates it with Socrates. He says that Socrates λόγῳ ἀληθεῖ καὶ
ἐξεταστικῶς had tried to bring into light the whole conspiracy
of the demons. We encounter a similar phrase in Ap. 2,3 (κατὰ
τὸν ἀκριβῆ καὶ ἐξεταστικὸν λόγον τὴν κρίσιν ποιήσασθαι) as an
expression of something that the Christians require from the
Roman emperors. In Ap. 5,3 the adjective ἀληθὴς and the adverb

---

[64] E.g. ἄλογος ὁρμή (Philo, *Leg. All.* III, 185; III,
229; III, 249; *Poster. C.* 74; *Fug.* 158); ἄλογον πάθος (*Sacr.
AC.* 80; *Congr.* 56); ἀλόγως ζῆν (*Poster. C.* 69).

[65] Cf. Philo, *Sacr. AC.* 106.

[66] We may add also Athenagoras and Tatian. In
Athenagoras, for instance, one finds passages where ἄλογος
is connected to the belief in God (*Suppl.* 7) or to the
belief in idols (*Suppl.* 27), in other words in conceptual
associations similar to the Justinian ones. Cf. also Tatian,
Or. Graec. 5.

ἐξεταστικῶς are used in order to emphasize the fact that what is meant here is not just reasoning in general but reasoning which strives for the truth (or accuracy in Ap. 2,3).[67] The term λόγος in Ap. 5,4 seems to operate still on the same level as in Ap. 5,2 but with increased intensity.

2. At this point occurs the crucial passage in Ap. 5,4 with which we began. The first part of the passage declares that Ἕλλησι διὰ Σωκράτους ὑπὸ λόγου ἡλέγχθη ταῦτα. The phrase that follows reveals that λόγος here is a definite reference to the pre-existing Christ. In 5,4 then Justin envisages the λόγος in his function of ἐλέγχειν. Philo has already ascribed a similar function to λόγος. In *Deus Imm.* 182 he says: ἐπιστάντος ἐλέγχου -- λόγος δ' ἐστὶ θεῖος, ἄγγελος ποδηγετῶν καὶ τὰ ἐν ποσὶ ἀναστέλλων, ἵνα ἄπταιστοι διὰ λεωφόρου βαίνωμεν τῆς ὁδοῦ.[68] Yet there is a difference between Philo and Justin. The former applies the concept of λόγος-ἔλεγχος in individual cases, whereas the latter utilizes it in general situations.

The christological idea behind Ap. 5,4 is that Christ the pre-existing Λόγος spoke through Socrates. The scope, however, of this speaking is defined and limited: Christ the Λόγος acted as ἔλεγχος in the specific issue of laying bare the guile of the demons and the true nature of the idols. There is no doubt that demonology is here instrumental in connecting the pre-existing Christ to Socrates,[69] although this connection might have been facilitated by the Philonic notion of λόγος-ἔλεγχος possibly known to Justin.

The christological frame of Ap. 5,4 is the bipartite

---

[67] It is not accidental that Celsus' basic work has as title the term *Alethes Logos*. C. Andresen has convincingly argued in his book *Logos und Nomos* (Berlin, 1955), pp. 308ff. that Celsus writes in fact an answer to Justin. See also A. D. Nock's review of Andresen's book in *Journ. Theol. Stud.* 7 (1956), pp. 314-17, who agrees with the thesis of Andresen.

[68] Cf. Philo, *Det. Pot. Ins.* 146: [ὁ θεός] τὸν σωφρονιστὴν ἔλεγχον, τὸν ἑαυτοῦ λόγον, εἰς τὴν διάνοιαν ἐκπέμψας, δι' οὗ δυσωπήσας καὶ ὀνειδίσας περὶ ὧν ἐπλημμέλησεν αὐτὴν ἰάσεται.

[69] Cf. C. I, K. Story, *op. cit.*, pp. 57-58.

schema of pre-existence and incarnation (τοῦ λόγου μορφωθέντος καὶ ἀνθρώπου γενομένου) which, as we often said, might
be a form of the humiliation and exaltation pattern. It is
worth noting that in Ap. 5,4 the concept of pre-existence does
not appear independently but as part of a schema. One could
contend that such a schema, by tying together pre-existence and
incarnation, favors--if not causes--connections and parallel-
isms like the one met in Ap. 5,4: the Logos who became man
could very well have used Socrates as a spokesman on a specific
issue. The incarnational reality is strongly felt here as a
factor which leads to a particular understanding of the function of the pre-existent Christ within the pagan world.

E. *Justin, Apology 46,1-5*

Ap. 46,2-3: τὸν Χριστὸν πρωτότοκον τοῦ θεοῦ εἶναι
ἐδιδάχθημεν καὶ προεμηνύσαμεν λόγον ὄντα, οὗ πᾶν γένος ἀνθρώπων μετέσχεν. Καὶ οἱ μετὰ λόγου βιώσαντες χριστιανοὶ εἰσί,
κἂν ἄθεοι ἐνομίσθησαν.[70]

This passage is Justin's answer to an allegation that
there cannot be a universal judgment since the people who
lived before Christ did not know Christ's teaching and consequently are not morally responsible (Ap. 45,1: καὶ ἐπικαλῶσιν ὡς ἀνευθύνων ὄντων τῶν προγεγενημένων πάντων ἀνθρώπων).
The Apologist, because of his firm eschatological-judgmental
orientation, cannot accept such a claim and responds to it by
the affirmation of Ap. 46,2-3: [Χριστοῦ-Λόγου] πᾶν γένος
ἀνθρώπων μετέσχε.

1. The crucial term in the first part of Justin's
statement (Ap. 46,2) is the verb μετέχειν. Justin uses it
six more times.[71] In Dial. 6,1-2 when he speaks about the
human soul and its having the attribute of life says: εἰ δὲ
ζῇ [ἡ ψυχή], οὐ ζωὴ οὖσα ζῇ ἀλλὰ μεταλαμβάνουσα τῆς ζωῆς·
ἕτερόν δέ τι τὸ μετέχον τινος ἐκείνου οὗ μετέχει . . . Οὕτως

---

[70]One might find in R. Holte, *op. cit.*, pp. 135 ff.,
some of the plausible connections of Ap. 46,2-3 to the relevant Platonic or Stoic teachings and formulations. Cf. J. H.
Waszink, *Bemerkungen zu Justins Lehre . . .*, pp. 387ff.

[71]Ap. 57,2; 66,1; Dial. 6,1-2; 20,3; 63,5; 86,3.

114

ἄρα καὶ οὐ μεθέξει ποτέ, ὅταν [ὁ θεός] αὐτὴν μὴ θέλοι ζῆν.
The verb μετέχειν in the present passage means partake, not by
any inborn quality or any right the soul has of itself but
because of the will of God: Ζωῆς δὲ ψυχὴ μετέχει ἐπεὶ ζῆν
αὐτὴν ὁ θεὸς βούλεται. This partaking accentuates, does not
efface, the otherness of the soul with respect to God.[72]

In Dial. 20,3 μετέχειν is used in the sense of
laying hands on and taking to eat, whereas in Ap. 57,2 the
same term is related to διοίκησις and simply means participat-
ing in the government.

Μετέχειν in Dial. 63,5 and 86,3 moves into the
christological realm. Justin says in Dial. 63,5 that all
Christians belong τῇ ἐκκλησίᾳ τῇ ἐξ ὀνόματος αὐτοῦ [Χριστοῦ]
γενομένη καὶ μετασχούσῃ τοῦ ὀνόματος αὐτοῦ (χριστιανοὶ γὰρ
πάντες καλούμεθα). The term μετέχειν describes here a relation between the Christians and Christ, which is based on
association by name. Something similar is also applicable in
the case of Dial. 86,3. Here Justin interprets Ps. 44,8 (LXX)
as indicating that οἱ βασιλεῖς πάντες καὶ οἱ χριστοὶ ἀπὸ
τούτου [Χριστοῦ] μετέσχον καὶ βασιλεῖς καλεῖσθαι καὶ χριστοί.
Thus the kings of old "participated in Christ" simply by being
kings and anointed, two realities or titles given actually by
the Father of all to the Son. One readily sees in this case,
how the word μέτοχοι of Ps. 44,8 (LXX), by receiving a literal
exegesis, produced the phrase οἱ βασιλεῖς πάντες καὶ οἱ
χριστοὶ ἀπὸ τούτου [Χριστοῦ] μετέσχον (Dial. 86,3). In view
of the frequent usage of Ps. 44 (LXX) by Justin,[73] and the
significance of association by name in Dial. 86,3, one might
assume that Ps. 44,8 might be one of the texts behind the
μετέχειν christological passages in Justin.[74]

[72]Note the emphasis in the phrase ἕτερον δέ τι τὸ
μετέχον τινὸς ἐκείνου οὗ μετέχει (Dial. 6,1). R. Holte is
right in assuming that here Justin follows Plato's terminology
but he has changed its sense thus emphasizing the distinction
more strongly (*op. cit.*, pp. 154-55).

[73]The passage Ps. 44,8 (LXX) occurs four times: Dial.
38,4; 56,14; 63,4; 86,3. These are the only instances when
the word μέτοχος appears in the Justinian texts.

[74]If one takes into account the usage and meaning of
μετέχειν in passages like Dial. 63,5 and 86,3, one cannot

We encounter the verb μετέχειν one more time, in the
christological-eucharistic passage Ap. 66,1: καὶ ἡ τροφὴ
αὕτη καλεῖται παρ᾽ ἡμῖν εὐχαριστία ἧς οὐδενὶ ἄλλῳ μετασχεῖν
ἐξόν ἐστιν ἢ τῷ πιστεύοντι. Here Justin approximates, if not
follows directly, the terminology of 1 Cor. 10,17 ἐκ τοῦ ἑνὸς
ἄρτου μετέχομεν, and 1 Cor. 10,21 οὐ δύνασθε τραπέζης κυρίου
μετέχειν, where the meaning of μετέχειν is determined by
christological liturgical concepts.[75]

It is worth noticing that in the sentence which
immediately precedes Ap. 66,1 Justin uses the verb μεταλαμβάνειν as a synonym for μετέχειν within a eucharistic context.
If we now turn to Dial. 6,1 we will see that the verbs
μετέχειν and μεταλαμβάνειν have been used synonymously side by
side in a philosophical context.[76] One could suggest that
even in the philosophically oriented passage Dial. 6,1 the
μετέχειν-μεταλαμβάνειν vocabulary might be of christological-
eucharistic origin, at least in part.

The survey of μετέχειν passages in Justin helps us to
discern in our passage Ap. 46,2, two lines of thought:

a) The first one is encountered in Dial.
63,5 and 86,3. These two passages present the concept of
μετέχειν as being based on the name or titles of Christ
(Χριστός-χριστιανοί,the first case; Χριστός-βασιλεῖς,
χριστοί, the second) as we have already explained. This line
of thought is perhaps encountered in Ap. 46,2 too. In this
passage the name is Λόγος. We have previously seen that an
immediate derivative of λόγος, viz. λογικὸς has been used with
reference to men (Ap. 10,4; 28,3)[77] and that the same

_____

easily agree with Holte's contention that "when, in Justin, we
meet the terminology μετέχω, μέθεξις, we should . . . interpret
this in a Platonic way" (op. cit., p. 143).

[75]Cf. H. Lietzmann, An die Korinther I-II, Hand. zum N.
Test. (Tübingen, 1949⁴), pp. 48-50. See also the article
μετέχω in Kittel's Theol. Diction. of the New Testament, Engl.
trans., Vol. II, pp. 830-32.

[76]Dial. 6,1: [ἡ ψυχή] οὐ ζωὴ οὖσα ζῇ ἀλλὰ μεταλαμβάνουσα τῆς ζωῆς . . . Ζωῆς δὲ ψυχὴ μετέχει ἐπεὶ ζῆν αὐτὴν ὁ
θεὸς βούλεται.

[77]J. C. T. Otto, op. cit., vol. I, p. 129, has already
made the connection between λόγου . . .μετέσχεν (Ap. 46,2)

adjective is employed for Christ too (App. 10,1; Dial. 61,1;
62,2). We also noticed that λογικός for men in Ap.
28,3 is an attribute connected directly to the question of moral responsibility and susceptibility to judgment which is exactly the
case also in Ap. 46,2. So then what Justin states by his
phrase λόγον ὄντα, οὗ πᾶν γένος ἀνθρώπων μετέσχεν is a relationship of partaking, analogous to that expressed in Dial.
63,5 and 86,3, and based on the pair λόγος-λογικοί with
clearly defined limits of application (i.e. moral responsibility and inescapable judgment).[78]

　　　　　b) The second line of thought is encountered
in Ap. 66,1. Here μετέχειν (also μεταλαμβάνειν in Ap. 65,5)
has a eucharistic basis. I am not contending that this line
of thought is immediately discernible in Ap. 46,2. But I surmise that it helped the formulation of Ap. 46,2 in a specific
way, which I shall explain presently. The μετέχειν eucharistic
terminology in Justin is directly related to the incarnation.[79]
Μετέχειν in the eucharistic idiom conveys the idea of a poten-
tially maximum participation of the people in the flesh and
blood of the incarnate Λόγος. The event of partaking of the
eucharist would therefore render the usage of the verb μετέ-
χειν--as a term descriptive of a relationship between Christ
and men--rather easy.

　　　　　2. Justin has introduced in Ap. 46,2 the declaration
λόγου . . . οὗ πᾶν γένος ἀνθρώπων μετέσχε in order to uphold
the moral responsibility of men who lived prior to the

___

and λογικοί (Ap. 28,3).

[78]The occurrence of the term πρωτότοκος in Ap. 46,2
could be an additional evidence for our interpretation.
Justin might not have known Rom. 8,29 εἰς τὸ εἶναι αὐτὸν
πρωτότοκον ἐν πολλοῖς ἀδελφοῖς (cf. also Hebr. 12,22-23) but
he knows well and he makes extensive Christological utilization of Deut. 33,13-17 in Dial. 91. The Old Testament
passage contains the phrase δοξασθεὶς ἐν ἀδελφοῖς πρωτότοκος
which is quoted by Justin in Dial. 91,1. It is plausible
that a term like πρωτότοκος would be suggestive of an idea
of kinship because of its connection to ἀδελφός.

[79]Cf. Ap. 66,2: (in the eucharist) οὐ γὰρ ὡς κοινὸν
ἄρτον οὐδὲ κοινὸν πόμα ταῦτα λαμβάνομεν· ἀλλά . . . ἐκείνου
τοῦ σαρκοποιηθέντος ᾿Ιησοῦ καὶ σάρκα καὶ αἷμα ἐδιδάχθημεν
εἶναι.

incarnation of Christ. What follows in Ap. 46,3-4 constitutes
a further elaboration of the same concept. The key phrases in
Ap. 46,3-4 are μετὰ λόγου βιοῦν [ζῆν] and ἄνευ λόγου βιοῦν
and, as the context indicates, they should be viewed as
directly connected to the issue of moral responsibility and
susceptibility to judgment. In that respect the expressions
μετὰ λόγου βιοῦν and ἄνευ λόγου βιοῦν belong to a group of
Justinian formulations which join together the constants βιοῦν
(or ζῆν) and λόγος with several variants in order to spell out
the same idea (either in an affirmative or in a negative form).
Some of the phrases used are e.g., κατὰ λόγον βιοῦν (App. 8,2),
ἀλόγως βιοῦν (Ap. 12,5), σωφρόνως καὶ μετὰ λόγου βιοῦν
(App. 2,2).[80] In most cases the context is explicitly
eschatological-judgmental, in some implicitly.

What Justin wants to express in Ap. 46,3 is a relationship much stronger and closer than the one expressed in
Ap. 46,2. In the latter case the people are portrayed as
having a share in the Logos because they are λογικοί (Ap.
28,3). In Ap. 46,3, however, some of the people are given a
special place and are called χριστιανοί (like Socrates,
Heraclitus, Abraham a.o.) because they have lived μετὰ λόγου.
We have shown that the term μετὰ λόγου βιοῦν is a basic concept in Justin directly related to Christ the Logos.[81] Hence
the people who lived μετὰ λόγου-Χριστοῦ could be called
χριστιανοί.[82] Needless to say that the area of application of
this concept is strictly ethics.

3. In Ap. 46,1-5 and its immediate context we again
encounter christological formulations which one could presumably associate with a humiliation and exaltation Christology.

---

[80]Cf. also App. 9,1 ἐναρέτως βιοῦν; Ap. 21,6 ὁσίως
καὶ ἐναρέτως ἐγγὺς θεῷ βιοῦν; Dial. 4,3 ἐν δίκῃ βιοῦν; Ap.
19,8 ἀδίκως βιοῦν etc.

[81]Goodenough, *op. cit.*, p. 214, seems to associate the
formulations μετὰ λόγου and ἄνευ λόγου, in Justin, with reason
rather than with Christ. Such an association, however, is not
favored by Ap. 46,2-3.

[82]For an analogous way of thinking in Philo with
regard to Abraham who was νόμος before the written law (*Abr.*
275-76) see H. Koester, *Nomos Physeos*, pp. 535-36.

Ap. 45 begins with an exaltation statement[83] followed by the locus classicus Ps. 109,1-3 (LXX), and ends with a declaration of unavoidable punishment of all those who will not accept the word of Christ. Ap. 46,1-4 continues the thrust of thought of Ap. 45 and concludes with another humiliation and exaltation statement: [Χριστός] διὰ παρθένου ἄνθρωπος ἀπεκυήθη καὶ ᾿Ιησοῦς ἐπωνομάσθη καὶ σταυρωθεὶς ἀποθανὼν ἀνέστη καὶ ἀνελήλυθεν εἰς οὐρανόν (Ap. 46,5). Thus Ap. 46,1-4 is framed within a humiliation and exaltation Christology which directly affects it.[84] One could propose that the reality of incarnation (Ap. 46,5) is instrumental in Justin's affirmation that Christ is the Logos of whom every race of men were partakers (Ap. 46,2). Here the concept of pre-existence is defined to a considerable degree by the event of the incarnation. This becomes apparent in the application of the name χριστιανός to persons who lived before Christ. They were χριστιανοὶ because they lived with the pre-existing Logos, the incarnate Christ. On the other hand the idea of Christ's exaltation (Ap. 45,1; 46,5), which affirms his lordship and power, functions as an assurance that the defeat of the demons and the final eschatological judgment will definitely and undoubtedly take place.

F. *Justin, 2 Apology 8,1-5*

The passage under examination contains two statements related to the general problem which we are discussing: (a) διὰ τὸ ἔμφυτον παντὶ γένει ἀνθρώπων σπέρμα τοῦ λόγου (App. 8,1), and (b) τοὺς οὐ κατὰ σπερματικοῦ λόγου μέρος, ἀλλὰ κατὰ τὴν τοῦ παντὸς λόγου ὃ ἐστι Χριστοῦ γνῶσιν καὶ θεωρίαν (App.

[83]Ap. 45,1: ὅτι δὲ ἀγαγεῖν τὸν Χριστὸν εἰς τὸν οὐρανὸν ὁ πατὴρ τῶν πάντων θεὸς μετὰ τὸ ἀναστῆσαι ἐκ νεκρῶν . . . καὶ κατέχειν ἕως ἂν πατάξῃ τοὺς ἐχθραίνοντας αὐτὸν δαίμονας.

[84]Both R. Holte and J. H. Waszink have perhaps overlooked the presence and function of the christological formulations in Ap. 45,1 and Ap. 46,5. Hence their handling of Ap. 46,2 seems to be incomplete.

8,3).[85] A basic fact that should be remembered is that
pronounced conceptual restrictions are at work in App. 8,1-5.
They are imposed by the wider context to which chapter 8
belongs, namely chs. 7 through 9. In these chapters Justin
defends the αὐτεξούσιον of men and simultaneously upholds their
full responsibility for their ideas or actions. With the same
stroke he attacks the theories and the agents militating
against the principle of responsibility (εἱμαρμένη, demons,
relativity of laws et al.). Obviously App. 8,1-5 as a part
of the section App. 7-9 is conditioned by the set of ideas and
the thrust of thought of that section.

1. Within the context described above, and in order
to strengthen his thesis, Justin makes the remark that even
some of the Stoics,[86] despite their theories in other realms,[87]
ἐπειδὴ κἂν τὸν ἠθικὸν λόγον κόσμιοι γεγόνασι, have been persecuted (App. 8,1). They are κόσμιοι according to Justin διὰ
τὸ ἔμφυτον παντὶ γένει ἀνθρώπων σπέρμα τοῦ λόγου.

The term ἔμφυτος occurs also in App. 6,3 and 13,5.
The modifiers of ἔμφυτος in App. 6,3, ἔμφυτος τῇ φύσει τῶν
ἀνθρώπων, and in App. 13,5, ἐνούσης ἐμφύτου, help to understand
the meaning of ἔμφυτον in App. 8,1. It denotes something
implanted or inborn into the human γένος something which
accompanies human nature from the very beginning of its
creation and existence.[88]

---

[85]For an analysis of the concepts involved in App.
8,1-5 see R. Holte, *op. cit.*, pp. 135-59. For an evaluation
of Holte's analysis see N. Hyldahl, *op. cit.*, pp. 70-85.

[86]Justin mentions in addition to the Stoics the poets
in some of their particulars.

[87]E.g. the theory of εἱμαρμένη (App. 7,4; 7,9), the
theory of ἐκπύρωσις (App. 7,3).

[88]The term ἔμφυτος could be connected with the Stoic
ἔμφυτοι προλήψεις or the ἔμφυτοι φυσικαὶ ἔννοιαι of the
Middle-Platonists (see R. Holte, *op. cit.*, pp. 136-37). One
might suggest, however, that Justin uses it in the way in
which it has been used by several authors, viz. as a designation of something that is inherent to human nature. Numerous
examples of such a usage are given in Henricus Stephanus,
Thesaurus Graecae Linguae, ed. C. B. Hase, G. Dindorfius et
L. Dindorfius, Vol. III (Parisiis, 1835), col. 953.

120

What is ἔμφυτον παντὶ γένει ἀνθρώπων is the σπέρμα
τοῦ λόγου. How should we interpret this last expression?
Justin employs the word σπέρμα many times. In most cases it
denotes progeny and occurs within Scriptural quotations.[89]
Next, in frequency of usage, the word appears in the phrase
σπέρμα ἀνθρώπειον and it signifies the human semen.[90] In
another case it means simply germs (Ap. 19,4). There are
three more passages which contain the word σπέρμα. One of
them is a special case.[91] In the remaining two, namely Ap.
44,10 and App. 13,6, σπέρμα means small part, fragment, since
the context in both Ap. 44,10 and App. 13,6 suggests that
σπέρμα has been used in contradistinction to the concept of
fullness (quantitatively but also qualitatively).[92] In App.
13,6 for instance the statement ἕτερον γάρ ἐστι σπέρμα τινὸς
καὶ μίμημα . . . καὶ ἕτερον αὐτό, οὗ . . . ἡ μετουσία καὶ
μίμησις γίνεται establishes precisely the sharp distinction
about which we are talking.

Contextual and terminological similarities render
plausible that σπέρμα in App. 8,1 might have been used in the
way of Ap. 44,10 and App. 13,6.[93] Then σπέρμα τοῦ λόγου in
App. 8,1 could mean seed of λόγος in the sense of something

---

[89]Cf. Ap. 32,14; 51,3; 53,7; Dial. 13,8; 55,3; 58,12;
106,2; 123,5 etc.

[90]Cf. Ap. 19,1,2; 32,9; Dial. 54,2; 76,1 etc.

[91]It is the passage Ap. 32,8 where Justin says οἱ
πιστεύοντες in Christ are the people in whom οἰκεῖ τὸ παρὰ
τοῦ θεοῦ σπέρμα, ὁ λόγος. This is an unusual expression
which crops up unexpectedly. Could it be an echo of 1 John
3, 9? Cf. the astonishing similarity between Ap. 32,8 and
a patristic comment on 1 John 3,9 (cited by J. A. Cramer in
Catenae Gr. Patrum in N.T., VII, 126): σπέρμα θεῖόν ἐστι ὁ
Χριστὸς, ὃς ἐνοικῶν ἐν τοῖς πιστοῖς . . . .

[92]It should be pointed out that the occurrences of
such a usage are rather sparse. (In Philo, e.g., we do not
find even one relevant example.) There are, however, not
equal to zero. Clement of Alexandria offers two examples
where σπερματικῶς has the sense of "very briefly" (*Paedag.*
III.12/=Migne P. Gr. 8.673B/ and *Stromat.* VII.13/=Migne P.
Gr. 9.516D/).

[93]Cf. H. Chadwick, *op. cit.*, p. 295. Cf. Holte, *op.
cit.*, p. 142.

which is an elementary part, an imitation [μίμημα] of the real
and original, but at the same time something which partakes in
a certain way (μετουσία App. 13,6) of the real and original.
This seed of λόγος which is implanted or inborn in every human
being has a clearly defined function directly related to
ἠθικὸς λόγος viz. to problems of moral responsibility and
behavior.

At this juncture a short digression might offer some
help for a better understanding of App. 8,1. In Dial. 45,3-4
Justin affirms that ἐν τῷ Μωυσέως νόμῳ τὰ φύσει καλὰ καὶ
εὐσεβῆ καὶ δίκαια νενομοθέτηται πράττειν and that the
people who τὰ καθόλου καὶ φύσει καὶ αἰώνια καλὰ ἐποίουν are
going to be saved by Christ, together with those who acknowl-
edge Christ as the Son of God. The statement identifies the
φύσει καλὰ with what Moses legislated. Consequently τὸ κατὰ
νόμον Μωυσέως πολιτεύεσθαι (Dial. 45,3) corresponds to τὰ
καθόλου καὶ φύσει καὶ αἰώνια πράττειν (Dial. 45,4).[94] Justin
firmly believes that Christ is the eternal and last νόμος
(Dial. 11,2 αἰώνιός τε ἡμῖν νόμος καὶ τελευταῖος ὁ Χριστὸς
ἐδόθη) which invalidates the Mosaic Law and which constitutes
a universal expectation (Dial. 11,4). If only in Christ, the
whole Λόγος we have, according to Justin, the full, perfect
and supreme νόμος, it follows that any other law--either
mosaic or φύσει--must be something elementary and fragmentary.

This idea is implied by Justin in his usage of the
term σπέρμα τοῦ λόγου within ethical contexts, as, for
example, in App. 8,1.

2. The second fundamental statement of the pericope
App. 8,1-5 is that of verse 3: οὐδὲν δὲ θαυμαστόν, εἰ τοὺς
οὐ κατὰ σπερματικοῦ λόγου μέρος ἀλλὰ κατὰ τὴν τοῦ παντὸς λόγου
ὅ ἐστὶ Χριστοῦ γνῶσιν καὶ θεωρίαν . ... μισεῖσθαι οἱ δαίμονες
. . . ἐνεργοῦσι.

Two specific questions may be raised here: what is
the meaning of σπερματικὸς λόγος? And what is the relationship between the terms σπερματικὸς λόγος and σπέρμα τοῦ
λόγου?

---

[94]The same identification occurs already in Philo as
H. Koester, *Nomos Physeos*, pp. 535-36 has shown.

There is no doubt that the phrase σπερματικὸς λόγος
is of Stoic provenance[95] and that it occurs frequently in Stoic
texts. As we have seen Andresen has tried to prove that it has
come to Justin via Middle-Platonism.[96] But as R. Holte contends, "Andresen has not succeeded in finding the actual term
Logos Spermatikos in the Middle Platonic idiom." He further
argues that "in Philo we are able to show what Andresen did
not succeed in showing in Middle Platonism, i.e., that the very
term Logos Spermatikos has been symbolically used to describe
the transcendent and immaterial Logos as a principle of Man's
spiritual life."[97] Holte, however, does not adequately
elaborate on this statement.[98]

The term σπερματικὸς λόγος occurs four times in Philo.
In two of them it is to be found within a context where Philo
discusses and criticizes the Stoic tenets, and particularly the
theory of ἐκπύρωσις.[99] Σπερματικὸς λόγος here is unquestion-
ably and deliberately Stoic.

The scene changes entirely with the other two Philonic
passages. In *Leg. All.* III, 150 we encounter the phrase δια-
πίπτει . . . τῇ ψυχῇ καὶ ὁ σπερματικὸς καὶ γεννητικὸς τῶν
καλῶν λόγος ὀρθός. This λόγος is called ὑγιῆς καὶ ἡγεμὼν
λόγος and as νόμιμος ἀνὴρ τῆς ψυχῆς helps it to be fertile and
produce φρόνησιν, δικαιοσύνην καὶ σύμπασαν ἀρετήν (*ibid.*).
In *Rer. Div. Her.*, 119 Philo by allegorizing Exodus 13,1-2
says that it is the ἀόρατος καὶ σπερματικὸς καὶ τεχνικὸς θεῖος

---

[95]Cf. entry σπερματικὸς λόγος in von Armin's *Stoic.
Veter. Fragmenta*, vol. IV. Athenagoras, the only other early
Christian apologist who utilizes the term (only once and in
plural), quotes it within a statement in which he is trying
to refute a Stoic doctrine (*Suppl.* 6).

[96]C. Andresen, *Justin u. mittl. Plat.*, pp. 170-79.

[97]R. Holte, *op. cit.*, pp. 145 f.

[98]Goodenough, *op. cit.*, pp. 220-24, long before Holte,
analyzed the Philonic doctrine on Logos Spermatikos and showed
its significance for the understanding of Justin's usage of
Logos Spermatikos .

[99]Philo, *Aet. Mund.* 85 and 93. Here a third passage
ought to be quoted (viz. *Leg. Gaj.* 55) where we encounter
the phrase σπερματικοὶ λόγοι employed in a Stoic sense.

λόγος, ὃς προσηκόντος ἀνακείσεται τῷ πατρί, who opens the womb
of the mind, the speech, the senses and the body. The two
Philonic passages just cited are decisively important for the
following reasons: (a) In them Philo uses the term σπερματικὸς λόγος--despite its semantically monistic tint--in a transcendent sense. (b) σπερματικὸς λόγος is related to the Father
in a way which equals him to Λόγος-υἱός. (c) He is the same
with ὀρθὸς λόγος. (d) He is called σπερματικὸς λόγος because
of his seminal function (symbolically understood). (e) He is
connected etiologically to σύμπασα ἀρετή, i.e., he functions
within the realm of ethics (but note also that he "opens the
womb" of νοῦς πρὸς τὰς νοητὰς καταλήψεις).

One can readily see the approximation between the
Philonic σπερματικὸς λόγος[100] and the Justinian one in the
two cases where it has been utilized, namely App. 8,3 and
13,3.[101] It should be pointed out, nonetheless, that in the
passages of Philo the adjective σπερματικὸς refers mainly to
the sowing ability and activity of the Logos. In Justin,
although such a meaning is present,[102] one can discern also a
clear reference to the notion of σπέρμα as part and as
μίμημα. This suggestion is reinforced by the contradistinction
between σπερματικοῦ λόγου and παντὸς λόγου in App. 8,3.[103]
In this case the translation of the term σπερματικὸς λόγος in

---

[100]As the term appears in the two passages *Leg. All.*
III, 150 and *Rer. Div. Her.*, 119.

[101]Even terminologically we encounter in both authors
a common third component, i.e., θεῖος added to the term (App.
13,3; *Rer. Div. Her.*, 119).

[102]R. Holte (*op. cit.*, p. 128), J. H. Waszink
(*Bemerkungen zu Justins Lehre*, p. 390) and H. Chadwick (*op.
cit.*, p. 295) find an echo of the parable of the Sower (Mt.
13,3) in Justin's λόγος σπερματικός. Such an assumption,
however, cannot be strongly supported by the texts. The main
objection arises from the fact that in Justin, the term λόγος
σπερματικός is related exclusively to the pagans.

[103]I presuppose here that μέρος in App. 8,3 does not
mean part but share, as I explain in section G of this
chapter. Hence I surmise that the logical antithesis to
πᾶς [λόγος] is the term σπερματικός [λόγος].

124

App. 8,3 and 13,3, by "Logos the sower"[104] is apparently incomplete, if not misleading.

The grammatical and conceptual parallelism between ὁ σπερματικὸς λόγος and ὁ πᾶς λόγος in App. 8,3 and the explanatory phrase, ὅ ἐστι Χριστός, that accompanies the latter suggest that the former too is related to Christ. Thus Christ is called σπερματικὸς λόγος in his connection to pagans because they know the Logos only ἐν σπέρματι, viz. as part and μίμημα of the whole. The term σπερματικὸς λόγος is employed by Justin only in relation to pagans and only within contexts which emphasize the notion of fragmentariness. From this standpoint the expression σπερματικὸς λόγος is not identical in meaning with the term σπέρμα τοῦ λόγου. On the other hand the distance between the two is not of the magnitude that Holte thinks.[105]

G. *Justin, 2 Apology 10,1-8*

App. 10 begins with a general christological formulation in which Justin asserts the superiority of the Christian doctrine over against human philosophy. The superiority is founded on the fact that the whole Logos, (τὸ λογικὸν τὸ ὅλον) appeared in Christ and, consequently, through him the whole truth has been revealed.

Next follows a series of statements related to our general problem. One must examine them, keeping always in mind the initial affirmation in App. 10,1.

1. In App. 10,2 Justin contends that whatever the philosophers or lawgivers rightly said and found κατὰ λόγου μέρος δι᾽ εὑρέσεως καὶ θεωρίας ἐστὶ πονηθέντα αὐτοῖς. The word μέρος could have two basic meanings: (a) part (opposite

---

[104] So R. Holte, *op. cit.*, pp. 133, 135.

[105] J. H. Waszink, *Bemerkungen zu Justins Lehre*, pp. 387-90 has correctly criticized Holte for overemphasizing the difference between the two terms. Goodenough, *op. cit.*, p. 215 has convincingly argued that the whole discussion about distance and difference between the said terms forces upon Justin schemata of thought and metaphysical frameworks that he never had imagined. Cf. also N. Hyldahl, *op. cit.*, pp. 76-77.

to whole) and (b) share.[106] The term μέρος occurs several
times in Justin.[107] There are passages like Dial. 91,2 or
127,3 where the meaning is undoubtedly "part." In other
instances, however, as for example in App. 8,2, App. 10,2,8,
App. 13,3 and Dial. 4,3, there is the possibility of either
"part" or "share."[108] I would suggest, on both grammatical
and conceptual grounds, that the primary meaning of μέρος in
the passages under discussion is "share." In that case the
expressions κατὰ σπερματικοῦ λόγου μέρος (App. 8,3), κατὰ
λόγου μέρος (App. 10,1), Χριστῷ . . . ἀπὸ μέρους γνωσθέντι
(App. 10,8) and ἀπὸ μέρους τοῦ σπερματικοῦ θείου λόγου (App.
13,3), correspond precisely to the statement Ap. 46,2, τὸν
Χριστὸν . . . λόγον ὄντα οὗ πᾶν γένος ἀνθρώπων μετέσχε. The
difference is that in the passages of the second Apology the
statement of the partaking of the Logos is related to individual cases. But here again as in Ap. 46,2 there is a strongly
emphasized distance between Christians and pagans as far as
their respective relationship to Logos is concerned.

If we now return to the text of App. 10,2 we will
readily see that the meaning "share" for μέρος is fitting indeed. Everything which is well said (in the sense of correct-
ness and truth) by the philosophers and lawgivers of old is
the result of their sharing in the λόγος. The statement aims
primarily at ascribing to Christ all positive διδασκαλίαι of
the past.[109]

---

[106]See Lidell-Scott, *Greek-English Lexicon, s.v.*
Both meanings occur in the New Testament usage of the word
μέρος. Cf. J. Schneider, art. μέρος in Kittel, *Theol. Diction.
of the New Test.*, English trans., Vol. IV, pp. 594-98. The
same holds true for the Apostolic Fathers. Cf. *Barn.* 1,5;
I Clem. 29,1; Ign. *Pol.* 6,1.

[107]App. 8,3; 10,2; 10,8; 13,3; Dial. 4,2; 91,2; 127,3;
in plural: App. 7,9; D. 40,3; 110,4.

[108]Goodenough, *op. cit.*, p. 217 selects "partial
sense" for App. 10,8 and "share" for App. 13,3. Daniélou,
Message Evangélique, p. 43 prefers "partiellement" for all
cases. Holte, *op. cit.*, pp. 133-35 uses various expressions
in translating the relevant passages but they all point to the
notion of part. J. H. Waszink, *Bemerkungen zu Justins Lehre*,
pp. 385-86, despite valuable remarks, appears ambivalent.

[109]The christological thrust of the thought of Justin
becomes more evident by a comparison with a passage of

App. 10,3 advances further the argument of App. 10,1
and 10,2. The heathen thinkers and lawmakers had a share in
the Logos, but did not know πάντα τὰ τοῦ λόγου. Hence they
arrived at a point of contradictions: καὶ ἐναντία ἑαυτοῖς
πολλάκις εἶπον. So Justin is in a position to show that while
sharing to a certain degree the critique of the Sceptics
against the various philosophical systems, he nonetheless
appropriates all the good elements produced by philosophy
through the idea of the pre-existing Λόγος. The formulation
in App. 10,3 identifies λόγος with Christ in such a way as to
leave no room for doubt that Justin's ultimate reference for
λόγος is Christ. It is through this identification that Justin
is able to overcome the radical critique of philosophy by
Scepticism.

2. Our second point of special interest is App.
10,4-7. Here the problem of the persecution of Socrates and
of other persons prior to Christ is taken up again. The
argument in App. 10,4-7 follows a pattern similar to that of
Ap. 5,2-4: Socrates is depicted as trying to expose through
the λόγος the demons hiding behind the names of various gods
(Ap. 5,3; App. 10,4-6); he is consequently accused as ἀσεβὴς
and persecuted exactly as the Christians are;[110] what, however,
Socrates was unable to achieve, namely, to convince the people
about those truths, Christ the Λόγος who became man succeeded
(Ap. 5,4; App. 10,7-8).

Even a brief view of App. 10 leads to the conclusion
that the section App. 10,4-7 is not what one should expect as
a natural continuation of App. 10,1-3. Besides, Justin has
just finished expounding the idea of persecution in App. 8,1-3.
The recurrence of the same theme in the middle of App. 10, and
its connection with demonological considerations, reveals
Justin's orientation of thought, and corroborates the

Athenagoras (Suppl. 7) which deals with the same problem:
ποιηταὶ καὶ φιλόσοφοι . . . κινηθέντες μὲν κατὰ συμπάθειαν
τῆς παρὰ τοῦ θεοῦ πνοῆς ὑπὸ τῆς αὐτὸς αὐτοῦ ψυχῆς ἕκαστος
ζητῆσαι εἰ δυνατὸς εὑρεῖν καὶ νοῆσαι τὴν ἀλήθειαν. Διὸ καὶ
ἄλλος ἄλλως ἐδογμάτισεν.

[110]Cf. App. 5,3 καὶ ὁμοίως ἐφ' ἡμῖν τὸ αὐτὸ ἐνεργοῦσιν to App. 10,5 Σωκράτης τὰ αὐτὰ ἡμῖν ἐνεκλήθη.

assumption that in his dealing with the pre-existing Logos in relation to the pagan world he is strongly influenced by demonology. The last section of App. 10 contains the remark Χριστῷ δὲ τῷ καὶ ὑπὸ Σωκράτους ἀπὸ μέρους γνωσθέντι (λόγος γὰρ ἦν καὶ ἔστιν ὁ ἐν παντὶ ὤν) (App. 10,8). Here ἀπὸ μέρους should again be understood in terms of "having a share," not of "in part." The parenthetical phrase λόγος γὰρ ἦν . . . ὁ ἐν παντὶ ὤν explains precisely the notion of sharing by declaring that Christ the Logos is in every man.

Grammatically there is a possibility of taking the παντὶ in App. 10,8 as neutral.[111] If so, then the Justinian statement means that the λόγος is present in everything. Consequently we move to a cosmological level, and the phrase λόγος γὰρ ἦν καὶ ἔστιν ὁ ἐν παντὶ ὤν becomes a reference to the natural revelation through which Christ the Λόγος was known by Socrates. Such an idea, nonetheless, does not occur elsewhere in Justin. On the other hand, if one takes παντὶ as masculine, the phrase λόγος γὰρ ἦν καὶ ἔστιν ὁ ἐν παντὶ ὤν becomes a formulation which conceptually is on a par with basic Justinian expressions such as λόγου . . . πᾶν γένος ἀνθρώπων μετέσχεν (Ap. 46,2), ἔμφυτον παντὶ γένει ἀνθρώπων σπέρμα τοῦ λόγου (App. 8,1) et al.

3. At the beginning and at the end of App. 10 we encounter christological formulations which resemble many others which we have already found in Justin. The pattern is unmistakably the same, viz. pre-existence and incarnation, although the terminology is somehow different. Here again the bipartite pattern pre-existence and incarnation has a central function within the whole context of App. 10. The reality of incarnation in which, for Justin, the sublime and supreme christian doctrine (μεγαλειότερα μὲν οὖν πάσης διδασκαλίας φαίνεται τὰ ἡμέτερα App. 10,1) has been taught by the Logos who became full man (λόγου . . . δι' ἑαυτοῦ ὁμοιοπαθοῦς γενομένου καὶ διδάξαντος ταῦτα App. 10,8), affects the terminology of pre-existence. The concept of human beings sharing in the Logos (App. 10,2,8) is not impossible when the

---

[111]Cf. the pertinent discussion in J. C. T. Otto, *op. cit.*, p. 228, n. 13, who, however, shows that παντὶ is preferably masculine, not neutral.

128

Logos became man, that is, when the barrier of absolute transcendence has been abolished.   Christ in App. 10 is portrayed
as the revealer and teacher of the full truth to humanity by
his incarnation.   Why could he have not let humanity have
glimpses of this truth even before the incarnation?   In this
perspective the statements in App. 10 which refer to the partaking of men in the Logos should not be viewed as a product
of a pantheistically tinted philosophical speculation, but
rather as the result of Justin's adherence to a christological
pattern which contemplates simultaneously pre-existence and
incarnation.

H. *Justin, 2 Apology 13,1-6*

Chapter 13 of the Second Apology is parallel to
chapter 10.   It repeats the same ideas, sometimes verbatim.
The repetitions, however, accompanied by a certain amount of
modifications shed more light on some ambiguous points.

1.   In App. 13,5 we encounter the statement, οἱ γὰρ
συγγραφεῖς διὰ τῆς ἐμφύτου τοῦ λόγου σπορᾶς ἀμυδρῶς ἐδύναντο
ὁρᾶν τὰ ὄντα.   Justin uses here the adverb ἀμυδρῶς as a
modifier to the verb ὁρᾶν in the sense of "dimly."   This usage
recalls that of Philo.   In more than one instance Philo
employed the phrase ἀμυδρῶς ὁρᾶν.[112]   In the passage *Congr.*
140 we encounter in addition to ἀμυδρῶς ὁρᾶν another concept
which also appears in App. 13:   ἐπιστῆμαι τηλαυγῶς καὶ
σφόδρα ἐναργῶς καταλαμβάνουσι·   ἐπιστήμη γὰρ πλέον ἐστι τέχνης
τὸ βέβαιον καὶ ἀμετάπτωτον ὑπὸ λόγου προσειληφυῖα.   Here Philo
affirms the absolute clarity and the unfailing stability of
ἐπιστήμη due to the λόγος.   Justin in App. 13,3 says that the
authors contradicted themselves even in the principal doctrines because they did not possess ἐπιστήμην τὴν ἄποπτον
καὶ γνῶσιν τὴν ἀνέλεγκτον.   The conceptual closeness of the
two passages and the appearance of the term ἀμυδρῶς ὁρᾶν
(a ἅπαξ λεγόμενον in Justin) renders plausible the suggestion
of a connection between them.

[112]Cf. Philo, *Sacr. AC.* 30; *Congr.* 135, 140 etc.   The
term ἀμυδρῶς is of Platonic origin (cf. Daniélou, *Message
évangélique,* p. 44).

In App. 13,6 Justin offers an explanation for his
statement in v. 5. He says that ἕτερον γάρ ἐστι σπέρμα τινος
καὶ μίμημα κατὰ δύναμιν δοθὲν καὶ ἕτερον αὐτὸ οὗ κατὰ χάριν
τὴν ἀπ᾽ ἐκείνου ἡ μετουσία καὶ μίμησις γίνεται. Thus the
word σπέρμα (or σπορά) is placed on the same conceptual level
with μίμημα and sharply distinguished from the reality to
which its ultimate reference pertains. App. 13,5-6 establishes
the otherness of the σπέρμα τοῦ λόγου in relation to the Λόγος
himself,[113] and its weakness to offer anything more than a
help to ἀμυδρῶς ὁρᾶν τὰ ὄντα.

The σπέρμα τοῦ λόγου is κατὰ δύναμιν δοθέν. The
expression apparently refers to the wide range of human
response and to the varying degrees of approximation between
the Christian doctrines and the tenets of the philosophers.
The phrase κατὰ δύναμιν δοθὲν should not be viewed over against
the expression κατὰ χάριν γίνεται (v. 6). The terms are not
antithetical but complementary: the σπορὰ τοῦ λόγου is an
event which always takes place κατὰ χάριν τὴν ἀπ᾽ ἐκείνου
(i.e. Λόγου).

2. In App. 13,3 Justin repeats the idea of App. 10,2
that everything correct which the pre-Christian philosophers
have said is a result of their sharing in the σπερματικὸς
λόγος. The formulation in App. 13,3 contains the expression
τὸ συγγενὲς ὁρῶν.[114] The only other place where Justin employs
the words συγγενῆς-συγγένεια is Dial. 4,1-3[115] where he discusses some Platonic tenets. The context in Dial. 4 suggests
that Justin would not agree with the Platonic understanding of
συγγενῆς-συγγένεια as applied to the problem of the human

---

[113]But note at the same time their intimate relation
expressed in the usage of the term μετουσία.

[114]For a discussion on the term συγγενὴς and the
whole passage App. 13,3 see J. H. Waszink, *Bemerkungen zu
Justins Lehre*, pp. 385-87. Cf. *idem.*, "Bemerkungen zum Einfluss des Platonismus im frühen Christentum," *Vigiliae
Christianae* 19 (1965), p. 148. Cf. also N. Hyldahl, *op. cit.*,
p. 77.

[115]Cf. Dial. 4,2: τίς οὖν ἡμῖν, ἔλεγε, συγγένεια
πρὸς τὸν θεὸν ἐστί; ἢ καὶ ἡ ψυχὴ θεία καὶ ἀθάνατός ἐστι καὶ
αὐτοῦ ἐκείνου τοῦ βασιλικοῦ νοῦ μέρος; ὡς δὲ ἐκεῖνος ὁρᾷ τὸν
θεόν, οὕτω καὶ ἡμῖν ἐφικτὸν etc.

possibility of knowing God.[116] In App. 13,3, however, he is
using, one could argue, συγγενὲς in a Platonizing sense but
with reference to λόγος, not to God. Justin could do that
because with Christ the problem of transcendence was solved.

Since the philosophers of old could know only ἀπὸ
μέρους τοῦ σπερματικοῦ θείου λόγου (App. 13,3) and ἀμυδρῶς
(App. 13,5),[117] it follows that they could not teach exactly
what the Christians teach who have τὴν τοῦ παντὸς λόγου ὅ ἐστὶ
Χριστοῦ γνῶσιν καὶ θεωρίαν (App. 8,3). Justin did not hesitate to assert οὐχ ἀλλότριά ἐστι τὰ Πλάτωνος διδάγματα τοῦ
Χριστοῦ ἀλλ' ὅτι οὐκ ἔστι πάντη ὅμοια, ὥσπερ οὐδὲ τὰ τῶν
ἄλλων, Στωϊκῶν τε καὶ ποιητῶν καὶ συγγραφέων (App. 13,2). It
is interesting to note that apologetic motivations did not lead
Justin to try to establish an agreement between philosophy and
Christian teaching. He is firm in insisting on the difference
in order to show the superiority of Christianity. Under no
circumstances would Justin equate the illumination given by the
σπερματικὸς λόγος to the pagan thinkers with the full revelation in Christ. Everything well and rightly uttered in the
past belongs to us (App. 13,4) but the heathen antiquity did
not, rather could not, know the fullness of our teaching,
because οὐ πάντα τὰ τοῦ λόγου ἐγνώρισαν, ὅς ἐστι Χριστός
(App. 10,3).[118]

3. a) The demonological element is present again in
App. 13 as in most of the passages that we have examined so
far. This time the demons are accused of distorting the
Christian teaching in order to turn men aside from joining it.

---

[116]On a parallel case Athenagoras states τὸ μὲν θεῖον
. . . νῷ μόνῳ καὶ λόγῳ θεωρούμενον (*Suppl.* 4) or τὸν ἀγέννητον
καὶ ἀίδιον (θεόν) . . . νῷ μόνῳ καὶ λόγῳ καταλαμβανόμενον
(*Suppl.* 10). The vocabulary and the concepts are unquestion-
ably Platonic. Justin, because of his strong christological
presuppositions, did not utter such an affirmation.

[117]Or, according to App. 10,3 ἐπειδὴ οὐ πάντα τὰ τοῦ
λόγου ἐγνώρισαν.

[118]The lack of the full knowledge of Christ accounts
for the contradictions encountered in the teachings of the
pre-Christian philosophers (App. 10,3; App. 13,3).

Here one witnesses once more Justin's keen sense of the
immediacy of the demonic interference with Christ's work, both
before and after his incarnation.

    b) App. 13,4 offers an important statement of
the type "pre-existence and incarnation." The nucleus of it
is the basic bipartite phrase λόγος-ἄνθρωπος γενόμενος. Here,
however, the formulation is developed so as to include some
additional concepts: τὸν γὰρ ἀπὸ ἀγεννήτου καὶ ἀρρήτου θεοῦ
λόγον μετὰ τὸν θεὸν προσκυνοῦμεν καὶ ἀγαπῶμεν ἐπειδὴ καὶ δι᾽
ἡμᾶς ἄνθρωπος γέγονεν, ὅπως καὶ τῶν παθῶν τῶν ἡμετέρων συμμέτοχος γενόμενος καὶ ἴασιν ποιήσηται. In this statement the
divine status and origin of the Logos is contemplated simultaneously with the absolute transcendence of the Father, and
is connected with worship (προσκυνοῦμεν). The wording refer-
ing to the incarnation emphasizes human weakness (τῶν παθῶν
τῶν ἡμετέρων συμμέτοχος), that is, it betrays traces of a
humiliation language. Finally, the statement is soteriologically oriented (ἴασιν ποιήσηται).

    This is a brilliant example of Justin's ability to use
a creedal formulation of pre-existence and incarnation
(ultimately of humiliation and exaltation) Christology,
plausibly of liturgical origin, within a complicated theological discussion. We don't need to explain how the approximation
of pre-existence and incarnation affects the whole passage
App. 13,1-6 both conceptually and dialectically. We have
done so with a similar case, namely, App. 10,1-8. The particular aspect that ought to be emphasized in App. 13 is the
soteriological implications of the incarnation with regard
to the truth. The Logos who became man did not only teach
mankind the fulness of truth--whereas the pagan philosophers
taught only part of it--but he also brought healing (ἴασιν
ποιήσηται). The last phrase, as the context indicates, is a
reference to the effecting of change in man by the incarnate
Logos, so that he may have a better and more substantial
access (μετουσία) to the truth and ultimately to the Logos.
Here the pre-existence and incarnation schema is instrumental
in establishing not only the accessibility of the truth but
the accessibility of God himself in the person of the Logos.

132

I. *Final Remarks*

1. The first subject to which we should direct our
attention is the problem of terminology. We pointed out
already that attempts have in the past been made to attribute
the Justinian words and concepts employed in the theory of the
σπερματικὸς λόγος to Stoic or Middle-Platonic sources. In
the present chapter we have demonstrated, I believe, that the
theory of the σπερματικὸς λόγος is not an isolated phenomenon
but a part of a whole complex of ideas and concepts which
refer to the more complicated problem of the relationship
between the pre-existent Christ-Λόγος and the pagan world.
This problem because of its magnitude and complexity gave us
the opportunity to examine a larger number of terms and concepts and consequently to collect more data for a linguistic
assessment.

The exegetical data presented in sections B through
H lead to the conclusion that the Justinian terminology is,
to be sure, ultimately of Stoic provenance (e.g. σπερματικὸς
λόγος, ὀρθὸς λόγος, κοιναὶ φυσικαὶ ἔννοιαι, κατὰ λόγον ζῆν,
ἔμφυτος, φύσις, ἄλογος, θεωρητικὸς, ἀπάθεια).[119] We noticed,
however, that such terminology occurs already in Philo--and
in other authors who are by no means Stoics. We also observed
that in Philo one could detect clear traces of a process of
convergence in which some of the basic terms tend to approximate the concept of λόγος (cf. an example of this process in
section C concerning the four concepts) and that in the
Philonic tradition Stoic terminology conveys concepts and
ideas which are not Stoic any more. The similarities, not
only in vocabulary but also in concepts, between Justin and
Philo render plausible the assumption that the former is
related terminologically and conceptually to the latter. So
then one could surmise that Justin, in his handling of the
problem of the connection between the pre-existent Λόγος and
the pagan world, utilizes a terminology which, though originally Stoic, comes to him conceptually altered--and conforming
to his own patterns of thought--via the Philonic writings.

---

[119]But note also the appearance of some Platonic
terms, like συγγενής, μίμημα, ἀμυδρῶς.

2. According to Justin the pre-existent Λόγος was a living and powerful agent within pagan societies, and more precisely:

a) He was present in every case where demonic activity, directed against God or against ἀρετή, was opposed and fought against. This could happen either in individual (Socrates, Musonius, Ap. 5,3, App. 8,1) or in general cases (πάντας τοὺς κἂν ὁπωσδήποτε κατὰ λόγον βιοῦν σπουδάζοντας καὶ κακίαν . . . φεύγειν App. 8,2).

b) He was present as Λόγος (who sows the σπέρμα τοῦ λόγου and somehow is in it) in every human soul so that it may be able to discern between virtue and wickedness and to act accordingly (Dial. 141,1). He was, and still is, standing behind the concept of ὀρθὸς λόγος which is a universal criterion for the recognition and the acute differentiation between good and evil (Ap. 9,4; App. 7,7). In that sense every human being--all heathen included--μετέσχε τοῦ λόγου and consequently is morally responsible and susceptible to judgment when Christ comes in his παρουσία.

c) Finally he was present as an agent of illumination among the philosophers, lawgivers and authors. Everything rightly said by them came from the pre-existing Christ (ὅσα γὰρ καλῶς ἐφθέγξαντο καὶ εὗρον οἱ φιλοσοφήσαντες καὶ νομοθετήσαντες κατὰ λόγου μέρος . . . App. 10,2). This illumination, nevertheless, is not comparable to the Christian revelation. It is partial (μέρος) and dim (ἀμυδρῶς . . . ὁρᾶν τὰ ὄντα App. 13,5).

Demonology and eschatology are strongly operative in the configuration of christological ideas in cases (a) and (b) respectively. Obvious apologetic purposes are at work in case (a) where the persecution stirred by demons is viewed as alternating continuously between Christians and pagans. Apologetic motivations are also traceable in case (c) where the emphasis is both on the fact that pagans in whatever they have rightly said were illumined by the Λόγος and on the fragmentariness of their attaining to the truth in comparison to the full knowledge of the truth given to the Christians (App. 10,1-3; 13,1-5). It is not difficult to see that the whole nexus of christological ideas in (a), (b) and (c) is produced not as an answer to the problem of "pre-existent Λόγος and

ancient philosophy" but as an outcome of Justin's attempt to
cope with specific problems such as the persecution of the
Christians prompted by demons, the moral responsibility of the
people before and after the incarnation of Christ, the possibility of and the yearning for a full knowledge of God,
et al.

Within such a framework it is understandable that
Justin does not seem to contemplate the problem of a panthe-
istic interpretation of the Logos' function in the pagan world
or any similar theoretical problem. The Apologist does not
ponder the function of the pre-existing Λόγος in abstract
terms. He brings the Λόγος into specific situations without
thinking that he should at the same time answer questions pertaining to the exact nature of the function of the Logos and
his precise connection to the human λόγος or to ὀρθὸς λόγος.
Hence Justin's texts present a pronounced ambiguity on that
subject and sometimes one is not in a position to say with
certainty whether our author is speaking of the pre-existing
Λόγος or the human λόγος or both (e.g. Ap. 5,4; App. 9,4).
This is perhaps another major case where the Apologist did not
make terminological clarifications and did not define with
precision the basic terms with which he works. (We have seen
another case with the term θεὸς applied to both the Father and
the Son but with reservation as regards to transcendence.)
But then this might have been simply not his purpose, since he
obviously deals with particular cases, and not with a general
theoretical system.

3. Justin's decision to introduce the pre-existing
λόγος in situations described in cases (a), (b) and (c) of
the previous paragraph might have been prompted or facilitated by the concept of λόγος itself. One could suggest, however, that christological ideas relating to the humiliation
and exaltation christological pattern play as well an important
role in our author's attitude. As we have pointed out in the
course of interpreting the five fundamental passages, there
is a common feature in four of them (viz. Ap. chs. 5 and 46;
App. chs. 10 and 13): a creedal formulation in which the pre-
existence and incarnation of the Λόγος--sometimes his exaltation too--are rehearsed. The terminology varies considerably
in each case but pre-existence and incarnation are constantly

there.[120] The fact should not escape unnoticed that incarnation in two of the pertinent passages is described in language influenced by humiliation terminology (App. 10,8 ὁμοιοπαθοῦς γενομένου; App. 13,4 τῶν παθῶν τῶν ἡμετέρων συμμέτοχος γενόμενος). Attention should be drawn also to the fact that in three of the passages (App. 10,1; 10,8 and 13,4) the statements emphasize that in incarnation the Λόγος became full and true man.

One could argue then, that Justin views the activity of the pre-existent Λόγος among the heathen also through his incarnation. The incarnation as full humanity is unequivocal evidence that the Λόγος could and was willing to become man, and actually did. If he did the greater, he could all the more do the lesser, namely to be in some kind of direct connection with the pagan people. The connection was related to areas of activity which are also outstanding areas of activity of the incarnate Christ. Hence the projection of the incarnational reality backwards to the phase of pre-existence could be accomplished quite easily. The presence of creedal statements which associate the incarnation to the pre-existence within the basic Justinian passages Ap. 5 and 46, App. 10 and 13, and the specific content and wording of these statements indicate that the conept and the reality of incarnation are instrumental in Justin's christological ideas which refer to the relationship between the pre-existent Λόγος and the pagan world. They also indicate that it is in fact an older pre-existence and exaltation Christology which Justin interprets by means of a somewhat more philosophical terminology.

---

[120]Ap. 5,4 . . . αὐτοῦ τοῦ λόγου μορφωθέντος καὶ ἀνθρώπου γενομένου καὶ Ἰησοῦ Χριστοῦ κληθέντος.

Ap. 46,5 διὰ δυνάμεως τοῦ λόγου κατὰ τὴν τοῦ πατρὸς πάντων καὶ δεσπότου βουλὴν διὰ παρθένου ἄνθρωπος ἀπεκυήθη καὶ Ἰησοῦς ἐπωνομάσθη.

App. 10,1 διὰ τοῦ τὸ λογικὸν τὸ ὅλον τὸν φανέντα δι᾿ ἡμᾶς Χριστὸν γεγονέναι καὶ σῶμα καὶ λόγον καὶ ψυχήν.

App. 10,8 λόγος . . . δι᾿ ἑαυτοῦ ὁμοιοπαθοῦς γενομένου καὶ διδάξαντος ταῦτα.

App. 13,4 λόγος . . . δι᾿ ἡμᾶς ἄνθρωπος γέγονεν ὅπως καὶ τῶν παθῶν τῶν ἡμετέρων συμμέτοχος γενόμενος καὶ ἴασιν ποιήσηται.

CHAPTER FOUR

THE PRE-EXISTING CHRIST
AND HIS INCARNATION

A. *Introductory Remarks*

1. The subject of this chapter is the study of the
conceptual and terminological relationship between the pre-
existence of Christ and his incarnation, as it is presented in
the writings of Justin. The focus is on incarnation but we
shall not deal with everything that belongs to it. Although
we have surveyed all the relevant passages we will report
basically on those which directly or indirectly relate to both
pre-existence and incarnation. Our objective is to examine
in what way and to what degree the concepts and the language
of the pre-existence Christology in Justin affect--if they do
so--his dealing with the incarnation of Christ.

There are three major areas in Justin where one could
study this problem:

a) The first area is the terminology used by
the Apologist in order to express the transition from pre-
existence to incarnation: terms like μορφοῦσθαι, παραγίγνεσθαι, σαρκοποιεῖσθαι, σωματοποιεῖσθαι, φανεροῦσθαι, ἄνθρωπος
γίγνεσθαι, employed by Justin in various combinations but
always as indicators of the transition from the pre-existential
to the incarnational phase. The examination of these terms
within their contextual framework will be the content of
section B of the present chapter.

b) The second major area concerns the virgin
birth. This subject occurs frequently in Justin and constitutes a definite and outstanding point of connection between
pre-existence and incarnation. Hence it offers an invaluable
opportunity for research pertinent to our main theme. We

138

shall take up the question of the virgin birth for a detailed study in section C.

c) The third area pertains to the terminology which displays the humiliation element. Here one may find words which describe the incarnation as humiliation, e.g. adjectives like ἄτιμος, ἄδοξος, παθητός, verbs like ὑπομένειν, and phrases such as ἐξουθενημένη πρώτη παρουσία et al. Section D of this chapter is devoted to the specific discussion of the humiliation element which can be detected in the language used by Justin for the incarnation of the Logos.

B. *Terminology Used for the Transition*
from Pre-existence to Incarnation

1. Justin employs a variety of terms in order to describe the transition of the Λόγος from his status of pre-existence to the incarnational one. The predominant expression is ἄνθρωπος γενόμενος[1] but other terms like μορφωθείς (Ap. 5,4), παραγενόμενος,[2] σαρκοποιηθείς,[3] σωματοποιηθείς (Dial. 70,4), φανερωθείς,[4] et al. are also used. Let us first study this last group and then proceed to the examination of the basic phrase ἄνθρωπος γενόμενος.

a) The verb μορφοῦν[5] occurs twice in Justin. In Ap. 9,1 it appears in connection with the idols (οὖς ἄνθρωποι μορφώσαντες καὶ ἐν ναοῖς ἱδρύσαντες θεοὺς προσωνόμασαν) whereas in Ap. 5,4 it describes the incarnation of the Λόγος (λόγου μορφωθέντος καὶ ἀνθρώπου γενομένου). One might think of Gal. 4,19 as an antecedent of Ap. 5,4 with respect to the use of μορφοῦν. But a closer study of the two

---

[1]Ap. 5,4; 23,2; 50,1; 53,2; 63,10; App. 13,4; Dial. 8,4; 38,1; 48,1; 57,3; 64,7; 67,2; 85,2; 100,2; 105,1; 125,4 etc.

[2]Ap. 49,5; 53,6; 54,2; Dial. 49,3; 52,1 etc.

[3]Ap. 32,10; 66,2; Dial. 45,4; 84,2; 87,2; 100,2.

[4]Ap. 56,1. Cf. Ap. 32,2,3; 56,1; Dial. 49,3 etc.

[5]On μορφοῦν see J. Behm, "μορφή-μορφόω", in Kittel, *Theol. Dict. New Test.*, Engl. trans., Vol. IV, pp. 742-55, esp. 752-54.

texts shows that the semantic distance between Gal. 4,19 and
Ap. 5,4 is noticeable. There are in Philo two passages which
approximate the Justinian ones. In *Spec. Leg.* II,255 Philo
uses the verb μορφοῦν with reference to the idols[6] and in *Abr.*
117-118 he employs the same term in order to describe the
appearance of the angels to Abraham during the theophany at
Mamre.[7] It is characteristic that both Clement of Alexandria
and Origen who knew the Philonic texts use the verb μορφοῦσθαι
in connection with the Old Testament theophanies.[8] Clement,
in particular, speaks in the same instance about the Λόγος
and his ἐπιδημία and thus offers an example of how the
Philonic μορφοῦν of *Abr.* 117-118 could be transferred to the
level of incarnation, a case which might well be applicable
to the Justinian passages, too.[9]

One might see the incarnational use of μορφοῦν in Ap.
5,4 as a result of Justin's understanding of the term μορφή.
Our author uses it in various passages. However, he employs
consistently μορφή in order to describe the appearance of the
Logos in the Old Testament theophanies.[10] Yet Justin does not
use μορφή in phrases which denote incarnation.[11] This could
be demonstrated by reference to Dial. 75,4 where Old Testament
theophanies and incarnation are placed on the same level but

---

[6]*Spec. Leg.* II, 255: ὅσα θνητοὶ δημιουργοὶ κατεσκεύ-
ασαν ξύλα καὶ λίθους, ἅπερ εἰς ἀνθρωποειδεῖς τύπους
ἐμορφώθη.

[7]*Abr.* 117-118: ἀσωμάτους ὄντας . . . εἰς ἰδέαν
ἀνθρώπων μεμορφῶσθαι.

[8]Clement of Alexandria, *Paedagog.* 2,8 (Migne P. Gr.
8,488A); Origen, *Selecta in Genesim* (Migne P. Gr. 12,93B).

[9]The terms μορφή-μορφοῦσθαι occur also in the
Excerpta ex Theodoto (31,34,45,50,59 et al.) where they have
a special theological meaning related to γνῶσις (opp. ἀγνω-
σία καὶ ἀμορφία). There seems to be no connection between
Exc. ex Theodoto and Justin at this point.

[10]Cf. Ap. 63,16; Dial. 61,1; 75,4; 128,2.

[11]Tatian (*Or. Graec.* 21) utilizes the expression θεὸν
ἐν ἀνθρώπου μορφῇ γεγονέναι. Such a formulation never occurs
in Justin.

μορφῇ is restricted only to the former whereas for the latter the terminology used is ἄνθρωπον γεννηθῆναι.

b) The verb σαρκοποιεῖσθαι as a term denoting the incarnation of the Logos occurs six times in Justin. This verb is unusual. Within the Christian literature of the second century σαρκοποιεῖσθαι is encountered only in Justin, as far as we know. Outside of this literature one finds the verb in Plutarch where it implies a materialistic understanding of man (*Suav. viv. Epic.* 14 [Moral. 1096E]: σαρκοποιεῖν τὸν ὅλον ἄνθρωπον, ὥσπερ ἔνιοι ποιοῦσι τὴν τῆς ψυχῆς οὐσίαν ἀναιροῦντες) and consequently cannot be related to the Justinian usage. One might assume that σαρκοποιεῖσθαι is the term equivalent to the Johannine σὰρξ γίνεσθαι (John 1,14), or to the ἐν σαρκὶ ἔρχεσθαι of the *Epistle of Barnabas* (5,10-11). We should note, however, that in most cases, Justin does not leave the term isolated but he associates it with the phrase ἄνθρωπος γέγονεν (e.g. Ap. 32,10; Dial. 100,2 etc.). It should also be pointed out that in all cases the verb appears in its participial form σαρκοποιηθείς. This observation could lead to the conjecture that σαρκοποιηθείς belonged to some sort of a creedal formulation (a predecessor of the term σαρκωθείς of the Nicean Creed?) or that it belonged to a liturgical text. Such an assumption finds support in the passage Ap. 66,2-3 where σαρκοποιηθεὶς occurs twice within a thoroughly eucharistic context. It also finds support in Dial. 70,4 where Justin uses the verb σωματοποιεῖσθαι possibly as a synonym of σαρκοποιεῖσθαιwithin a eucharistic context.[12]

c) Παραγίγνεσθαι as a word describing the actualization of the incarnation appears in both the First Apology (Ap. 49,5; 53,6; 54,2; 54,7; 57,1) and the Dialogue (Dial. 49,3; 52,1; 126,1). In all probability Justin took it from the Septuagint since it occurs there in passages which

---

[12]In the fourth century A.D. we encounter in Macarius the Egyptian a similar usage of σωματοποιεῖσθαι: σωματοποιεῖ ἑαυτὸν καὶ εἰς βρῶσιν καὶ πόσιν (i.e. eucharist) ὁ Κύριος (*Homiliae spirituales* 4,12, Migne P. Gr. 34,481B). Σωματοποιεῖσθαι as a term for incarnation occurs also in Hippolytus in his account on the heretics called Περάται (*Ref.* V, 17): υἱός . . . . ἄνωθεν μετενηνεγμένος ἐνθάδε σωματοποιηθείς.

141

have been used christologically by Justin.[13] The Apologist
employs the verb as a general term for both the incarnation of
the Son (e.g. Ap. 57,1) and his eschatological coming (Dial.
49,3). The former usage occurs also in the *Testament of
Benjamin* X,8 (ὅτι παραγενόμενον θεὸν ἐν σαρκί) whereas the
latter is found also in Tatian (*Or. Graec.* 12: . . . καὶ ὁ
δικαστὴς παραγένηται, viz. in the eschatological consummation).
The coincidence of both usages in Justin could be an indication
of his tendency to view the basic christological events as
phenomena of the same nature, namely, as manifestations of a
direct relationship of the Logos-Son to mankind.

Such a hypothesis is corroborated by the Justinian
usage of another term, viz. the word παρουσία. This word in
the New Testament books denotes "nearly always" the eschatological coming of Christ.[14] Justin is the first to utilize
the term extensively and deliberately for both the incarnation
of the Logos and the eschatological coming of Christ (Ap.
52,3; Dial. 14,8; 49,2,7; 52,1,4; 110,2; 121,3 etc.).[15] He
differentiates the two cases by introducing the adjectives
πρώτη and δευτέρα but these adjectives show precisely the
inner association of the two cases.

The terms φανεροῦσθαι-φανέρωσις constitute an additional evidence for our hypothesis. Justin utilizes them in
order to denote the event of the manifestation of the Logos
via incarnation (Ap. 32,2; 56,1; Dial. 52,4 etc.). He also
uses them for the eschatological coming of Christ (Dial. 49,3;
note the characteristic phrase πρώτη φανέρωσις which corresponds to the term πρώτη παρουσία). But, more importantly, he
also employs them for the Old Testament theophanic appearances
(Dial. 60,4; 75,4). The New Testament offers evidence for a
usage of the verb φανεροῦν on both the incarnational and the

---

[13]E.g. Josh. 5,13 quoted in Dial. 62,5; Is. 62,11 and
63,1 quoted in Dial. 26,3.

[14]Cf. Bauer-Arndt-Gingrich, *A Greek-English Lex. New
Test.*, p. 635, s.v.

[15]Ignatius of Antioch has a passage in which παρουσία
might be an equivalent for incarnation (*Philad.* 9,2):
ἐξαίρετόν τι ἔχει τὸ εὐαγγέλιον τὴν παρουσίαν τοῦ σωτῆρος . . .
τὸ πάθος αὐτοῦ καὶ τὴν ἀνάστασιν.

eschatological christological level.[16] In the Apostolic
Fathers the verb is restricted only to the incarnation[17] and
the noun φανέρωσις is totally absent. Yet in Justin we not
only have both the verb and the noun but we also encounter
their use for the description of the Old Testament theophanies
as well. Thus the particular terms for the transition from
pre-existence to incarnation, which we are examining in this
paragraph, are also utilized for the theophanic appearances
and for the eschatological coming of Christ. A plausible
explanation for this phenomenon is that Justin looks at the
above mentioned christological events from the standpoint of
the pre-existence of Christ.

　　　2. Nonetheless close similarity does not mean
identity. Justin is aware of the uniqueness of the incarnation
of the Logos. Therefore for the description of that particular christological event he uses the expression ἄνθρωπος
γενόμενος accompanied often by the phrase διὰ παρθένου
γεννηθείς (Dial. 57,3; 85,2; 101,1 et al.). The last phrase
will be examined in the following section.

　　　The expression ἄνθρωπος γενόμενος occurs twenty-four
times in the works of Justin.[18] Although the participial form
appears in the majority of the cases, other forms of the verb
γίγνεσθαι are also encountered in combination with the noun
ἄνθρωπος (e.g. ἄνθρωπος γέγονεν et al.).

　　　The expression under examination does not occur in the
New Testament. The closest example provided by the New Testament is Phil. 2,7 where we find the formulation ἐν ὁμοιώματι
ἀνθρώπου γενόμενος (if we read ἀνθρώπου instead of ἀνθρώπων
according to P 46 and other manuscripts). Justin might have
known the formulation of Philippians and used it by

---

[16]E.g. Col. 3,4; 1 Tim. 3,16; Hebr. 9,26; 1 Petr.
1,20; 1 Jo. 2,28; see R. Bultmann-D. Lührmann, "φανερόω", in
Kittel, *Theologisches Wört. zum N. Test.*, Vol. IX (Stuttgart,
1969), pp. 4-6.

[17]Cf. *Barn.* 5,6; 6,9; Ign. *Eph.* 19,3; Ign. *Magn.*
8,2 etc.

[18]Ap. 5,4; 23,2; 50,1; 53,2; 63,10,16; App. 13,4;
Dial. 38,1; 48,1; 57,3; 64,7; 67,2; 67,6; 68,1; 76,1; 85,2;
98.1; 99,2; 100,2,4; 101,1; 105,1; 125,3,4.

eliminating the term ἐν ὁμοιώματι.[19]

A second possible New Testament antecedent for Justin's ἄνθρωπος γενόμενος might be the Johannine καὶ ὁ λόγος σὰρξ ἐγένετο (Jo. 1,14). This phrase, however, does not occur in the works of Justin. One cannot be sure whether or not the Apologist knew it. From his christological use of the verb σαρκοποιεῖσθαι and the noun σάρξ, nonetheless, one could surmise that Justin would perhaps be reluctant to substitute σὰρξ ἐγένετο for ἄνθρωπος ἐγένετο. Studying the usage of σαρκοποιεῖν in Justin we noticed that the term is usually complemented by other expressions within the christological statements (e.g. Ap. 32,10; Dial. 100,2 etc.), a fact suggesting that the Apologist regards σαρκοποιεῖσθαι as only an aspect of incarnation. Furthermore the word σάρξ with reference to Christ is used by Justin in the phrase σάρκα ἔχειν,[20] in other words in a formulation which defines a part or a constituent, not a whole.

The term ἄνθρωπος γενόμενος is found in an interpretative connection to the Johannine καὶ ὁ λόγος σὰρξ ἐγένετο (Jo. 1,14) in a Valentinian teaching recorded in *Excerpta ex Theodoto*.[21] This Valentinian passage points to the possibility that the term ἄνθρωπος γενόμενος might have been in circulation among gnostic authors. Justin's use of the term could then reflect his acquaintance with gnostic texts. The christological concept, however, denoted by the

---

[19]Such a process is not implausible if we take into account that Justin employs the word ὁμοίωμα only in two passages and then in connection with Exod. 20,4 οὐ ποιήσεις σεαυτῷ εἴδωλον οὐδὲ παντὸς ὁμοίωμα (Dial. 94,1,3 and 112,1). One is allowed to surmise that Justin would be reluctant to utilize the word ὁμοίωμα--because of its negative Old Testament reference--within a fundamental christological formulation.

[20]Dial. 48,3: ὁ Χριστός . . . προϋπῆρχε καὶ γεννηθῆναι ἄνθρωπος ὁμοιοπαθὴς ἡμῖν σάρκα ἔχων. Cf. Ap. 66,2 . . . ὁ σωτὴρ ἡμῶν καὶ σάρκα καὶ αἷμα ὑπὲρ σωτηρίας ἡμῶν ἔσχεν.

[21]*Excerpta ex Theodoto*, 19 (Migne P. Gr. 9.665D): καὶ ὁ λόγος σὰρξ ἐγένετο οὐ κατὰ τὴν παρουσίαν μόνον ἄνθρωπος γενόμενος, ἀλλὰ καὶ ἐν ἀρχῇ ὁ ἐν ταυτότητι λόγος, κατὰ περιγραφὴν καὶ οὐ κατ' οὐσίαν γενόμενος [ὁ] υἱός. Καὶ πάλιν σὰρξ ἐγένετο διὰ προφητῶν ἐνεργήσας· τέκνον δὲ τοῦ ἐν ταυτότητι λόγου ὁ σωτὴρ εἴρηται.

expression ἄνθρωπος γενόμενος in Justin is radically different
from that encountered in the gnostic passage just quoted.
For Justin, to mention one point, the σωτήρ is not τέκνον
τοῦ λόγου but the Λόγος himself γενόμενος ἄνθρωπος.

There is a passage in Ignatius of Antioch where the
term ἄνθρωπος γενόμενος occurs. He says in *Smyrn.* 4,2
πάντα ὑπομένω αὐτοῦ [Χριστοῦ] με ἐνδυναμοῦντος τοῦ τελεί-
ου ἀνθρώπου γενομένου.[22] This passage seems to have something in common with Phil. 2,7 and this is the participial
form γενόμενος associated with the noun ἄνθρωπος. It is
beyond doubt that the Philippian passage belongs to hymnic
texts of a creedal nature. The Ignatian phrase is of a somehow similar nature, since it is included in a chain of statements which seem to rehearse the basic christological events.
One could therefore contend that the phrase ἄνθρωπος γενόμενος was part of a christological creedal statement or hymn
or both and that Justin happened to know it in that creedal
form.

The texts of Justin support, I think, this contention.
In Dial. 85,2, for instance, we meet the phrase γενόμενος
ἄνθρωπος as a part of an elaborate creedal statement: τοῦ
υἱοῦ τοῦ θεοῦ καὶ πρωτοτόκου πάσης κτίσεως, καὶ διὰ παρθένου
γεννηθέντος καὶ παθητοῦ γενομένου ἀνθρώπου, καὶ σταυρωθέντος
ἐπὶ Ποντίου Πιλάτου . . . καὶ ἀποθανόντος, καὶ ἀναστάντος ἐκ
νεκρῶν καὶ ἀναβάντος εἰς . . . οὐρανόν. Here γενομένου seems
to be an integral part of the statement and follows the mode
and tense of the other basic verbs which are participles of
the aorist. The whole statement is cited with reference to
exorcism and expulsion of the demons. It is not unlikely that
here is a creedal formula used perhaps in exorcisms, and that

---

[22]In Ign. *Smyrn.* 1-7 one encounters some other
phrases besides ἄνθρωπος γενόμενος which have parallels in
Justin. Thus *Smyrn.* 1,1 γεγεννημένος ἀληθῶς ἐκ παρθένου is
comparable to Dial. 84,2 διὰ παρθενικῆς μήτρας . . . ἀληθῶς
παιδίον γενέσθαι, and *Smyrn.* 2,1 [Χριστός] ἀληθῶς ἔπαθεν to
Dial. 99,2 ἀληθῶς παθητὸς ἄνθρωπος γεγέννηται. From these
similarities the inference could be drawn that Justin uses
traditional material relating to incarnation used also by
Ignatius.

Justin is quoting it.[23]

    3. Three major conclusions could be drawn from the examination of the material in this section:

    a) Some of the terms (φανεροῦσθαι, παραγίγνε-σθαι, μορφοῦσθαι, μορφή, παρουσία) are used by Justin not only for the incarnation of the pre-existent Christ but also for his eschatological coming and for his manifestation in the Old Testament theophanies as well. As a plausible explanation for this phenomenon, it has been suggested that Justin views all christological events, where Christ appears in a visible form, against the background of his pre-existence as God. Such a juxtaposition is expected where a christological schema of pre-existence and incarnation is operative.

    b) Most of the verbs designating the transition from pre-existence to incarnation occur in participial form within the Justinian texts.[24] This might well be an indication of the hymnic-creedal provenance of these terms. Justin could have found them in brief creedal formulations or in traditional hymnic material as we have already suggested. He, however, transposes all this hymnic-creedal terminology into the theologico-apologetic discussion.

    c) A recurring phenomenon has been observed in the passages which contain the expression ἄνθρωπος γε-νόμενος or a variant of it: in sixteen out of the twenty-four relevant cases this expression is preceded by various

---

[23]A particular terminology for the designation of the transition from pre-existence to incarnation is encountered in App. 10,1: μεγαλειότερα μὲν οὖν πάσης ἀνθρωπείου διδασκα-λίας φαίνεται τὰ ἡμέτερα διὰ τοῦ τὸ λογικὸν τὸ ὅλον τὸν φανέντα δι᾽ ἡμᾶς Χριστὸν γεγονέναι καὶ σῶμα καὶ λόγον καὶ ψυχήν. C. Semisch has advanced the hypothesis that the phrase τὸν Χριστὸν γεγονέναι καὶ σῶμα καὶ λόγον καὶ ψυχήν betrays a Christology of the type of Apollinaris where logos takes the place of νοῦς. F. Bosse (*op. cit.*, p. 38), shows that this hypothesis is ill-founded. E. Goodenough (*op. cit.*, pp. 240-42) agrees with Bosse and argues convincingly that eventually the statement in App. 10,1 is nothing else than an elaborate and more explicit form of the basic phrase ἄνθρωπος γενόμενος. Cf. also C. I, K. Story, *op. cit.*, p. 105.

[24]E.g. ἄνθρωπος γενόμενος (majority of cases), σαρκο-ποιηθείς (all cases), παραγενόμενος (seven out of eight cases) etc.

statements which declare the pre-existence of the Son and, often, his divinity.[25] This holds true for the other terms discussed in the present section. Here is likely evidence that Justin's terminology for the actualization of the incarnation is developed within a christological pattern of pre-existence and incarnation, which could ultimately belong to a humiliation and exaltation Christology. Such a hypothesis is corroborated by the fact that in some of the relevant passages the christological statement contains also an exaltation formula as for example in Dial. 38,1 (καὶ ἀναβεβηκέναι εἰς τὸν οὐρανόν . . . καὶ προσκυνητὸν εἶναι) Dial. 85,2 (καὶ ἀναβάντος εἰς τὸν οὐρανόν, πᾶν δαιμόνιον . . . νικᾶται καὶ ὑποτάσσεται) Dial. 126,1 (καὶ παραγενόμενον . . . καὶ ἀναβάντα εἰς τὸν οὐρανόν) et al. Thus one can presume that a humiliation and exaltation Christology is in the background of the Justinian use of the terms which describe the incarnation of the Logos.

C. *The Virgin Birth*

A basic and constantly recurring element in Justin's statements relating to the incarnation of the Son is the virgin birth. It is encountered in more than thirty cases either in the simple form διὰ παρθένου γεννηθεὶς or in a more elaborate variation.[26]

1. The biblical text upon which Justin depends for his virgin birth christological concept is Is. 7,14.[27] He quotes the passage several times (Ap. 33,1; Dial. 43,4-8;

---

[25]Ap. 5,4; 23,1-3; 53,1-3; 63,10,16; App. 13,4; Dial. 48,1; 64,7; 68,1; 125,3 etc.

[26]E.g. Ap. 22,5; 32,14; 33,1; 46,5; Dial. 23,3; 43,7; 45,4; 50,1; 57,3; 63,1; 75,4; 84,2; 100,2; 127,4 etc. Cf. C. I. K. Story, *op. cit.*, p. 103.

[27]For the relevant Old Testament texts used by Justin see P. Prigent, *Justin et l'Ancien Testament*, pp. 145-57. It should be noted, however, that Prigent deals mainly with Is. 7,10-17 (and Is. 8,4,7) and touches only lightly upon the other Old Testament passages. For a detailed discussion on the text of Is. 7,10-17 with particular emphasis on Is. 7,14 see H. Koester, *Septuaginta und Synoptischer Erzählungsstoff im Schriftbeweis Justins*, pp. 12-16 and 76-84.

66,2-4; 68,6; 71,3; 77,2; 84,1) and comments on it.   Is. 7,14
is cited in Mt. 1,23 and Justin presumably knows the whole
Matthean passage which contains Is. 7,14, namely, Mt. 1,18-25,
as it becomes obvious in Ap. 33 and Dial. 78. Justin also
knows the annunciation passage in Lk. 1,35 which he quotes in
relation to the virgin birth in both Ap. 33 and Dial. 100,5.

The way in which Justin deals with Is. 7,14 proves
that for him the σημεῖον about which Isaiah speaks is the
virgin birth.   In Dial. 84,1, for instance, after quoting Is.
7,14, he asks: εἰ γὰρ μὴ ἐκ παρθένου οὗτος . . . εἰ γὰρ
ὁμοίως τοῖς ἄλλοις ἅπασι πρωτοτόκοις καὶ οὗτος Χριστὸς
γεννᾶσθαι ἐκ συνουσίας ἔμελλε, τί καὶ ὁ θεὸς σημεῖον ὃ καὶ
μὴ πᾶσι τοῖς πρωτοτόκοις κοινόν ἐστι ἔλεγε ποιεῖν.[28] In order
to uphold his thesis, Justin has to fight not only against any
interpretation of Is. 7,14, other than that supporting the
virgin birth of Christ,[29] but also against a textual variant
of Is. 7,14 which reads νεᾶνις instead of παρθένος.[30] The
Apologist accuses the Jewish exegetes of changing the original
Septuagintal text in order to eliminate a strong christological
evidence: πολλὰς γραφὰς τέλεον περιεῖλον ἀπὸ τῶν ἐξηγήσεων
τῶν . . . παρὰ Πτολεμαίῳ . . . πρεσβυτέρων (Dial. 71,2).[31]

---

[28]Cf. Ap. 33,4: τὸ οὖν ἰδοὺ ἡ παρθένος ἐν γαστρὶ
ἕξει σημαίνει οὐ συνουσιασθεῖσαν τὴν παρθένον συλλαβεῖν· εἰ
γὰρ ἐσυνουσιάσθη ὑπὸ ὁτουοῦν οὐκέτι ἦν παρθένος. Tertullian
in *Adversus Marcionem* III, 13 quoting Is. 7,14 follows precisely the argument used by Justin concerning the interpretation of the term σημεῖον.

[29]Justin time and again attacks the Jewish interpretation according to which Is. 7,14 relates to the king Hezekiah
(Dial. 43,7; 67,1; 71,3 etc.).

[30]Cf. Dial. 43,4-8; 67,1; 71,3; 84,1 etc.

[31]D. Barthélémy, "Redéconverte d'un chaînon manquant
de l'histoire de la Septante," *Revue Biblique* 60 (1953), pp.
18-29, has produced evidence that Justin, in all probability,
uses "une recension rabbinique de la Septante qui avait cours
entre 70 et 135" (*ibid.*, p. 21). This points to the possibility that Justin uses basically a text employed also by his
Jewish opponents. Hence he is in a position to criticize them
for altering it. Cf. also F. M. Cross, Jr., "The History of
the Biblical Text in the Light of Discovering in the Judaean
Desert," *Harv. Theol. Rev.* 57 (1964), pp. 281-99, esp. 282,
284; W. Shotwell, *op. cit.*, pp. 69-70; J. Daniélou, *Message
évangélique*, pp. 200-201.

148

Justin's argument against the reading νεᾶνις is based on the premise that with such a reading the passage Is. 7,14 does not make any sense, since there is no σημεῖον any more. Shortly after, Irenaeus following Justin would repeat the same argument and would name the exegetes who translated νεᾶνις instead of παρθένος.[32] But Justin was the first extensively to discuss Is. 7,14 and to insist on the Septuagintal reading as a decisive and unequivocal witness to the virgin birth of Christ, and ultimately to his divine pre-existence.[33]

Justin did not exhaust his proof-texts concerning the virgin birth with Is. 7,14. He takes a phrase from Is. 53 (v. 8: τὴν γενεὰν αὐτοῦ τίς διηγήσεται) and uses it as evidence for the virgin birth. Is. 53 is often quoted in the New Testament. It has been interpreted messianically as a prophecy of the sufferings and death of the Messiah. Justin is aware of this interpretation (Dial. 32,2; 72,3; 114,2 et al.), and defends it, but in addition he discerns in Is. 53,8 an indication of Christ's virgin birth. He says in Dial. 76,2: καὶ τὸ ᾿Ησαΐαν φάναι· τὴν γενεὰν αὐτοῦ τίς διηγήσεται [Is. 53,8] ἀνεκδιήγητον ἔχοντα τὸ γένος αὐτὸν ἐδήλου· οὐδεὶς γὰρ ἄνθρωπος ὢν ἐξ ἀνθρώπων ἀνεκδιήγητον ἔχει τὸ γένος.[34] Thus the Apologist is able to draw from Is. 53,8 the conclusion that Christ is not ἄνθρωπος ἐξ ἀνθρώων and consequently that he was born of a virgin.

---

[32]Iren., *Adv. Haer.* III. 21,1: ὁ θεός . . . δοὺς τὸ τῆς παρθένου σημεῖον, ἀλλ᾿ οὐχ ὡς ἔνιοί φασιν τῶν νῦν τολμώντων μεθερμηνεύειν τὴν γραφὴν "ἰδοὺ ἡ νεᾶνις" . . . ὡς Θεοδοτίων ἡρμήνευσεν ὁ ᾿Εφέσιος καὶ ᾿Ακύλας ὁ Ποντικός. To Aquila and Theodotion one should add also Symachus. See J. Ziegler, "Isaias," in *Septuaginta Vetus Testamentum Graecum*, Vol. XIV (Göttingen, 1967²), p. 147.

[33]For the readings παρθένος or νεᾶνις in Is. 7,14 see J. Ziegler, *op. cit.*, p. 147. Cf. also K. Stendahl, *The School of St. Matthew* (Philadelphia, 1968), pp. 97-98 and 181-182; W. Shotwell, *op. cit.*, pp. 69-70. For a review of the exegesis of the passage see J. Coppens, "L'interprétation d' Is. VII,14 à la lumière des études les plus recentes," in *Lex Tua Veritas* (Festschrift H. Junker) (Trier, 1961), pp. 31-45.

[34]Cf. Dial. 63,2: ἔφη ᾿Ησαΐας τὴν γενεὰν αὐτοῦ τίς διηγήσεται . . . οὐ δοκεῖ σοι λελέχθαι ὡς οὐκ ἐξ ἀνθρώπων ἔχοντος τὸ γένος; cf. also Dial. 68,4.

Justin does something similar with Gen. 49,11. He quotes the text in connection with the passion of Christ (Ap. 32,1-11; Dial. 54,1; 63,2). But at the same time he picks out the phrase αἷμα σταφυλῆς and he reads in it a foretelling of the virgin birth: τὸ δὲ εἰρημένον αἷμα σταφυλῆς σημαντικὸν τοῦ ἔχειν μὲν αἷμα τὸν φανησόμενον ἀλλ' οὐκ ἐξ ἀνθρωπείου σπέρματος ἀλλ' ἐκ θείας δυνάμεως (Ap. 32,9). It is difficult to determine the precise process by which Justin arrives at this conclusion. The only explanation that he offers is this: ὃν γὰρ τρόπον τὸ τῆς ἀμπέλου αἷμα οὐκ ἄνθρωπος ἐγέννησε ἀλλὰ θεός, οὕτως καὶ τὸ τοῦ Χριστοῦ αἷμα οὐκ ἐξ ἀνθρωπείου γένους ἔσεσθαι ἀλλ' ἐκ θεοῦ δυνάμεως προεμήνυσε (Dial. 54,2. Also Ap. 32,11 and Dial. 76,2). The argument depends on an interpretation of the phrase τὸ τῆς ἀμπέλου αἷμα, which interpretation might have emerged out of a liturgical-eucharistic context. The significant thing here is the disclosure of Justin's christological intentions.

Another Old Testament text which Justin adduces as an evidence for the virgin birth is Dan. 2,34 in combination with Dan. 7,13-14. In Dial. 76,1, commenting upon the phrase ὡς υἱὸν ἀνθρώπου of Dan. 7,13, he says: τὸ γὰρ ὡς υἱὸν ἀνθρώπου εἰπεῖν, φαινόμενον μὲν καὶ γενόμενον ἄνθρωπον μηνύει, οὐκ ἐξ ἀνθρωπίνου δὲ σπέρματος ὑπάρχοντα δηλοῖ.[35] And immediately after this statement he quotes freely Dan. 2,34 as a witness to the same truth: καὶ τὸ λίθον τοῦτον εἰπεῖν ἄνευ χειρῶν τμηθέντα, ἐν μυστηρίῳ τὸ αὐτὸ κέκραγε [i.e. Daniel]˙ τὸ γὰρ ἄνευ χειρῶν εἰπεῖν αὐτὸν ἐκτετμῆσθαι, ὅτι οὐκ ἔστιν ἀνθρώπινον ἔργον ἀλλὰ τῆς βουλῆς τοῦ προβάλλοντος αὐτὸν πατρὸς τῶν ὅλων θεοῦ (Dial. 76,1). Such a novel interpretation of Dan. 2,34 and 7,13-14 enters the field of Christian literature for the first time with Justin.[36]

---

[35]Justin employs several times the expression οὐκ ἐξ ἀνθρωπίνου σπέρματος in order to designate the supernatural and virgin birth of Christ. Cf. Ap. 32,9,11; Dial. 54,2; 63,2; 76,1.

[36]Irenaeus also uses Dan. 2,34 as a proof for the virgin birth of Christ: Propter hoc autem et Daniel previdens eius adventum "lapidem sine manibus abscisum" (ait) advenisse in hunc mundum . . . hoc est non operante in eum Ioseph, sed sola Maria cooperante dispositioni (*Adv. Haer.* III,21,7). It

150

The Old Testament passages which Justin uses in order
to defend the virgin birth sometimes appear in a series in the
Justinian texts. In Dial. 63,2 for example we find Is. 53,8
followed by Gen. 49,11. In Dial. 76,1-2 one finds Dan. 7,13-
14, Dan. 2,34, Is. 53,8 and Gen. 49,11 quoted in succession.
Is this an indication that Justin employs an already existing
source, a kind of testimonia? Such a possibility should be
seriously considered. However, it is not unlikely that Justin
himself selected the texts which, in a discussion with the
Jews, would give support to the idea of Christ having been
born from a virgin.

2. Next to the Old and the New Testament passages, one
might surmise that Justin, in his discussion of the virgin
birth, presupposes some other texts.

In his Apology to the Emperor Hadrian--or Antonius--
Aristides of Athens says that Christ ἐκ παρθένου ἀγίας γεννηθεὶς ἀσπόρως τε καὶ ἀφθόρως σάρκα ἀνέλαβεν (Apol. 15,1).
Knowing the adventures of Aristides' text[37] one might argue
that the passage from Apology 15 as it stands, does not preserve the original wording. The terms ἀσπόρως and ἀφθόρως in
particular, belong to a late third century christological
terminology and could hardly be ascribed to Aristides himself.
Nevertheless the nucleus of the passage is the virgin birth,
regardless of the specific terminology which was later super-
imposed on it. Here then we have a passage where the virgin
birth seems to be a part of a concise presentation of the
Christian faith. Since Aristides' Apology must have been
written between the years 117-138 (according to Eusebius,
Eccl. Hist. 4,3) or between 138-161 (according to the Syriac
translation), it attests to a very early inclusion of the
virgin birth into the creedal formulations.

Ignatius of Antioch is another early Christian author
who speaks about the virginity of Mary in terms of a creedal
statement. In *Eph.* 19,1 he places the virginity of Mary among

---

is difficult, however, to ascertain whether Irenaeus depends
here on Justin or whether he follows another source.

[37]See J. Quasten, *Patrology*, Vol. I (Utrecht, 1962),
pp. 191-92.

the three μυστήρια κραυγῆς (the other two: ὁ τοκετὸς αὐτῆς
καὶ ὁ θάνατος τοῦ κυρίου) and in *Smyrn*. 1,1 he declares
Christ γεγεννημένον ἀληθῶς ἐκ παρθένου (cf. also Ign. *Eph*.
18,2). The last passage is of importance because it belongs
to a context which presumably is of creedal nature.

In view of the Ignatian passages and the text from
Aristides, one might assume that when Justin wrote he had at
his disposal already existing written formulations of the
doctrine of the virgin birth.

The Justinian works validate such an assumption.
Several of the passages where Justin makes a statement relating
to the virgin birth display unmistakable chracteristics of
comprehensive christological confessions of faith. Dial.
85,1-9, for example, reads: τοῦ υἱοῦ τοῦ θεοῦ καὶ πρωτοτόκου
πάσης κτίσεως καὶ διὰ παρθένου γεννηθέντος καὶ παθητοῦ
γενομένου ἀνθρώπου καὶ σταυρωθέντος ἐπὶ Ποντίου Πιλάτου . . .
καὶ ἀποθανόντος καὶ ἀναστάντος ἐκ νεκρῶν καὶ ἀναβάντος εἰς
τὸν οὐρανόν. It is interesting to see how the same elements
of a christological faith are presented as a result of
prophetic foretelling, because of apologetic purposes, in Ap.
31,7.[38] There is no doubt that Justin, in passages like those
cited above, works on the basis of given traditional material.
In that case the statements referring to Christ's birth from
the Virgin could possibly have been a part of the same
material.

The possibility then exists that next to the scriptural texts Justin presupposes also a certain amount of early
Christian traditional material which relates to the subject of
the virgin birth.

---

[38]Ap. 31,7: ἐν δὴ ταῖς τῶν προφητῶν βίβλοις εὕρομεν
προκηρυσσόμενον, παραγινόμενον, γεννώμενον διὰ παρθένου καὶ
ἀνδρούμενον . . . καὶ ἀγνούμενον καὶ σταυρούμενον Ἰησοῦν τὸν
ἡμέτερον Χριστὸν καὶ ἀποθνήσκοντα καὶ ἀνεγειρόμενον καὶ εἰς
οὐρανοὺς ἀνερχόμενον. See also Ap. 63,15-16 as another
example for Justin's free usage of a creedal framework in which
he retains, however, only the items necessary for the specific
argument. Note that the virgin birth occurs here in spite of
the fact that it does not serve any dialectical purpose.
Presumably it has been quoted because of its association with
creedal statements.

152

3. The Apologist, however, did not restrict himself
to the role of simply repeating in a mechanical fashion bits
of tradition or biblical texts. One could on good grounds
assume that the virgin birth is one of the themes with which
he deals seriously and extensively. Reading through the
Justinian texts one is immediately impressed by the ample
number of references to the virgin birth. The relevant references are more than forty,[39] and they occur within diversified
contexts. Even the specific terminology presents a variety of
formulations:

διὰ παρθένου γεγεννῆσθαι (Ap. 22,5).

διὰ παρθένου . . . διὰ δυνάμεως θεοῦ ἀπεκυήθη
(Ap. 32,14).

δύναμις θεοῦ . . . κυοφορῆσαι παρθένον οὖσαν πεποίηκεν
(Ap. 33,4).

τὸ πνεῦμα ἐλθὸν ἐπὶ τὴν παρθένον καὶ ἐπισκιάσαν οὐ
διὰ συνουσίας ἐγκύμονα κατέστησε (Ap. 33,6).

διὰ παρθένου ἄνθρωπος γενόμενος (Ap. 63,16).

διὰ Μαρίας . . . τῆς παρθένου γεννηθέντα (Dial. 23,3).

ὁ τῷ Ἀβραὰμ ὀφθεὶς θεός . . . διὰ τῆς παρθένου γεννηθεὶς ἄνθρωπος (Dial. 57,3).

διὰ παρθενικῆς μήτρας . . . ἀληθῶς παιδίον γενέσθαι
(Dial. 84,2).

A phenomenon that attracts the attention of the reader
is the steady usage of the expression διὰ παρθένου. Both
Aristides of Athens (*Apology* 15,1) and Ignatius of Antioch
(*Smyrn.* 1,1) employ the phrase ἐκ παρθένου. The preposition
ἐκ seems to be the standard one utilized with the noun
παρθένος in order to designate the virgin birth, from
Irenaeus onwards.[40] Why does Justin use διὰ παρθένου instead
of ἐκ παρθένου?

One could suggest that Justin has deliberately chosen

_____

[39]E.g. Ap. 21,1; 22,5; 32,8-11,14; 33,1-6; 63,16;
Dial. 23,3; 43,1; 54,2; 63,1; 76,1-2; 84,1-2; 100,2-6; 113,4;
127,4 etc.

[40]Irenaeus, *Adv. Haer.* III. 21,4:   credentes in eum
qui ex Virgine natus est Emmanuel; . . . generationem eius
quae est ex Virgine; III. 21,5: hic est qui ex Virgine . . .
generatus est.

the preposition διά instead of ἐκ because he wanted to keep
totally clear the idea of the divinity of the Logos in his
incarnational stage. With διά the origin of Christ would
definitely be sought beyond the Virgin. Of course the διά
could facilitate the rise of docetism[41] but Justin, as we
will see, had found ways to overcome this danger. In the
usage of the term διά παρθένου instead of ἐκ παρθένου one
might discern Justin's orientation towards a Christology which
contemplates the incarnation sub specie pre-existentiae.

Such an assumption is sustained by the fact that the
phrase διά παρθένου occurs in Justin more than twenty times,
and so it prevails in an almost absolute way. Over against
this high frequency we have only two passages where the term
ἀπό παρθένου appears (Dial. 43,7 and 66,4) and two more where
the term ἐκ παρθένου has been used (Dial. 66,1 and 84,1). A
closer look at Dial. 43,7 and 66,4 easily leads to the conclusion that the second passage is a duplicate of the first and
that both follow immediately after the quotation of Is. 7,10-
17. So here we have a verbatim repetition of the same piece.
In other words, we have actually only one case where we
encounter the term ἀπό παρθένου. The occurrence of that term
in Dial. 43,7 (and 66,4) might be accidental. It should be
noted, however, that in the same chapters Justin employed the
expression διά παρθένου (Dial. 43,1 and 66,1) which would help
interpret correctly the ἀπό παρθένου. It also ought to be
pointed out that Dial. 43,7 (and 66,4) is a comment formulated
by way of exclusion,[42] at the end of which Christ is introduced, and not a direct christological statement.

If we now turn to the phrase ἐκ παρθένου (Dial. 66,1

---

[41]As a matter of fact the preposition διά has been
used by the Valentinians in a docetic sense. Irenaeus (*Adv.
Haer.* I.7,2) quotes them as teaching that εἶναι δὲ τοῦτον
[Χριστόν] τὸν διὰ Μαρίας διοδεύσαντα, καθάπερ ὕδωρ διὰ
σωλῆνος ὁδεύει. Hippolytus in his account on the Valentinians
attests to their usage of the term διὰ Μαρίας (cf. *Ref.* VI,
35-36, where the term is mentioned four times!).

[42]Dial. 43,7: ὅτι μὲν οὖν ἐν τῷ γένει τῷ κατὰ σάρκα
τοῦ Ἀβραὰμ οὐδεὶς οὐδέποτε ἀπὸ παρθένου γεγέννηται οὐδὲ
λέλεκται γεγεννημένος . . . πᾶσι φανερὸν ἐστίν. See also
Dial. 66,4.

154

and 84,1) we will see that in Dial. 66,1 the term ἐκ παρθένου
is immediately followed by the term διὰ παρθένου: . . . ἀποδεικνύων ὅτι ἐκ παρθένου γεννητὸς καὶ διὰ παρθένου γεννηθῆναι
αὐτὸν διὰ ᾽Ησαΐου ἐπεπροφήτευτο.[43] One could think that here
Justin utilizes the preposition ἐκ for purely stylistic
reasons, in order to avoid an annoying repetition. In the
second passage, namely Dial. 84,1, the phrase ἐκ παρθένου
might have been used because it was simply a traditional term.
It is, nonetheless, noticeable that the passage, where the
term ἐκ παρθένου occurs, is the initial statement of a con-
centrated argument in defense of the miraculous birth (σημεῖον)
of the Logos. This argument concludes in Dial. 84,2 with a
statement in which the διὰ formulation appears: διὰ παρθενικῆς
μήτρας τὸν πρωτότοκον τῶν πάντων ποιημάτων σαρκοποιηθέντα
ἀληθῶς παιδίον γενέσθαι. Thus the term ἐκ παρθένου in Dial.
84,1 is qualified by the following argumentation and finally
by the phrase διὰ παρθενικῆς μήτρας of Dial. 84,2.

Justin utilizes once more the phrase ἐκ παρθένου. But
this time the reference is to the Greek mythology: ἐκ παρθένου γεγεννῆσθαι τὸν Περσέα (Dial. 70,5). In two more
instances the Apologist makes a reference to Perseus as having
been born of the virgin Danae according to the myth (Ap. 21,2
and Dial. 67,2). In both cases the preposition used is ἐκ
never διά.[44] The phenomenon cannot be accidental. In all
three instances where Perseus is mentioned, and in spite of
the difference in wording, the preposition ἐκ steadily appears.
This is probably due to Justin's decision to differentiate
sharply the virgin birth of Christ from any other alleged
virgin birth.

A further investigation of the Justinian texts shows
that for the Apologist the preposition ἐκ indicates a substantial origin. Thus, when Justin speaks about the Son being

---

[43]A. L. Williams, *op. cit.*, p. 138 is wrong when he
translates both διὰ παρθένου and ἐκ παρθένου of this passage
by the same term, i.e. "of a virgin." J. C. T. Otto, *op. cit.*,
Vol. II, pp. 234-35, correctly uses the expressions ex virgine
and per virginem respectively.

[44]Dial. 67,2: ἐν δὲ τοῖς τῶν λεγομένων ᾽Ελλήνων
μύθοις λέλεκται ὅτι Περσεὺς ἐκ Δανάης, παρθένου οὔσης . . .
γεγέννηται. Cf. Ap. 21,2: τὸν ἐκ Δανάης Περσέα.

begotten by the Father he utilizes the preposition ἐκ.[45] An
example of the differentiation between ἐκ and διὰ with reference to Christ is encountered in Ap. 22,2-5. There, in v. 2
Justin says εἰ δὲ καὶ ἰδίως παρὰ τὴν κοινὴν γένεσιν, γεγεννῆσθαι αὐτὸν ἐκ θεοῦ λέγομεν. A few verses later (v. 5) he
continues: εἰ δὲ διὰ παρθένου γεγεννῆσθαι φέρομεν. The contradistinction between ἐκ θεοῦ and διὰ παρθένου is here fully
manifested. The previous observations explain also Justin's
emphatic statements in which the preposition ἐκ has been
employed: οὐκ ἔστιν ὁ Χριστὸς ἄνθρωπος ἐξ ἀνθρώπων κατὰ τὸ
κοινὸν τῶν ἀνθρώπων γεννηθείς (Dial. 54,2).[46]

The preceding discussion leads to the conclusion that
in dealing with the virgin birth of Christ Justin avoids the
phrase ἐκ παρθένου and uses διὰ παρθένου instead. He does so
because for him the origin of Christ is divine, an event which
is upheld linguistically by the usage of the preposition ἐκ
utilized exclusively with reference to God the Father as the
substantial and ultimate cause of Christ's incarnation through
the virgin. In this case we have, one might contend, an
example of how the concept of the pre-existence of Christ as
God affects the terminology of incarnation.

4. The virgin birth is a basic doctrine for Justin
precisely because of its direct connection to the divinity of
the Son.[47] Hence the Apologist does not refrain from employing

---

[45]E.g. Dial. 105,1: μονογενὴς γὰρ ὅτι ἦν τῷ πατρὶ τῶν
ὅλων οὗτος, ἰδίως ἐξ αὐτοῦ λόγος . . . γεγεννημένος: Ap. 22,2:
γεγεννῆσθαι αὐτὸν ἐκ θεοῦ λέγομεν λόγον θεοῦ.

[46]Cf. also Ap. 30,1; Dial. 48,1,3; 49,1; 67,2; 76,2
where the phrase ἄνθρωπος ἐξ ἀνθρώπων is utilized. In Dial.
76,1-2 where Justin discusses some Old Testament passages
which relate to the virgin birth, he introduces two formulations that run parallel to the phrase οὐκ ἔστιν ἄνθρωπος
ἐξ ἀνθρώπων. They are ὅτι αἷμα μὲν ἔχειν αὐτόν [Χριστόν]
ἀλλ' οὐκ ἐξ ἀνθρώπων (v. 2), and φαινόμενον μὲν καὶ γενόμενον
ἄνθρωπον μηνύει, οὐκ ἐξ ἀνθρωπίνου δὲ σπέρματος ὑπάρχοντα
δηλοῖ (v. 1).

[47]F. Bosse (op. cit., p. 34), even without making any
analysis of the texts, had a right insight into the matter
when he maintained that Justin dealt with the virgin birth
not because of its being an article of the Community's faith
but because of its immediate connection to the pre-existence
of Christ.

156

a plain vocabulary in order to make clear his thesis. Thus
the expression διὰ παρθένου means without human intercourse.[48]
In Ap. 33,4, for instance, he says τὸ οὖν ἰδοὺ ἡ παρθένος ἐν
γαστρὶ ἕξει σημαίνει οὐ συνουσιασθεῖσαν τὴν παρθένον συλλαβεῖν·
εἰ γὰρ ἐσυνουσιάσθη ὑπὸ ὁτουοῦν, οὐκέτι ἦν παρθένος (cf. Ap.
33,6; Dial. 78,3; 84,1). Justin is the only one among the
second century Apologists and the Apostolic Fathers to use the
terms συνουσία and συνουσιάζεσθαι, in order to reject them,
with reference to the virgin birth. In Ap. 21,1 he employs
the word ἐπιμιξία for the same purpose: ἄνευ ἐπιμιξίας φάσκειν
ἡμᾶς γεγεννῆσθαι ᾿Ιησοῦν Χριστόν.[49]

          Justin knows that he should explain how Christ was
conceived and born since he was not born κατὰ τὸ κοινὸν τῶν
ἀνθρώπων (Dial. 54,2). His explanation is built on Mt. 1,18-
25 and Lk. 1,35. In Ap. 33,1-5 the Apologist, having used
phrases from Mt. 1,18-25 and Lk. 1,35 which he integrates into
his own statements, concludes by saying ὡς οἱ ἀπομνημονεύσαν-
τες πάντα τὰ περὶ τοῦ σωτῆρος ἡμῶν ᾿Ιησοῦ Χριστοῦ ἐδίδαξαν
οἷς ἐπιστεύσαμεν. It is then apparent that here Justin is
following the New Testament texts mentioned above. What he
takes from them is the phrase τὸ γὰρ ἐν αὐτῇ γεννηθὲν ἐκ
πνεύματός ἐστιν ἁγίου (Mt. 1,20) and the angelic message
πνεῦμα ἅγιον ἐπελεύσεται ἐπὶ σὲ καὶ δύναμις ὑψίστου ἐπισκιάσει
σοι (Lk. 1,35). Justin then fuses these phrases and formulates
his own statements like τοῦτο [πνεῦμα] ἐλθὸν ἐπὶ τὴν παρθένον
καὶ ἐπισκιάσαν οὐ διὰ συνουσίας ἀλλὰ διὰ δυνάμεως ἐγκύμονα
κατέστησεν (Ap. 33,6), or δύναμις θεοῦ ἐπελθοῦσα τῇ παρθένῳ
ἐπεσκίασεν αὐτὴν καὶ κυοφορῆσαι παρθένον οὖσαν πεποίηκε (Ap.
33,4). Actually Justin's formulations repeat the New Testament

---

[48]In order to eliminate any possibility of misinterpretation Justin does not hesitate to make a change in the
accounts of Matthew and Luke as regards the ancestral line of
Christ. As E. R. Goodenough appropriately states (*op. cit.*,
p. 239) Justin "traces the Davidic line of Christ not through
Joseph but through Mary." Goodenough, however, fails to
evaluate properly the change.

[49]The word ἐπιμιξία for intercourse occurs in Philo
(*Decal.* 127) and later on in Clement of Alexandria (*Strom.*
2.23, Migne P. G. 8,1089A). Justin is the only Christian
author prior to Clement to use the word.

statements, with an emphasis on the virginal conception and birth, rather than on explaining them. Justin's own particular contribution is the identification of πνεῦμα and δύναμις with the Logos: τὸ πνεῦμα οὖν καὶ τὴν δύναμιν τὴν παρὰ τοῦ θεοῦ (of Lk. 1,35) οὐδὲν ἄλλο νοῆσαι θέμις ἢ τὸν λόγον, ὃς καὶ πρωτότοκος τοῦ θεοῦ ἐστί . . . τοῦτο ἐλθὸν ἐπὶ τὴν παρθένον etc. (Ap. 33,6). The relationship between the Logos and the πνεῦμα in Justin is a special subject which falls outside of the present study and so we shall not deal with it here. The introduction of the Logos as the divine agent for the impregnation of the Virgin Mary is in full agreement with Justin's basic theological presuppositions. As we have observed in the previous chapters Justin ascribes the divine activities which come in contact with the world to the Logos-Son because he wants God the Father to remain in absolute transcendence.[50] Therefore the Son has to be the agent who acts in the incarnational process, as he acted in the theophanies, not only as the one who should be born διὰ παρθένου but as the one who would bring about the whole event.

5. During the assessement of the data pertaining to Justin's handling of the concept of the virgin birth we have observed a persisting fact: In most cases the statement of the virgin birth is accompanied by a statement of the pre-existence of Christ, sometimes in an elaborate form:

Ap. 21,1: τὸν λόγον, ὃ ἐστι πρῶτον γέννημα τοῦ θεοῦ ἄνευ ἐπιμιξίας φάσκειν ἡμᾶς γεγεννῆσθαι, ᾿Ιησοῦν Χριστόν.

Ap. 32,10-14: ἡ δὲ πρώτη δύναμις μετὰ τὸν πατέρα πάντων καὶ δεσπότην θεὸν καὶ υἱὸς ὁ λόγος ἐστιν· ὃς τίνα τρόπον σαρκοποιηθεὶς ἄνθρωπος γέγονεν ἐροῦμεν . . . διὰ γὰρ παρθένου . . . ἀπεκυήθη.

Ap. 63,15-16: ὃς [υἱός] καὶ λόγος πρωτότοκος ὢν τοῦ θεοῦ καὶ θεὸς ὑπάρχει . . . νῦν δέ . . . διὰ παρθένου ἄνθρωπος

---

[50] Justin is not anxious to show in the case of the impregnation of the virgin Mary that the δύναμις of the Logos is not of his own but of the Father, as Goodenough seems to believe (*op. cit.*, p. 236f.). The central issue here is the relationship between the Father and the Son, not in terms of subordination, but in terms of transcendence. Cf. Daniélou, *Message évangélique*, p. 153.

158

γενόμενος.

Dial. 45,4: ὃς (Χριστός) καὶ πρὸ ἑωσφόρου καὶ σελήνης ἦν
καὶ διὰ τῆς παρθένου ταύτης . . . γεννηθῆναι.

Dial. 48,2: προϋπῆρχε υἱὸς τοῦ ποιητοῦ τῶν ὅλων, θεὸς ὤν,
καὶ γεγέννηται ἄνθρωπος διὰ τῆς παρθένου.

Dial. 57,3: ὁ τῷ Ἀβραὰμ ὀφθεὶς θεός . . . διὰ τῆς παρθένου
γεννηθεὶς ἄνθρωπος.

Dial. 84,2: διὰ παρθενικῆς μήτρας τὸν πρωτότοκον τῶν
πάντων ποιημάτων σαρκοποιηθέντα ἀληθῶς παιδίον γενέσθαι.

Dial. 85,2: τοῦ υἱοῦ τοῦ θεοῦ καὶ πρωτοτόκου πάσης
κτίσεως καὶ διὰ παρθένου γεννηθέντος.

Dial. 127,4: θεὸν ὄντα, υἱὸν αὐτοῦ, καὶ ἄγγελον ἐκ τοῦ
ὑπηρετεῖν τῇ γνώμῃ αὐτοῦ· ὃν καὶ ἄνθρωπον γεννηθῆναι διὰ
τῆς παρθένου βεβούληται.[51]

The evidence is unmistakable that a christological
pattern of pre-existence and incarnation is operative here.
This pattern belongs to early creedal traditions, to be sure.
But Justin develops it by interpreting it theologically. His
terminological and conceptual elaborations centered around
the virgin birth are probably the outcome of such a theological interpretation.

D. *The Humiliation Element*

Justin's various statements relating to the
incarnation of Christ are couched in language which contains
a number of "humiliation" terms.[52] The provenance of these
terms could be sought in the area of "suffering-cross-death-
of-Christ" early traditions. The concept of the pre-existence
of Christ, on the other hand, might have contributed to the
humiliation terminology in Justin. Let us examine this

---

[51]Cf. also Dial. 50,1; 75,4; 87,2; 100,4; 105,1; 113,4.

[52]E.g. ἄδοξος, ἄτιμος, ἀειδής, παθητός, ὁμοιοπαθὴς
ἡμῖν, ταπεινὸς ἄνθρωπος occur often in the Justinian texts
with reference to the incarnate Son.

alternative.

     1. The first elements of a humiliation language in
Justin are to be discerned in his description of the incarnation as the πρώτη παρουσία.[53] Justin characterizes this first
παρουσία as ἄτιμος καὶ ἀειδής καὶ ἐξουθενημένη (Dial. 121,3)
and ἄδοξος (Dial. 49,7). The argument could be made that the
incarnation is characterized so because it is compared to the
δευτέρα παρουσία, i.e., the glorious eschatological coming
of Christ (Dial. 31,1; 35,8; 121,4). In addition one might
contend that the Apologist describes the incarnation as ἄτιμος
καὶ ἄδοξος πρώτη παρουσία in conformity with the scriptural
terminology, in order to win his Jewish opponents.[54] In that
case the humiliation language employed in the πρώτη παρουσία
passages seems to be the result of apologetic and exegetical
reasoning, not of christological reflection based on the pre-
existence of Christ. The latter, however, should not be
excluded as a formative factor. Justin portrays Christ in his
first παρουσία as ἄτιμος, ἀειδής καὶ θνητὸς (Dial. 14,8), as
ἄτιμος καὶ παθητὸς ἄνθρωπος (Apol. 52,3) or as ταπεινὸς
ἄνθρωπος (Dial. 33,2) without any reservation. He does not
make any attempt to mitigate such a description, to say e.g.
that this is applicable mainly to the passion of Jesus. This,
one might argue, could not be so if the πρώτη παρουσία was not
viewed also from the standpoint of pre-existence.

     2. Justin betrays an understanding of the incarnation
as humiliation by using the adjectives ἄτιμος, ἄδοξος, ἀειδὴς
and παθητὸς for Christ. They occur several times mostly
together as a group of characterizations.[55] There is no doubt
that Justin, as he often says, has taken these adjectives from
Isaiah 53, a chapter which he extensively utilizes.[56] Ἄτιμος
appears in Is. 53,3 (τὸ εἶδος αὐτοῦ ἄτιμον καὶ ἐκλεῖπον).

---

[53]Dial. 14,8; 36,1; 49,7; 52,1 etc.

[54]Cf. Trypho's theory in Dial. 32,1 to Justin's thesis
expressed in a variety of occasions (Apol. 52,3; Dial. 14,8;
40,4; 49,2; 52,1; 110,2; 111,1).

[55]Ap. 52,3; Dial. 32,1; 49,2; 85,1; 100,2; 110,2 etc.

[56]Cf. N. Brox, *op. cit.*, pp. 126-27. Passages from
Isaiah 53 are quoted by Justin in more than twenty instances
(e.g. Ap. 50,3-11; Dial. 32,1; 42,2,3; 68,4; 72,3; 76,2 etc.)

῎Αδοξος and ἀειδής are apparently a rendering in adjectival
form of the expression οὐκ ἔστιν εἶδος αὐτῷ οὐδὲ δόξα (Is.
53,2). Finally παθητὸς seems to be the central concept of
Is. 53 which is the chapter of suffering. The term does not
occur in Is. 53, neither does the verb πάσχειν but the whole
pericope abounds with verbs of pain and suffering (ὀδυνᾶσθαι,
εἶναι ἐν πόνῳ, τραυματίζεσθαι, ἐν πληγῇ εἶναι, κεκακῶσθαι et
al.). Here then the humiliation vocabulary is borrowed from
texts related to the passion and is not prompted by the concept
of pre-existence.

        a) That the words ἄτιμος et al. originated
from texts connected with the sufferings and the death of
Christ no one could deny. It is interesting to note, however,
that these terms appear in statements of the type "pre-existence and incarnation," where pre-existence is present side by
side with these adjectival indicators of the humiliation of
the incarnate Son. We have an example of this kind in Dial.
100,2: Γνόντες αὐτὸν [Χριστόν] πρωτότοκον μὲν τοῦ θεοῦ καὶ
πρὸ πάντων τῶν κτισμάτων, καὶ τῶν πατριαρχῶν υἱόν, ἐπειδὴ διὰ
τῆς ἀπὸ τοῦ γένους αὐτῶν παρθένου σαρκοποιηθείς, καὶ ἄνθρωπος
ἀειδὴς καὶ ἄτιμος καὶ παθητὸς ὑπέμεινε γενέσθαι. The passage
speaks only about pre-existence and incarnation. In the
immediately following text (Dial. 100,3), even a reference to
the passion from Mk. 8,31 is employed because of the expression
υἱὸς ἀνθρώπου contained in it which is related by Justin to
the birth of Christ, i.e., to incarnation.[57] In the same
chapter the Apologist returns again to the theme of the virgin
birth preceded by the theme of the pre-existence (Dial. 100,4),
a fact which reveals the thrust of his thought. In Dial.
100,2 one could observe how a passion vocabulary has unreservedly been used for the incarnation possibly because of the
juxtaposition of the latter to pre-existence.[58]

---

[57]J. Howton, *op. cit.*, p. 238, believes that in Dial.
100,3, and specifically in Justin's interpretation of the
phrase υἱὸς ἀνθρώπου there is a "small pointer" to the fact
that Justin understood υἱὸς in terms of the Old Testament concept of Israel. Dial. 100,3, however, does not seem to favor
Howton's contention.

[58]The ἄτιμος-ἄδοξος-ἀειδὴς vocabulary in Justin is
not only related to the pre-existence but also to the

b) Among the adjectives of humiliation the
term παθητός deserves special attention. It is frequently met
in the Justinian works.[59] Sometimes it appears as part of the
group ἄτιμος-ἄδοξος-ἀειδής, sometimes it stands all by itself
or in conjunction with other words.

The word παθητός related to the Messiah occurs
already in Acts (26,23: εἰ παθητὸς ὁ Χριστός) where the context suggests that the term is used with reference to the
passion. In Ignatius of Antioch παθητός appears twice. A
remarkable change, however, occurs. The term παθητός in the
Ignatian passages is placed over against the term ἀπαθής:
τὸν ἄχρονον τὸν ἀόρατον τὸν δι᾿ ἡμᾶς ὁρατόν, τὸν ἀψηλάφητον
τὸν ἀπαθῆ τὸν δι᾿ ἡμᾶς παθητόν (Ign. Polyc. 3,2).[60] The passage does not leave any room for doubt that παθητός has as its
main point of connection the christological categories of pre-
existence expressed by the terms ἀπαθής and ἀψηλάφητος (also
ἄχρονος and ἀόρατος). A peculiar coincidence of the Ignatian
terminology in a totally different conceptual setting is met
in a gnostic passage. According to Irenaeus (Adv. Haer. I.
6,1) the Valentinians taught that ἀπὸ δὲ τοῦ δημιουργοῦ
ἐνδεδύσθαι τὸν ψυχικὸν Χριστόν, ἀπὸ δὲ τῆς οἰκονομίας περι-
τεθεῖσθαι σῶμα ψυχικὴν ἔχον οὐσίαν, κατεσκευασμένον δὲ
ἀρρήτῳ τέχνῃ πρὸς τὸ καὶ ἀόρατον καὶ ἀψηλάφητον καὶ παθητὸν
γεγεννῆσθαι. Here ἀόρατον, ἀψηλάφητον καὶ παθητὸν belong
together, contrary to the Ignatian usage. The interesting
thing, nonetheless, is that with Adv. Haer. I.6,1 we are even
more removed from a passion context. Far more important is a

---

exaltation of Christ as Dial. 36,5-6 shows. This points to a
humiliation and exaltation Christology behind the said
vocabulary. Cf. J. T. Brothers, op. cit., p. 131-32.

[59]Παθητός occurs twenty times in eighteen Justinian
passages: Ap. 52,3; Dial. 34,2; 36,1; 39,7; 41,1; 49,2;
52,1; 68,9; 70,4; 74,1; 76,6; 85,2; 89,2; 99,2; 100,2; 110,2;
111,2; 126,1.

[60]Cf. Ign. Eph. 7,2 καὶ ἐκ Μαρίας καὶ ἐκ θεοῦ πρῶτον
παθητὸς καὶ τότε ἀπαθής. Here ἀπαθής is a consequence of
exaltation after death.

162

gnostic text from *Excerpta ex Theodoto*.[61] In this passage
the adjective παθητός is used as a basic interpretative term
of the humiliation phrase in Phil. 2,7 μορφὴν δούλου λαβών.
At the same time the terminology takes on a philosophical
coloration.[62] The antithesis ἀπαθής-παθητός occurs also in
Plutarch where the reference is to the divine things in juxtaposition to the earthly.[63]

Justin utilizes the adjective παθητός with scriptural
references to the passion when he relates it, e.g., to Is.
53.[64] Thus he is able to advance his discussion with Trypho
or the Jewish exegetes on a biblical basis. Yet Justin's use
of παθητός might be ascribed also to the connection of this
term with the concept of the pre-existence of Christ. Such
a connection is evident in several instances. In Dial. 85,2,
for instance, it is expressed in a creedal formulation: τοῦ
υἱοῦ τοῦ θεοῦ καὶ πρωτοτόκου πάσης κτίσεως καὶ διὰ παρθένου
γεννηθέντος καὶ παθητοῦ γενομένου ἀνθρώπου καὶ σταυρωθέντος.
In Dial. 34,2 the term παθητός seems to be part of a statement
which displays undeniable traces of a humiliation and exaltation Christology: ὁ γὰρ Χριστὸς βασιλεὺς καὶ ἱερεὺς καὶ θεὸς
καὶ κύριος . . . καὶ παιδίον γεννώμενον καὶ παθητὸς γενόμενος

---

[61] *Excerpta ex Theod.* 19 (Migne P.G. 9.668B): ὅθεν
καὶ μορφὴν δούλου λαβεῖν εἴρηται, οὐ μόνον τὴν σάρκα κατὰ
τὴν παρουσίαν, ἀλλὰ καὶ τὴν οὐσίαν ἐκ τοῦ ὑποκειμένου, δούλη
δὲ ἡ οὐσία ὡς ἂν παθητὴ καὶ ὑποκειμένη τῇ δραστηρίῳ καὶ κυριω-
τάτῃ αἰτίᾳ.

[62] Cf. Dionysius of Halicarn, apud Eusebius, *Evang.
Praep.* 7.19,1: οὐδ᾽ ἐκεῖνοι μὲν γὰρ ὅσιοι οἱ τὴν ὕλην ὡς
ἀγέννητον ὑποχείριον εἰς διακόσμησιν διδόντες τῷ θεῷ·
παθητὴν γὰρ αὐτὴν καὶ τρεπτὴν ὑπάρχουσαν εἴκειν ταῖς θεοποιή-
τοις ἀλλοιώσεσι. 7.19,5: ὁ μὲν θεὸς ἀπαθὴς ἄτρεπτος . . .
ἡ δὲ [ὕλη] τὰ ἐναντία παθητή, τρεπτή . . . Cf. also
Apollodorus apud Diogenes Laertius VII,, 150: καὶ παθητὴ
γὰρ ἐστίν [ἡ οὐσία]· εἰ γὰρ ἦν ἄτρεπτος . . . Philo, too,
uses the adjective παθητός as a modifier for ὕλη (*Spec. Leg.*
III, 180: παθητὴ καὶ διαιρετὴ ὕλη) or for οὐσία in sharp
differentiation from God (*Ebr.* 73).

[63] Plutarch, *De anima procr. in Tim.* 27 (Moral. 1026D):
ἔκ τε τῆς θείας καὶ ἀπαθοῦς ἔκ τε τῆς θνητῆς καὶ περὶ τὰ
σώματα παθητῆς μερίδος. Cf. *Amat.* 19 (Moral. 765B).

[64] Dial. 126,1: καὶ παθητὸς καὶ ᾽Ιακὼβ καὶ ᾽Ισραὴλ
πάλιν διὰ ᾽Ησαίου κέκληται ὁ Χριστός . Cf. Dial. 89,2:
παθητὸν μὲν τὸν Χριστὸν ὅτι αἱ γραφαὶ κηρύσσουσι, φανερόν ἐστιν.

πρῶτον εἶτα εἰς οὐρανὸν ἀνερχόμενος.[65] On the basis of this
evidence one could contend that the word παθητὸς in Justin is
employed with reference not only to the passion of Christ, but
even more to his pre-existence and exaltation.

3. How the concept of pre-existence could affect the
language pertinent to incarnation might be seen in Justin's
handling of the verb ὑπομένειν. The New Testament contains
examples of a christological utilization of that verb.
Hebrews 12,2 speaks about Jesus ὃς ἀντὶ τῆς προκειμένης
αὐτῷ χαρᾶς ὑπέμεινε σταυρόν.[66] The reference is to the cross
and to the rejection of Christ by the "sinners."

The Apostolic Fathers follow the same line. The
author of *Barnabas* often speaks about the Lord who ὑπέμεινε
παθεῖν. He always means the passion and the death of Jesus.
So does the author of *Second Clement*.[67] Ignatius describes
Christ as κατὰ πάντα τρόπον δι' ἡμᾶς ὑπομείναντα (Ign., *Polyc.*
3,2) and Polycarp states that Χριστὸς . . . ὑπέμεινε ὑπὲρ
τῶν ἁμαρτιῶν ἡμῶν ἕως θανάτου καταντῆσαι (Pol., *Philip.* 1,2).

Justin knows this line of tradition, since he uses
the verb ὑπομένειν in conjunction with the passion of Christ:
[Χριστός] παθεῖν καὶ ἀτιμασθῆναι ὑπέμεινεν (Ap. 50,1), καὶ
ἐξουθενηθῆναι καὶ παθεῖν ὑπέμεινεν (Ap. 63,16) et al. The
Apologist, however, departs in a significant way from the type
of ὑπομένειν christological passages found in the New Testament and the Apostolic Fathers: he uses the verb ὑπομένειν
with reference to the comprehensive category of incarnation.
He makes the statement that the Son διὰ τῆς παρθένου ταύτης
. . . γεννηθῆναι σαρκοποιηθεὶς ὑπέμεινεν (Dial. 45,4) or that
γεννηθῆναι ἄνθρωπον γενόμενον ὑπομεῖναι (Dial. 48,1) or that

---

[65]Cf. the phrase παθητὸς γενόμενος πρῶτον εἶτα εἰς
οὐρανὸν ἀνερχόμενος to Dial. 33,2 ταπεινὸς ἔσται πρῶτον
ἄνθρωπος εἶτα ὑψωθήσεται. It is apparent that ταπεινὸς
ἄνθρωπος corresponds to παθητὸς and so the latter term seems
to characterize the incarnation in contradistinction to the
pre-existence and the exaltation.

[66]Cf. also Hebr. 12,3 τὸν τοιαύτην ὑπομεμενηκότα
ὑπὸ τῶν ἁμαρτωλῶν εἰς ἑαυτὸν ἀντιλογίαν.

[67]*Barn.* 5,1; 5,5; 5,6: 5,12; 14,4. *II Clem.* 1,2 ὅσα
ὑπέμεινεν ᾽Ιησοῦς Χριστὸς παθεῖν ἕνεκα ἡμῶν.

διὰ τῆς παρθένου ἄνθρωπος γεννηθῆναι κατὰ τὴν τοῦ πατρὸς αὐτοῦ βούλησιν ὑπέμεινεν (Dial. 63,1. Cf. Dial. 48,3; 50,1; 67,4).

Thus the verb ὑπομένειν in the sense of suffering or being subject to a condition of debasement becomes in Justin a term for characterizing the incarnation. The transference from the passion level to the incarnation level is evident here. Most of the passages where ὑπομένειν relates to the incarnation are christological formulations which exhibit a "pre-existence and incarnation" pattern. Furthermore, the pre-existence part in these formulations ascribes the title θεός to the pre-existing Christ: προϋπάρχειν θεὸν ὄντα πρὸ αἰώνων τοῦτον τὸν Χριστόν, εἶτα καὶ γεννηθῆναι ἄνθρωπον γενόμενον ὑπομεῖναι (Dial. 48,1); προϋπῆρχε καὶ ἄνθρωπος ὁμοιοπαθὴς ὑμῖν . . . ὑπέμεινε (Dial. 48,3); πῶς ἔχεις ἀπο-δεῖξαι ὅτι καὶ ἄλλος θεὸς παρὰ τὸν ποιητὴν τῶν ὅλων καὶ τότε ἀποδείξεις ὅτι καὶ γεννηθῆναι διὰ τῆς παρθένου ὑπέμεινε (Dial. 50,1); . . . ὅτι θεὸς ὑπέμεινε γεννηθῆναι (Dial. 68,1).[68] In view of these statements and of the preceding analysis one could assume that the usage of ὑπομένειν as a term referring to the incarnation is prompted by the simultaneous contempla-tion of incarnation and pre-existence through a christological pattern that combines them. A strong pre-existence terminology naturally leads to an emphasis of the humiliation aspect in the incarnation.

4. When exploring the expression διὰ παρθένου we pointed out the possibility of a docetic exploitation of it. We noticed, however, that Justin had means to render impossible a docetic interpretation of his texts. These means are the humiliation terms unreservedly used by the Apologist in his dealing with the incarnation. In the foregoing pages we have studied most of the relevant terms. Here we will report on additional ones which relate to the question of anti-docetism.

Justin uses the word ὁμοιοπαθὴς for the incarnate

---

[68]The most elaborate formulation of this type is met in Dial. 45,4: τὸν Χριστὸν τοῦτον τοῦ θεοῦ υἱόν, ὃς καὶ πρὸ ἐωσφόρου καὶ σελήνης ἦν, καὶ διὰ τῆς παρθένου ταύτης τῆς ἀπὸ τοῦ γένους τοῦ Δαυεὶδ γεννηθῆναι σαρκοποιηθεὶς ὑπέμεινε.

Christ in order to designate his full and real humanity.[69] In
a passage which we quoted already (Dial. 48,3) Justin says ὁ
Χριστὸς προϋπῆρχε καὶ γεννηθῆναι ἄνθρωπος ὁμοιοπαθὴς ἡμῖν
σάρκα ἔχων. In Dial. 57,3 he repeats the statement with
slight modifications: ὁ τῷ Ἀβραὰμ ὀφθεὶς θεός . . . διὰ
τῆς παρθένου γεννηθεὶς ἄνθρωπος ὁμοιοπαθὴς πᾶσι . . . γέγονεν.
The expressions ὁμοιοπαθὴς ἡμῖν σάρκα ἔχων and ὁμοιοπαθὴς
πᾶσιν as adjectival modifiers for ἄνθρωπος reveal Justin's
anti-docetic intentions.[70] In two more passages the word
ὁμοιοπαθὴς is employed by the Apologist in order to denote a
sharing of the same nature on a purely human level.[71] It
should not be overlooked that in both Dial. 48,3 and 57,3
ὁμοιοπαθὴς occurs within a context where the expression διὰ
παρθένου also appears.

Justin's overcoming of docetism via a humiliation
language is also manifested in Dial. 99,2 and 103,8. Commenting on Mt. 26,39 Justin says δηλῶν διὰ τούτων ὅτι ἀληθῶς
παθητὸς ἄνθρωπος γεγένηται [ὁ Χριστός] (Dial. 99,2). In
another comment on Lk. 22,42-44 he states more explicitly
that ὁ πατὴρ τὸν ἑαυτοῦ υἱὸν καὶ ἐν τοιούτοις πάθεσιν ἀληθῶς
γεγονέναι δι᾽ ἡμᾶς βεβούληται καὶ μὴ λέγωμεν ὅτι ἐκεῖνος τοῦ

---

[69]The term ὁμοιοπαθὴς occurs in Acts 14,15 and James
5,17. In both instances it is not a christological term and
it means having the same nature with someone, viz., being
human. There is a latent juxtaposition of the human and the
divine in these two passages (contrary to the opinion of E.
Haenchen, *Die Apostelgeschichte*, Meyer Komment. Göttingen,
1968, p. 369). The term ὁμοιοπαθὴς in a christological
context appears also in the spurious epistle of Ignatius to
the *Philippians* (ch. 9) and in the lengthier recension of
Ignatius' epistle to the *Trallians* (ch. 10). In both cases,
however, the word is connected to σῶμα in the phrase ὁμοιοπαθὲς σῶμα not to ἄνθρωπος.

[70]Cf. also App. 10,8 where ἄνθρωπος is omitted or
rather replaced by ὁμοιοπαθὴς: λόγος γὰρ ἦν καὶ ἔστιν . . .
διὰ τῶν προφητῶν προειπὼν τὰ μέλλοντα γίνεσθαι καὶ δι᾽ ἑαυτοῦ
ὁμοιοπαθοῦς γενομένου καὶ διδάξαντος ταῦτα.

[71]App. 1,1: ὑπὲρ ὑμῶν [ὦ Ῥωμαῖοι] ὁμοιοπαθῶν ὄντων
καὶ ἀδελφῶν; Dial. 93,3: πλησίον δὲ ἀνθρώπου οὐδὲν ἄλλο
ἐστὶν ἢ τὸ ὁμοιοπαθὲς καὶ λογικὸν ζῶον, ὁ ἄνθρωπος. Tatian
(*Or. Graec.* 35) utilizes ὁμοιοπαθὴς once on this human level
with reference to himself. This is the only occurrence of
ὁμοιοπαθὴς in the Apologists and the Apostolic Fathers.

θεοῦ υἱὸς ὤν, οὐκ ἀντελαμβάνετο τῶν γινομένων καὶ συμβαινόντων αὐτῷ.[72]

For Justin then the incarnation of Christ is real and complete just as the pre-existence in a divine status is real. Hence he does not have any scruples in using the διὰ παρθένου formula and at the same time in employing the humiliation terminology which we have analyzed in the present section. As the author of Hebr. 5,5-8 could proceed into an intensified humiliation language because of his firm belief in the pre-existing Christ, so Justin. But in addition Justin uses this opportunity for anti-docetic purposes.

5. Before closing the present section we should also report on one additional special term, and a particular passage with respect to the humiliation element in Justin.

a) The passage is Dial. 134,5 which among other statements contains also this: ἐδούλευσε καὶ τὴν μέχρι σταυροῦ δουλείαν ὁ Χριστὸς ὑπὲρ τῶν ἐκ παντὸς γένους ποικίλων καὶ πολυειδῶν ἀνθρώπων, δι᾿ αἵματος καὶ μυστηρίου τοῦ σταυροῦ κτησάμενος αὐτούς. The connection between δουλεύω-δουλεία and, on the other hand, the cross is clear in this passage, but not exclusive.[73] Grammatically examined the formulation καὶ τὴν μέχρι σταυροῦ δουλείαν means that the cross is the most extreme point which this δουλεία has reached, but not the exclusive one.[74] One could contend that δουλεύω-

---

[72]Dial. 103,8. Cf. Dial. 98,1 καὶ ἀποδεικνύων ὅτι ἀληθῶς γέγονεν ἄνθρωπος ἀντιληπτικὸς παθῶν. One more case should be mentioned. In App. 13,4 we have an additional "humiliation" statement: [ὁ λόγος] δι᾿ ἡμᾶς ἄνθρωπος γέγονεν, ὅπως καὶ τῶν παθῶν τῶν ἡμετέρων συμμέτοχος γενόμενος καὶ ἴασιν ποιήσηται. The context indicates that the passage was not written with anti-docetic intentions although it defends the real humanity of Christ. Here the orientation is soteriological.

[73]J. T. Brothers, *op. cit.*, p. 137 appears to over-state this connection and to make it exclusive when he argues that here "the δουλεία is the sacrificial offering on the Cross." He obviously overlooks the other references of δουλεύω-δουλεία in Dial. 134,5.

[74]A. L. Williams, *op. cit.*, p. 277 is right when he translates this passage: "Christ served His service even as far as the cross." Similarly G. Archambault, *op. cit.*, Vol. II, p. 283: "le Christ a servi aussi et jusqu'à la servitude de la croix."

δουλεία in Dial. 134,5 refers to the incarnation in general
with the cross as a culminating point. The Justinian texts
seem to support this contention.

           1) The verb δουλεύω occurs several times in
Justin. It means to be enslaved to the demons (Ap. 44,12;
Dial. 83,4), to serve (by doing an unpleasant and somehow
forced work, Dial. 134,3,5 ref. to Jacob with respect to
Laban), to be subjected to the Lord (Dial. 34,4 ref. to Ps.
71,11 [LXX]), to be subject and obedient to God (Dial. 28,6
ref. to Ps. 17,44-45 [LXX], Ap. 40,17 ref. to Ps. 2,11, Dial.
136,1 ref. to Is. 65,8), and, finally, to serve in a good
sense (the expression is εὖ δουλεύοντα found in Is. 53,11
which is quoted by Justin, in Ap. 51,4 and Dial. 13,7). The
verb δουλεύειν with reference to Christ occurs only in Dial.
134,3 and 134,5. In both instances the term is used exactly
as in the case of Jacob and Laban which is interpreted typologically (Dial. 134,2-5). The meaning is "to serve in a
painful and humiliating manner."[75] That this serving is not
limited to the cross is evidenced by the statement in Dial.
134,3: καὶ ὑπὲρ τούτων δουλεύει μέχρι νῦν ὁ Χριστός, which
means that Christ's humble condition of serving continues as
long as there are people in need of salvation.

           2) The word δουλεία in Dial. 134,5 reinforces
the humiliation element which is inherent in the verb δουλεύω.
The term δουλεία is found only three times in Justin. In
Dial. 134,4 and Dial. 139,4 δουλεία means bondage and refers
to the same Old Testament incident (Noah and his sons). The
third occurrence of the term is in Dial. 134,5: ἐδούλευσε
καὶ τὴν μέχρι σταυροῦ δουλείαν ὁ Χριστός. In view of the

---

[75]Attention ought to be drawn to the fact that
Justin's own usage of δουλεύω (i.e. outside of the scriptural
quotations), is conceptually restricted to two negative
meanings: (a) to be enslaved to the demons, and (b) to serve
in a painful and humiliating way. The same holds true for
his usage of the term δοῦλος. Outside of the scriptural
quotations (e.g. Dial. 87,6; 123,3; 135,4) Justin employs
the term δοῦλος always with negative connotations (Ap. 14,1;
Dial. 134,3; 140,1, etc.). In this sense Justin does not
follow the New Testament usage of the respective terms. Cf.
K. H. Rengstorf, "δοῦλος, δουλεύω, δουλεία etc." in Kittel,
Theol. Diction. New Testam., English trans., Vol. II,
pp. 261-80.

168

Justinian usage of δουλεύω-δουλεία in general, and in Dial.
134,3-5 in particular, one might assume that in the specific
passage Dial. 134,5 these terms imply an understanding of
Christ's incarnation as humiliation which reached its climax
at the crucifixion.

Various commentators have already noticed the similarity between Dial. 134,5 and Phil. 2,7-8.[76] One cannot
establish conclusively a dependence of Dial. 134,5 from Phil.
2,7-8. One might argue, nonetheless, that the mode of thought
is similar and that in both cases there is a humiliation
Christology discernible in the background.

b) The specific term is the word οἰκονομία.
Daniélou has shown that this is a basic term in Justin[77] which
designates God's plans for salvation centered around the incarnation. It relates more specifically to the virgin birth
and to the passion.[78]

Antecedents for the Justinian use of οἰκονομία could
be found in Eph. 1,10 and 3,9[79] but more closely in Ignatius.[80]
One also encounters a considerable number of gnostic passages
where the term οἰκονομία is used in formulations similar to
the Justinian ones.[81]

The frequency of occurrence and the particular usage
of the word οἰκονομία in Justin might reflect his knowledge
of gnostic texts. It might also reflect Justin's awareness of

---

[76] J. C. T. Otto, *op. cit.*, Vol. II, p. 478; G.
Archambault, *op. cit.*, Vol. II, p. 282.

[77] Dial. 30,3; 31,1; 45,4; 67,6; 87,5; 103,3; 120,1 etc.

[78] J. Daniélou, *Message évangélique*, pp. 148-49.

[79] See O. Michel, "οἰκονομία", in Kittel, *Theol.
Diction. New Testam.* Vol. V, pp. 151-53.

[80] Ignatius, *Eph.* 18,2: Ἰησοῦς ὁ Χριστὸς ἐκυοφο-
ρήθη ὑπὸ Μαρίας κατ' οἰκονομίαν θεοῦ. This passage shows an
early connection of the term οἰκονομία with the birth of
Christ. The whole statement in *Eph.* 18,2 betrays characteristics of a creedal formulation.

[81] Cf. Irenaeus *Adv. Haer.* I.15: ὁ κατ' οἰκονομίαν διὰ
τῆς Μαρίας to *Dial. 120,1* κατὰ τὴν οἰκονομίαν τὴν διὰ τῆς
παρθένου Μαρίας. See also Iren. *Adv. Haer.* I.10,3; *Excerpta
ex Theod.* 5 etc.

the fact that incarnation is something which evidently trans-
cends any description because it is the incarnation of the
pre-existing Logos-God. One could propose that the οἰκονομία
terminology with reference to the virgin birth and to the
passion is to a considerable degree the result of contemplating
these events from the angle of a pre-existence Christology.
The statement in Dial. 45,4 might be cited as a characteristic
example: ὃς [Χριστός] καὶ πρὸ ἑωσφόρου καὶ σελήνης ἦν καὶ διὰ
τῆς παρθένου ταύτης τῆς ἀπὸ τοῦ γένους τοῦ Δαυεὶδ γεννηθῆναι
σαρκοποιηθεὶς ὑπέμεινε, ἵνα διὰ τῆς οἰκονομίας ταύτης . . .
The notion of condescension--and ultimately of humiliation--
seems to be inherent in such a use of the term οἰκονομία
by Justin.

E. *Final Remarks*

1. The preceding analysis has shown that the incarnation terminology of Justin derives from, or exhibits similarities in vocabulary found in, the following groups of texts:

(a) Early Christian creedal formulations where
christological statements of the type γεννηθεὶς ἐκ παρθένου
or ἄνθρωπος γενόμενος might have been included.

(b) Gnostic texts (as they are quoted in the accounts
of Clement's *Excerpta ex Theodoto*, Irenaeus' *Adversus
Haereses*, and Hippolytus' *Refutatio*) in which one encounters
terms like παθητός, διὰ Μαρίας, ἄνθρωπος γενόμενος, οἰκονομία
et al.).

(c) Old Testament passages like Is. 7,14 and 52,13-
53,12, Dan. 2,34 and 7,13-14, Gen. 49,11 et al., where Justin
could read predictions of the virgin birth and the passion of
Christ.

(d) New Testament texts, primarily Mt. 1,18-25 and
Lk. 1,35 but possibly also Hebr. 12,2-3 and Acts 21,23.

(e) Passages from the Apostolic Fathers, especially
from *Barnabas* and the Ignatian Epistles, where terms of
humiliation (παθητός, ὑπομένειν) or references to the virgin
birth occur (Ign. *Eph*. 19,1; Ign. *Polyc*. 3,2; *Barnabas* 5,4-
12 et al.).

We have found that Justin, in several cases, utilizes
the material which we meet also in the above classified

groups, in a way similar to theirs. On the other hand we have noticed a considerable number of instances where Justin departs from his sources either by giving to some of the terms a particular nuance (e.g. ὑπομένειν in connection with incarnation), or by unusually increasing the frequency of occurrence (e.g. ἄνθρωπος γενόμενος 24 times; παθητὸς 20 times et al.) or by selecting a specific formulation instead of its traditional counterpart (e.g. διὰ παρθένου instead of ἐκ παρθένου). The study of those instances has produced a noteworthy number of indications that behind Justin's handling of incarnation terminology one might discern the concept of the pre-existence of Christ at work.

2. The main characteristic of the Justinian terminology used for the transition from pre-existence to incarnation is the phrase ἄνθρωπος γενόμενος. Even where other expressions are used, such as μορφωθείς, σαρκοποιηθείς, παραγενόμενος et al., the fundamental and recurrent formulation ἄνθρωπος γενόμενος qualifies all special words which relate to the incarnation. In Christ the pre-existing Logos-Son-God became man simply and fully.

By his emphasis on Christ's full humanity Justin checks any docetic interpretation of the incarnation. At the same time the continuity between pre-existence and incarnation, or rather the identity between Christ the pre-existing God and Christ the man, serves as an answer to the gnostic speculations on incarnation. The last point is readily substantiated by a comparison of the use of the phrase ἄνθρωπος γενόμενος by Justin and by the gnostic authors respectively. Furthermore the stress on Christ's humanity in inseparable connection with pre-existence unifies the activity of the incarnate Christ with all its manifestations prior to incarnation. The final outcome is the concept of an essential continuity between the Old and the New Testament. Such a continuity is of central theological and apologetic importance in Justin's confrontation with both the gnostics and the Jewish teachers.

3. Justin's formulations concerning the virgin birth betray unmistakable traces of the strong impact of the concept of pre-existence. In this case pertinent biblical texts, found possibly in Testimonia, and early creedal formulae have been

interpreted by Justin in the light of the belief in the pre-existing Logos-God. The result of such a process is both terminological (διὰ παρθένου instead of ἐκ παρθένου) and theological (the Logos was the One who caused the impregnation of the virgin Mary and who was born through her). The theologians of the succeeding generations, however, did not follow Justin. The formula διὰ παρθένου was viewed as easily susceptible to a docetic interpretation. The impregnation of the virgin Mary, on the other hand, was very early connected by other theologians, with the Holy Spirit rather than the Logos.

4. Because of the orientation towards pre-existence, Christ's human status could not viewed but as humiliation. This is precisely the case with the Justinian passages which refer to the incarnation as the human status of the Logos. Justin does not refrain from stretching even the passion vocabulary into the entire comprehensive category of incarnation. The reverberations of ἄτιμος, ἀειδής, ἄδοξος καὶ παθητὸς resound through the entire Justinian corpus. This humiliation vocabulary in Justin functions apologetically not only against the Jewish messianic ideas (as expressed by Trypho) but also against a docetic interpretation of the incarnation, as we have noted.

The concept of incarnation as humiliation in Justin seems to be couched in vocabulary borrowed from the Old Testament texts, which speak about the suffering righteous one, especially Is. 53. The concept in itself, however, is rather the result of the incarnation contemplated simultaneously with pre-existence and, one might add, exaltation and eschatological coming.

CONCLUDING DISCUSSION

1. In the course of the present study it became
evident that in Justin the concept of the pre-existence of
Christ occurs very rarely in isolated and autonomous form.
Nearly always it occurs as a part of a more general christological statement.[1] In all cases the statement makes an
explicit reference to the pre-existence and to the incarnation
of Christ. In some cases it contains also a formula relating
to his exaltation.[2] One could then conclude that Justin views
the pre-existence of Christ as a part of a christological
schema which integrates the three fundamental christological
concepts of pre-existence, incarnation and exaltation. Thus
Justin follows the line of the early creedal-hymnic traditions
found also in the New Testament christological statements of
the type of Phil. 2,6-11, John 1,1-14, Hebr. 1,1-12, Col.
1,15-20, where a similar schema is presupposed.[3] This observation should be emphasized because research has in the past
tended to regard the concept of Christ's pre-existence in
Justin's works as an autonomous notion imported through
philosophical speculation, and foreign to the early Christian
traditions.[4]

---

[1]E.g. Ap. 21,1; 63,16; Dial. 34,2; 38,1; 85,2;
126,1 etc.

[2]E.g. Ap. 31,7; 46,5; Dial. 34,2; 126,1 etc.

[3]There are of course differences between these passages.
But the mode of christological thought and the focal points in
them present an undeniable resemblance.

[4]What R. Holte has said for Justin in the special case
of the theory of spermatikos logos holds somehow true for his
whole dealing with the concept of the pre-existing Christ:

Justin's adherence, nonetheless, to a traditional
christological pattern does not mean that he simply repeated
the early creedal formulations. What he did was to interpret
them, and, while keeping the basic frame of pre-existence,
humiliation and exaltation, to bring these concepts into a
discussion of current theological problems. In this respect
he transformed the creedal-hymnic language of the early traditions such as the one preserved in Phil. 2,6-11, for instance,
into a language of theological explicitness.

The Apologist effected such a transformation mainly
on the level of the concept of Christ's pre-existence in a
status of God. Since, however, he worked always with a whole
schema, the other parts of this schema were also affected,
particularly the incarnation and also the exaltation.

2. As far as the concept of incarnation is concerned,
one could set down the following observations:

a) *The formula* ἐκ παρθένου *relating to the*
virgin birth. This formula is missing from the New Testament
texts but it was included in early creedal statements as one
could assume from the writings of Ignatius and of Aristides.[5]
Justin, as we have seen, makes the virgin birth an object of
extensive discussion, and also replaces the formula ἐκ
παρθένου with the formula διὰ παρθένου, or at least insists on
an exclusive usage of the expression διὰ παρθένου. This
insistence could be viewed as a result of Justin's awareness
of the christological significance of the concept of pre-
existence. If Christ is θεὸς προϋπάρχων then the virgin Mary
is only the one through (διά) whom Christ became man, whereas
his ultimate origin (ἐκ) should be sought in God the Father
of all.

b) *The formulation* ἄνθρωπος γενόμενος
designating the incarnation. The prevalence of this phrase
over any other expression (e.g. μορφοῦσθαι, παραγίνεσθαι, σάρξ

Justin shows an "unreserved attachment to the Christian doc-
trinal tradition (*theological traditionalism*)" (R. Holte,
op. cit., p. 112).

[5]Cf. Ign. *Sm.* 1,1; Aristides *Apol.* 15,1.

γίνεσθαι, φανεροῦσθαι) indicates that for Justin the pre-
existing Christ became full man in incarnation (App. 10,1).
Justin did not use phrases such as ἐν ὁμοιώματι ἀνθρώπων
γενόμενος or σχήματι εὑρεθεὶς ὡς ἄνθρωπος [ὁ Χριστός] (Phil.
2,7), phrases which could be interpreted docetically. Justin's
awareness of the implications of pre-existence for interpreting
the incarnation lead him to employ the phrase ἄνθρωπος γενόμενος stating unequivocally the full humanity of Christ in his
incarnation.

      c) *The statement referring to the cruci-
fixion* (Ap. 31,7; 46,5; Dial. 38,1; 85,2). The New Testament
passages which exhibit a humiliation and exaltation christological pattern include no doubt a reference to the cross.
Phil. 2,6-11, for example, mentions Christ's death on the
cross. In Phil. 2,6-11, however, the cross is mentioned, not
as a specific object-event of a confession of faith, nor as
an indispensable part of a "crucifixion and resurrection"
christological schema, but as the ultimate point of humiliation.
We have also encountered in Justin a case where the cross is
viewed as an ultimate point of humiliation (Dial. 134,5:
ἐδούλευσε καὶ τὴν μέχρι σταυροῦ δουλείαν ὁ Χριστός).[6] In the
vast majority of the Justinian passages, however, the crucifixion is reported as a special event, as a link in a chain of
creedal statements, usually connected to the death and resurrection of Christ in a formula of the type σταυρωθέντα καὶ
ἀποθανόντα καὶ ἀναστάντα (Ap. 21,1; cf. Ap. 31,7; 42,4; 46,5;
63,16; Dial. 85,2). This type of christological vocabulary
follows the line of 1 Cor. 15,3-4 (ὅτι Χριστὸς ἀπέθανε . . .
καὶ ὅτι ἐτάφη . . . καὶ ὅτι ἐγήγερται), or of 1 Thess. 4,14
(Ἰησοῦς ἀπέθανε καὶ ἀνέστη). Here we are in the presence of
a christological pattern based on "crucifixion and resurrection." This pattern in some of the Justinian passages seems
to be integrated into the other schema, viz. that of pre-
existence, incarnation, exaltation (Ap. 21,1; 31,7; Dial.
85,2). The integration or fusion of the two patterns has
occurred probably prior to Justin. But it is in the Apologist

---

   [6]But note the soteriological train of thought in this
passage: ὑπὲρ τῶν ἐκ παντὸς γένους ποικίλων καὶ πολυειδῶν
ἀνθρώπων, δι᾽ αἵματος καὶ μυστηρίου τοῦ σταυροῦ κτησάμενος
αὐτούς.

in whom one meets for the first time an explicit and complete
creedal formulation that preserves the principal elements of
the two patterns. One might cite as a characteristic example
Ap. 21,1: τὸν λόγον ὅ ἐστι πρῶτον γέννημα τοῦ θεοῦ, ἄνευ
ἐπιμιξίας φάσκειν ἡμᾶς γεγεννῆσθαι 'Ιησοῦν Χριστὸν τὸν
διδάσκαλον ἡμῶν, καὶ τοῦτον σταυρωθέντα καὶ ἀποθανόντα καὶ
ἀναστάντα ἀνεληλυθέναι εἰς τὸν οὐρανόν (cf. also Dial. 85,2).
Furthermore, the cross-death formula in Justin includes in
several cases the phrase ἐπὶ Ποντίου Πιλάτου (Ap. 13,1; Dial.
85,2 etc.). The inclusion of the name of Pontius Pilate in the
creedal statements belongs apparently to the early traditions
(cf. 1 Tim. 6,13; Ign. *Mg.* 11,1; Ign. *Tr.* 9,1; Ign. *Sm.* 1,2).
But Justin's mentioning of Pontius Pilate in many instances
and in different contexts[7] shows that the Apologist is
conscious of the fact that there is a concrete historical
reality within which the christological events took place.

There is no doubt that Justin, as a teacher faithful
to the traditions of the early Church (ἐδιδάχθημεν: Ap. 6,2;
13,1; 46,2; 66,2; δεδιδάγμεθα: Ap. 21,6; App. 4,2; δεδιδάγμεθα καὶ διδάσκομεν: Ap. 14,4), speaks about the cross
and the resurrection of Christ. He also declares his belief
in the soteriological significance of the passion of Jesus
(Dial. 11,4-5; 34,8; 41,1; 74,3; 86,6; 94,5; 106,1; 110,3;
117,5; 134,5; 137,1; 138,2), and in the redeeming power of his
blood (Ap. 32,7; Dial. 13,1; 54,1; 111,3-4). He does not
proceed, however, into something which is more than a mere
statement. He does not try to analyze the why and the how of
the salvation through the cross, nor to defend this doctrine.
His main aim is to show that all the series of events com-
prising the passion of Christ were foretold by Scripture. On
the other hand, Justin does not hesitate to speak about the
cross in a triumphant fashion and call it τὸ μέγιστον σύμβολον
τῆς ἰσχύος καὶ ἀρχῆς αὐτοῦ [Χριστοῦ] (Ap. 55,1-7). For the
Apologist, Christ the crucified one is by no means, as in
Paul, μωρία for the ἔθνη (1 Cor. 1,23) and power and wisdom of
God only for the κλητοί (1 Cor. 1,25). The cross is a

---

[7]Cf. Ap. 13,3; 35,9; rp,6; 46,1; 48,3; 61,13; App.
6,6; Dial. 30,3; 76,6; 85,2; 102,5; 103,4.

universal symbol of a supreme power. It is even the symbol
of might of the Roman emperors, although they do not know it
(Ap. 55,5: καὶ τὰ παρ' ὑμῖν δὲ σύμβολα τὴν τοῦ σχήματος τούτου [σταυροῦ] δύναμιν δηλοῖ, ἵνα ἀμελῶμεν καὶ τῶν τροπαίων δι'
ὧν αἱ πρόοδοι ὑμῶν πανταχοῦ γίνονται). One can here see how
the prevalence of the concept of pre-existence and exaltation
affects the interpretation of the death on the cross. The
traditional soteriological formulations are retained but the
presentation is replete with terms of glory and power. The
phenomenon is somehow analogous to that occurring in the
Gospel of John where the cross is viewed as exaltation. Justin
lacks, of course, the theological sublimity of the Johannine
presentation. He is, however, clearly on the same level as
far as the basic concept is concerned. The passion is only a
part within the grand schema of pre-existence, incarnation
and exaltation which seems to dominate completely Justin's
thought.

3. The fact that the schema of cross-resurrection is
eventually absorbed by the pattern of pre-existence, incarnation, exaltation could be substantiated by the way in which
Justin handles the concept of resurrection. The Apologist
refers to the resurrection in several passages (Dial. 41,4;
53,5; 100,1; 106,1; 107,1). These references, however, are
either proofs that what was foretold came to be true, or just
traditional expressions. One cannot find instances in Justin
where the resurrection in connection with the crucifixion is
the object of theological elaboration or a focal point of
christological discussion.

In addition to the passages mentioned above, one
encounters the concept of resurrection in eight special texts
of Justin. These seem to be developed christological statements of a creedal nature (Ap. 21,1; 31,7; 42,4; 46,5; 63,16;
Dial. 32,3; 36,5; 85,2) in which the resurrection is mentioned
immediately after the death on the cross such as in the
formula ἀποθανόντα καὶ ἀναστάντα (Ap. 21,1 etc.), or ἐκ νεκρῶν
ἀνέστη (Ap. 36,5). In seven out of these eight passages the
resurrection formula is followed by an exaltation statement
which is usually more elaborate and which attracts attention
as a final point of consummation. Under these circumstances

the resurrection appears to be a prelude to the exaltation or
perhaps an aspect of it, not a prominent, self-subsistent
point. This becomes obvious in Dial. 38,1 and Dial. 126,1
where from crucifixion and passion we move into exaltation
without any mention of the resurrection (Dial. 38,1: εἶτα
ἄνθρωπον γενόμενον σταυρωθῆναι, καὶ ἀναβεβηκέναι εἰς τὸν
οὐρανόν; Dial. 126,1: παραγενόμενον καὶ γεννηθέντα καὶ
παθόντα καὶ ἀναβάντα εἰς τὸν οὐρανόν). This is also evident
in the way in which Justin presents the ascension-exaltation
of Christ in Dial. 36,1-38,7 where, for example, the resurec-
tion is just mentioned whereas the ascension-exaltation covers
virtually the entirety of the passage.

Let us conclude this section:

a) Justin certainly knows a cross-resurrection
christological pattern, at least in its elementary form. However, this pattern does not appear to have a substantial
theological function within the writings of the Apologist,
and it is integrated in the wider schema of pre-existence,
incarnation, exaltation. No traces of tension between the two
schemata are discernible in the Justinian works, perhaps
because the cross-resurrection schema seems to operate on a
very low key.

b) The humiliation terms used by Justin with
reference to the incarnate Christ (παθητός, ἄτιμος, ἄδοξος
et al.), although connected directly to Is. 53, do not prove
that the Apologist works with a Christology of the type of the
suffering righteous one. The picture of the righteous one who
is humiliated but who finally is vindicated by God is absent
from Justinian christological thinking. Even when Justin says
that the Father raised Jesus from the dead (Dial. 106,1),
this is in no way connected to the preceding passion. The
etiological διὸ of Phil. 2,6-11 (διὸ καὶ ὁ θεὸς αὐτὸν ὑπερύψωσεν) is no part of Justin's interpretation of the exaltation. In this respect his christological schema is not the
humiliation and exaltation schema as E. Schweizer understands
it on the basis of the suffering righteous one. Justin's concept of humiliation as a characterization of Christ's incarnation is the result of his constant awareness of the pre-
existence of the Son in a status of God, as it has been
repeatedly indicated in the course of the present study.

Likewise Christ's exaltation is not the reward for, or the consequence of, his obedience to the Father (as in Philippians, John and Hebrews) but a result of his divine status. Christ did not become κύριος καὶ θεὸς after the resurrection. He was always κύριος καὶ θεός.

4. Justin's fundamental contribution is to be found in his extensive dealing with the first part of the christological schema of "pre-existence, incarnation, and exaltation," namely the pre-existence of Christ. The basic terminology used, as far as titles are concerned, is that of the New Testament: θεός, λόγος, υἱός, κύριος, πρωτότοκος. In addition Justin employs some titles or names taken from Old Testament texts which he interprets christologically: ἄγγελος, ἄνθρωπος, ἱερεύς, ἀρχιστράτηγος, et al.

As we have seen, Justin speaks extensively about the pre-existence of Christ (a) prior to creation, (b) in connection with the Old Testament theophanies, and (c) in relation to the pagan world.

a) *Pre-existence prior to creation.* Three points should be underlined here:

1) The Apologist in speaking about the mode of origin of the Son utilizes the term γεννᾶσθαι. Occasionally he employs other verbs, for example προβάλλειν, which shows his acquaintance with gnostic texts, but his main and controlling term is γεννᾶσθαι. This fact reveals Justin's adherence to the biblical language and to the biblical data in general. The last contention is supported by the fact that Justin does not proceed into any speculation pertaining to the life of and the relations within the deity. Scripture gives little information on this subject and Justin follows the same line. His attitude might also be the result of his reaction against the enormous gnostic speculations concerning the life of and events within the deity.

2) Justin rarely comments on the idea that the Son is the agent in the creation of the world. The case is very characteristic because, as we have reported, this idea was indeed ancient and included in most of the humiliation and exaltation statements of the New Testament (John 1,3, Col. 1,16-17, Hebr. 1,2 et al.). The Apologist deliberately avoids

emphasizing this issue possibly because of the Marcionite
teaching which separated God the Father from God the Creator
(Ap. 58,1).

3) The third point pertains to the
significance attached by Justin to the "numerical otherness"
of the Son. The Apologist is adamant against any modalistic
interpretation of the existence of the Son. The Son is not
an impersonal power, but another God next to the Father of all,
begotten by Him as a distinct person. Here Justin works on
the basis of an exegesis of the christological passages of the
Old Testament (Ps. 2, Ps. 109 [LXX], Prov. 8 et al). What the
early creedal formulations state in a somehow vague fashion
Justin makes explicit. By doing this the Apologist brings to
the fore the fundamental theological problems inherent in the
creedal statements. These problems would become the burning
issues of the fiery christological debates of the third,
fourth and fifth centuries A.D. For Justin, however, they are
not yet problems. The theory of the "numerical otherness" of
the Son and his real and distinctive existence in relation
to the Father is an example of Justin's skill of combining
early Christian creedal formulations with biblical exegesis
and current philosophical tenets. The early creedal formulations proclaim that the incarnate Son is the pre-existing God.
But the Platonic teaching on God, especially its interpretation by Philo and the Middle-Platonists, make it impossible
for the transcendent Father of all to change in any way, all
the more to become man. Thus it must be another God who could
do this, the Son. Scripture validates this idea because it
implicitly holds to the idea of the existence of another God,
the Son (Gen. 1,26, Gen. 19,24, Ps. 44,7-8 [LXX], Ps. 109,1
[LXX]). Such a dialectic may be neither convincing nor flaw-
less. It constitutes, nonetheless, a significant theological
step forward because it raises important christological
questions and shows a serious attempt to discuss and interpret
the creedal statements in a language of theological explicitness. Such a language contains to a certain degree a terminology which occurs also in Philo, the Middle-Platonists and
the gnostic theologians (προϋπάρχειν, κοσμεῖν, δύναμις,
γέννημα, προβάλλειν et al.). This might mean that Justin has
knowledge of the pertinent texts. It might also mean that he

shares the language used by the religious philosophers of his time who were directly or indirectly influenced by Plato.

b) *The pre-existence of Christ manifested in the Old Testament theophanies.* Justin's christological interpretation of the theophanies of the Old Testament has been facilitated by Philo, whose basic contribution is the introduction of the logos as the principal agent in them. But the Apologist moves in a different direction from Philo and emphasizes three points:

1) God who became man in the New Testament is none other than the pre-existing Christ who was also acting in the Old Testament theophanies and in the Old Testament history in general. Such an idea establishes an unbreakable continuity between the Old and the New Testament against the gnostic, more specifically the Marcionite tenets, which advocated a radical otherness and an unbridgeable gap between the two Testaments. With the same stroke the Apologist is in a position to show to the Jews that the Christians are the natural continuation of Israel since they follow the same God followed also by the Israelites of old.

2) Justin advances a conceptual approximation between the Old Testament theophanies and the incarnation. In both cases God is manifested in a visible way. This approximation has an apologetic function, particularly with regard to the Jews, because it shows that the incarnation is not such an unheard of and blasphemous novelty since it was already anticipated in the theophanic appearances to the patriarchs of Old Testament.

3) With the christological interpretation of the theophanies Justin places God, in the person of the pre-existing Christ, right in the center of the Old Testament history. The idea of the absolute transcendence of the one God in monotheism could create the danger of eventually leaving human reality and human history without God--in the sense of an immediate contact and a direct communication. Justin's introduction of the pre-incarnate Christ in the Old Testament history via the theophanies averts this danger. This is of significance in view of the gnostic tendencies to escape historical reality.

c) *The pre-existence of Christ in relation to the pagan world*. In presenting his opinion on this subject Justin employs a terminology which although originally Stoic comes to him as a language used already by Philo and Middle-Platonists, like Albinus and Plutarch.

The Apologist advances two basic ideas:

1) The pre-existing Christ is connected to the pagan world as the main agent in matters of morality and ethical responsibility. Justin's awareness of the increasing relativization of ethics and of the widespread belief in a moral determinism (εἱμαρμένη), prompts him to project into pagan history as well as into present reality the pre-existing Christ, the guarantor of an absolute ethic and the basis for the freedom of choosing and doing the good. Philo had already advanced a similar idea when he spoke about ὀρθὸς λόγος or νόμος φύσεως as H. Koester has shown. Rom. 2,14-15 moves along the same lines too. But Justin transforms a universal principle, an abstract concept, into a christological one. Via the concept of the pre-existence of the Son he brings Christ into an immediate and direct--though limited--contact with every man in matters of ethical decisions and behavior. Here again one can see how the "pre-Christian" history is placed by the Apologist under the "personal" action of Christ. At the same time by connecting the whole issue of ethics and freedom with the last judgment Justin projects this direct action of Christ on mankind into the future which will end at the δευτέρα παρουσία.

2) The pre-existing Christ is the protagonist of the battle against demons within the pagan world. This world has been the arena of a harmful activity and of a continuous fight of the demonic powers against man. Here Justin seems to share to a significant degree the demonological concepts of apocalyptic circles (Enoch, Jubilees et al.). History, however, is not at the mercy of the demons. Christ has conquered and defeated them through his incarnation, passion and exaltation (Dial. 30,3; 85,2 et al.). But he fought against them even before his incarnation by using Socrates and other wise men of old. Thus the concept of pre-existence functions in Justin as a battle motif. In other words, it is transferred from the level of a creedal-liturgical

setting to the level of interpretation and overcoming of the
contradictory, dark and tragic reality of the past and the
present.

5.   One could readily see why Justin works both
extensively and intensively with the christological concept of
pre-existence, as part of the more general schema of pre-
existence, incarnation and exaltation of Christ.   Through the
interpretation of this schema and the emphasis on pre-existence,
Justin is able simultaneously to confront the pagan thinkers,
the Jewish teachers and the gnostic theologians.

In facing the pagan philosophers and the pagan world
in general, he proposes solutions to crucial and burning
problems like the problem of the transcendence of God in
connection with human history, the problem of ethics in relation to the fatalistic doctrine of εἱμαρμένη, the problem of
knowing the truth of the real essence of beings (ὄντα), et al.

In facing the Jewish teachers, he shows the adherence
of Christians to a strict monotheism comparable to the Jewish
one by upholding the absolute transcendence of the Father of
all, while he solves the problem of the theophanies and the
divine activity in the Old Testament by introducing the Son as
the unique agent in all of these instances.   He further
demonstrates that the God of Christians is the God of Abraham,
Isaac and Jacob, because the pre-existing Logos who revealed
himself to the patriarchs is none other than the incarnate
Christ.

Finally, in facing the gnostic theologians Justin
maintains the unity between the Old and the New Testament,
the continuity of revelation in history, the identity of the
Father of all with the Creator.   Through his insistence on the
activity of the pre-existing Son during the course of the
entire history, the Apologist fights the negative gnostic
attitude toward the cosmos.

Justin perhaps does not succeed fighting in all these
fronts.   This would be an impossible task.   He succeeds, however, in pointing to a positive attitude toward the world and
in accepting the challenge of an open confrontation with his
contemporaries.   He succeeds all the more in showing that even
the specific and limited language of the early creedal-hymnic

formulations could become the matrix of linguistic and
conceptual developments through which the theologians of the
church could enter into a real dialogue with the intellectual
world of their time.

BIBLIOGRAPHY

A. *Texts*

Septuaginta, Vetus Testamentum Graece juxta LXX interpres,
        ed. A. Rahlfs, 2 vols., eighth edition, Stuttgart,
        1965.

Novum Testamentum Graece, Eb. Nestle-Erw. Nestle-K. Aland,
        25th edition, Stuttgart, 1965.

Arnim, J. V. Stoicorum Veterum Fragmenta, 4 vols., Stuttgart
        1964 (editio stereotypa editionis primae).

Babbitt, F. C., et al. Plutarch Moralia, 16 vols., The Loeb
        Classical Library, London-Cambridge, Mass., 1927-1969
        (so far publ. 15 vols.).

Baudry, J. Atticus Fragments de son Oeuvre, Avec introduction
        et Notes, Paris, 1931. Also apud Eusebius, Praeparatio
        Evangelica, ed. by K. Mras (GCS 43,1-2), Berlin,
        1954-56.

Charles, R. H. The Apocrypha and Pseudepigrapha of the Old
        Testament in English, Vol. II, Pseudepigrapha, Oxford,
        1966 (reprinted from the edition of 1913).

Cohn, L. and Wendland, P. Philonis Alexandrini Opera quae
        supersunt, 7 vols. Berlin, 1896-1926 (Vol. 7 indices
        by H. Leisegang).

Fowler, H. N., et al. Plato Works, 12 vols. The Loeb
        Classical Library, London-Cambridge, Mass., 1914-1935.

Froidevaux, L. M. Irénée de Lyon, Demonstration de la prédi-
        cation apostolique, Nouvelle traduction de l'arménien
        avec introduction et notes, Paris, 1959 (Sources
        Chrétiennes, 62).

Funk, F. X. and Bihlmeyer, K. Die Apostolischen Väter,
        Tübingen, 1956.

Goodspeed, E. J. Die ältesten Apologeten, Göttingen, 1914.

Harvey, W. W. Sancti Irenaei Episcopi Lugdunensis, Libros
        Quinque adversus Haereses, 2 vols., Cambridge, 1857

186

(Reprinted 1965). Note: In the division of chapters and paragraphs I follow Migne's numbering (Patrol. Graeca Vol. 7), not Harvey's.

Hermann, C. F. "Albinus, Εἰσαγωγὴ" and "Διδασκαλικὸς τῶν τοῦ Πλάτωνος δογμάτων" in Appendix Platonica (Vol. VI in "Platonis Dialogi," Leipzig, Teubner, 1921-1936), pp. 147-89.

Hobein, H. Maximus Tyrius, Philosophumena, Leipzig (Teubner), 1910.

Marcus, R. Philo, Supplement 2 vols. The Loeb Classical Library, Cambridge, Mass., 1961.

Nock, A. D. and Festugière, A. J. Corpus Hermeticum, 4 vols. Paris, 1945-54.

Otto, J. C. T. Corpus Apologetarum Christianorum Saeculi Secundi, 3rd ed. 5 Vols. Jena, 1876-81.

Wendland, P. Hippolytus Werke: Vol. 3, Refutatio omnium Haeresium (GCS, 26), Leipzig, 1916.

Stählin, O. Clemens Alexandrinus, Opera (GCS, 12, 15, 17), Berlin, 1909-39.

Voelker, W. Quellen zur Geschichte der christlichen Gnosis, Tübingen, 1932.

Vogel, C. J. de. Greek Philosophy, A Collection of Texts with Notes and Explanations, I-III, Leiden, 1953-59.

B. *Works of Reference*

Astius, F. Lexicon Platonicum sive vocum Platonicarum, I-III, Leipzig, 1835-38.

Bauer, W.-Arndt, W. F.-Gingrich, F. W. A Greek-English Lexicon of the New Testament, Chicago, 1957.

Goodspeed, E. J. Index Apologeticus sive Clavis Justini Martyris Operum aliorumque Apologetarum Pristinorum, Leipzig, 1912.

Kittel, G. (-Friedrich, G.). Theologisches Wörterbuch zum Neuen Testament, Vols. I-IX (A-Χάρις), Stuttgart, 1933-1971.

Kittel, G. (-Friedrich, G.). Theological Dictionary of the New Testament, trans. from the German by G. W. Bromiley, Vols. I-VII (A-Σ), Grand Rapids, Michigan, 1964-1971.

Kraft, H. Clavis Patrum Apostolicorum, München, 1963.

Lampe, G. W. H. A Patristic Greek Lexicon, Oxford, 1961-68.

Liddell, H. G.-Scott, R.-Jones, H. S. A Greek-English Lexicon, Oxford, 1966 (repr. from the 9th edition, 1940).

Stephanus, Henricus. Θησαυρὸς τῆς Ἑλληνικῆς Γλώσσης, Thesaurus Graecae Linguae, 8 vols., Paris, Ambr. Firmin Didot, 1831-65.

C. *Books and Articles*[#]

An asterisk in front of an author's name indicates a work which is directly connected to the writings of Justin.

*Aall, A. Die Geschichte der Logosidee, Vols. 2, Leipzig, 1899.

*Abbate, A. Filosofia e teologia, paganesimo e christianesimo nell' apologetica di S. Giustino (thesis), Univ. of Catane, 1947.

*Aeby, G. "Les missions divines de St. Justin à Origène," Paradosis 12, Freiburg, 1958.

d'Ales, A. "La Théophanie de Mambre devant la tradition des Pères," Rech. Sci. Rel. 20 (1930), pp. 150-60.

*Agourides, S. "Ἡ Χριστολογία τῶν Ἀπολογητῶν", Κληρονομία I (Thessalonike, 1969), pp. 39-62.

*Alfonsi, L. "Giustino, Apol. I.2,4," Vigil. Christ. 16 (1962), pp. 77-78.

*Alsten, L. Stoic and Christian in the Second Century, London, 1906.

Altaner, B. Patrology (Engl. trans. by H. C. Graef), Edinburgh-London, 1960.

*Anastasiou, J. Ἰουστῖνος ὁ Φιλόσοφος καὶ Μάρτυς περὶ τοῦ ἀρχαίου κόσμου, Thessalonike, 1959.

*Andresen, C. "Justin und der mittlere Platonismus," ZNW 44 (1952-3), pp. 157-95.

*_____. Logos und Nomos: Die Polemik des Kelsos wider das Christentum, Berlin, 1955.

*_____. "Justin," Religion in Gesch. u. Gegenw., third edition, Vol. III (Tübingen, 1959), col. 1076.

*Armstrong, G. T. Die Genesis in der alten Kirche: Die drei Kirchenväter [Justin, Irenaeus, Tertullian], Tübingen, 1962.

*Archambault, G. Justin, Dialogue avec Tryphon. Texte grec, traduction francaise, introduction, notes et index, Vols. I-II, Paris, 1909.

[#] The titles in Italian, Russian and Rumanian have been taken from an unpublished bibliographical list on Justin, compiled by Professor G. H. Williams.

188

*Aubé, B. Saint Justin, Philosophe et Martyr. Étude
    critique sur l'apologétique chrétienne au IIe siècle,
    Paris, 1861.

Aulen, G. Christus Victor, London, 1931.

*Aune, D. E. "Justin Martyr's Use of the Old Testament,"
    Bulletin of the Evangelical Theological Society 9
    (1966), pp. 179-97.

*Bacht, A. "Die Lehre des heiligen Justinus Martyr von der
    prophetischen Inspiration," Scholastik 26 (1951), pp.
    481-95; 27 (1952), pp. 12-33.

*Bammel, E. "Die Täufertraditionen bei Justin," Studia
    Patristica VIII (Berlin , 1966), pp. 53-61.

Barbel, J. Christos Angelos, in F. Dölger-Th. Klauser,
    Theophaneia III, Bonn, 1941, pp. 50-63.

*Bardy, G. "Saint Justin et la philosophie stoicienne,"
    Rech. Sci. Rel. 13 (1923), pp. 491-510 and 14 (1924),
    pp. 33-45.
_____. "La conversion dans les premiers siècles chrétiens,"
    Année théologique, 2 (1941), pp. 89-106 and 206-32.

*Barnard, L. W. Justin Martyr: his life and thought,
    Cambridge, 1967.

*Barnikol, E. "Verfasste oder benutzte Justin das um 140
    entstandene, erste antimarcionitische Syntagma gegen
    die Häresien?," Theol. Jahrbücher 6 (1938), pp. 17-19.

Barthélémy, D. "Redéconverte d'un chaînon manquant de l'
    histoire de la Septante," Revue Bibl. 60 (1953),
    pp. 18-29.

_____. "Les Devanciers d'Aquila," Supplements to V.T.,
    Vol. X, Leiden, 1963.

*Bayer, K. Justin Philosoph und Märtyrer: Die erste Apologie,
    Ausgewählt, herausgegeben und erläutert, München,
    1966.

*Bellini, E. "Dio nel pensiero di San Giustino," La Scuola
    Cattolica 90 (1962), pp. 387-406.

*Bellinzoni, A. J. The Sayings of Jesus in the Writings of
    Justin Martyr, Leiden, 1967.

Benoit, P. "Préexistence et Incarnation," Rev. Bibl. 77
    (1970), pp. 5-29.

*Benz, E. "Christus und Sokrates in der alten Kirche: Ein
    Beitrag zum altkirchlichen Verständnis des Märtyrers
    und des Martyriums," ZNW 43 (1950-51), pp. 195-224.

*Bery, A. St. Justin, sa vie et sa doctrine, Paris, 1911.

Beskow, P. Rex Gloriae: The Kingship of Christ in the Early Church, Stockholm-Göteborg-Uppsala, 1962.

Bietenhard, H. Die himmlische Welt im Urchristentum und Spätjudentum, Tübingen, 1951.

Betz, J. Die Eucharistie in der Zeit der griechischen Väter, Vol. I, 1, Freiburg in Br., 1955.

*Bishop, E. F. F. "Some Reflections on Justin Martyr and the Nativity Narratives," Evangl. Quarterly., 39 (1967), pp. 30-40.

*Blunt, A. W. F. The Apologies of Justin Martyr, Cambridge, 1911.

Bornkamm, G. "Zum Verständnis des Christus-Hymnus, Phil. 2,6-11," Studien zu Antike und Urchristentum, Vol. II, München, 1959.

*Bosse, F. Der präexistente Christus des Justinus Martyr, eine Episode aus der Geschichte des christologischen Dogmas (Inaug.-Diss.), Greifswald, 1891.

*Bousset, W. Die Evangeliencitate Justins des Märtyrers in ihrem Wert für die Evangelienkritik von neuem untersucht, Göttingen, 1891.

*_____. Jüdisch-christlicher Schulbetrieb in Alexandria und Rom: Literarische Untersuchungen zu Philo und Clemens von Alex., Justin und Irenaeus, Göttingen, 1915.

_____. Kyrios Christos, trans. from the German by J. E. Steely, Nashville and New York, 1970.

*Braun, H. "Entscheidende Motive in den Berichten über die Taufe Jesu von Markus bis Justin," ZTK 50 (1953), pp. 39-43.

Bréhier, É. Les idées philosophiques et religieuses de Philon d'Alexandrie, Paris, 1908.

Brideux, A. Le Stoicisme et son influence, Paris, 1966.

*Brothers, J. T. "The Interpretation of παῖς θεοῦ in Justin Martyr's Dialogue with Trypho," Studia Patristica IX (Berlin, 1966), pp. 127-38.

Brown, R. The Gospel according to John, Vol. I, Garden City, New York, 1966; Vol. II, Garden City, New York, 1970.

*Brox, N. "Zum literarischen Verhältnis zwischen Justin und Irenäus, ZNW 58 (1967), pp. 121-29.

*Buckley, E. R. "Justin Martyr's Quotations from the Synoptic Tradition," Jour. Theol. Stud. 36 (1935), pp. 173-76.

Bultmann, R. _Theology of the New Testament_, 2 Vols., trans. from the German by K. Grobel, London, SCM Press, paperback edition, 1965.

_____. _Das Evangelium des Johannes_, Meyer Komm., Göttingen, 1964. Engl. trans. by G. R. Beasley-Murray, Oxford, 1971.

*Campenhausen, H. F. v. _Die griechischen Kirchenväter_, Stuttgart, 1955, Engl. trans. _The Fathers of the Greek Church_, London, 1963.

_____. _Die Entstehung der christlichen Bibel_, Tübingen, 1968.

Carrington, P. _The Early Christian Church_, Vol. I, II, Cambridge, 1957.

_____. _The Primitive Christian Catechism_, Cambridge, 1940.

Carroll, K. L. "The Expansion of the Pauline Corpus," _Jour. Bibl. Lit._ 72 (1953), pp. 230-37.

Cerfaux, L. "L'hymne au Christ-Serviteur de Dieu," _Recueil L. Cerfaux, II: Etudes d'Exégèse et d'Histoire Religieuse_, Gembloux, 1954, pp. 425-37.

*Chadwick, H. _Early Christian Thought and the Classical Tradition_, Oxford, 1966.

* _____. "Justin Martyr's Defense of Christianity," _Bull. John Ryl. Libr._ 47 (1964-65), pp. 275-97.

Champomier, J. "Naissance de l'humanisme chrétien," _Bulletin de l'Association G. Budé_, NS 3 (1947), pp. 58-96.

*Chrestou, P. "'Ιουστῖνος", Θρησκευτικὴ καὶ 'Ηθικὴ 'Εγκυκλοπαιδεία, Vol. VI, Athens, 1965, cols. 972-85.

*Clemen, C. _Die religionsphilosophische Bedeutung des stoisch-christlichen Eudämonismus in Justins Apologie_, Leipzig, 1890.

Conzelmann, H. _An Outline of the Theology of the New Testament_, trans. from the German by J. Bowden, New York and Evanston, 1969.

Craddock, F. B. _The Pre-existence of Christ in the New Testament_, Nashville and New York, 1968.

*Cramer, J. A. "Die Logosstellen in Justins Apologien kritisch untersucht," _ZNW_ 2 (1901), pp. 300-30.

*Cross, F. L. _The Early Christian Fathers_, London, 1960.

Cullmann, O. The Christology of the New Testament, trans. from the German by S. C. Guthrie and C. A. M. Hall, Philadelphia, 1959.

*Daniélou, J. Message évangélique et culture hellénistique aux IIe et IIIe siècles, Tournai, 1961.

*Davey, J. M. "Justin Martyr and the Fourth Gospel," Scripture 17 (1965), pp. 117-22.

Dawe, D. G. "A Fresh Look at the Kenotic Christologies," Scott. Jour. of Theol. 15 (1962), pp. 337-49.

*Dembowski, H. Die Quellen der christlichen Apologeten, Leipzig, 1878.

Dodd, C. H. The Interpretation of the Fourth Gospel, Cambridge, 1963.

Dörrie, H. "Die Frage nach dem Transzendenten im Mittelplatonismus," Les Sources de Plotin, Entretiens sur l'Antiquité Classique V, Génève, 1960, pp. 191-223 and 224-41.

*Dunckler, L. Zur Geschichte der christlichen Logoslehre in den ersten Jahrhunderten: Die Logoslehre Justins des Märtyrers, Göttingen, 1848.

*Durproix, G. "Les influences littéraires dans la pensée de saint Justin," Revue des Études Latines, 1943-1944, p. 180.

*Ehrhardt, A. "Justin Martyr's Two Apologies," Jour. Eccl. Hist. 4 (1953), pp. 1-12.

Elze, M. Tatian und seine Theologie, Göttingen, 1960.

*v. Engelhardt, M. Das Christenthum Justins des Märtyrers, Erlangen, 1878.

*de Faye, E. "De l'influence du Timée de Platon sur la théologie de Justin," Bibl. de l'École des hautes études, Sciences Religieuses, VII (Paris, 1896), pp. 169-87.

*Feder, A. L. Justins des Märtyrers Lehre von Jesus Christus dem Messias und dem menschgewordenen Sohne Gottes, Freiburg in Br., 1906.

*Fedorkov, S. Justin Mucenik kak apologet i bogoslov, Moskow, 1958 (St. Justin as apologist and theologian).

Feuillet, A. "L'hymne christologique de l'épître aux Philippiens (II,6-11)," Rev. Bibl. 72 (1965-66), pp. 352-80, 481-507.

_____. Le Christ Sagesse de Dieu, d'après les Épîtres Pauliniennes, Paris, 1966.

192

*Franklin, C. F. Justin's Concept of Deliberate Concealment in the Old Testament, Harvard thesis, 1961.

Fuller, R. H. The Foundations of New Testament Christology, New York, 1965.

Gärtner, B. The Areopagus Speech and Natural Revelation, Uppsala, 1955.

*Ganszyniec, R. "In Justinum Martyrem," Eos 30 (1927), p. 26.

*Geffcken, J. Zwei griechische Apologeten, Leipzig u. Berlin, 1907.

Georgi, D. "Der vorpaulinische Hymnus Phil. 2,6-11," Zeit und Geschichte, Festschrift, R. Bultmann, ed. E. Dinkler, Tübingen, 1964, pp. 263-93.

*Gershenson, D. and Quispel, G. "Meristae," Vigil. Christ. 10 (1958), pp. 19-26.

*Gervais, J. "L'argument apologétique des prophéties messianiques selon saint Justin," Revue de l'Université d' Ottawa, 13 (1943), pp. 129-46, 193-208.

Gewiess, J. "Zum altkirchl. Verständnis der Kenosisstelle (Phil. II,5-11)," Theol. Quartalschr. 120 (1948), pp. 463-87.

*Gilbert, G. H. "Justin Martyr on the Person of Christ," Amer. Journ. Theol. 10 (1906), pp. 663-74.

*Gildersleeve, B. L. The Apologies of Justin Martyr, New York, 1904.

Gilg, A. Weg und Bedeutung der altkirchlichen Christologie, München, 1955.

*Gill, D. "A Liturgical Fragment in Justin, Dialogus 29,1," HTR 59 (1966), pp. 98-100.

*Giordani, I. S. Giustino Martire Apologie, Introd. e tradit., Roma Citta Nuova, 1962.

*Goguel, M. L'Eucharistie des origines à Justin Martyr, Paris, 1910.

*Goldfahn, A. H. "Justinus Märtyr und die Agada," Monatschrift für Geschichte und Wissenschaft des Judenthums 22 (1873), pp. 49-60, 104-15, 145-53, 193-202, 257-69.

*Gomez-Noguiera, A. "La inspiración biblico-profética en el pensamiento de San Justino," Helmantica 18 (1967), pp. 55-87.

*Goodenough, E. R. The Theology of Justin Martyr, Jena, 1923.

*Goodspeed, E. J. A History of Early Christian Literature, Revised and enlarged by R. M. Grant, Chicago, 1966.

*Grant, R. M. "The Chronology of the Greek Apologists," Vigiliae Christianae 9 (1955), pp. 25-33.

*_____. "Aristotle and the Conversion of Justin," Jour. Theol. Stud. 7 (1956), pp. 246-48.

*_____. "Studies in the Apologists," HTR 51 (1958), pp. 123-34.

Grillmeier, A. Christ in Christian Tradition, trans. from the German by J. S. Bowden, New York, 1965.

*Grube, K. L. "Die hermeneutischen Grundsätze Justin des Märtyrers," Der Katholik I (Mainz, 1880), pp. 1-42.

*_____. "Die typologische Schrifterklärung Justins des Märtyrers," Der Katholik II (Mainz, 1880), pp. 139-59.

Hahn, F. The Titles of Jesus in Christology: Their History in Early Christianity, trans. from the German by H. Knight and G. Ogg, New York and Cleveland, 1969.

*Haeuser, P. Des heiligen Philosophen und Märtyrers Justinus Dialog mit dem Juden Tryphon aus dem griechischen übersetzt und mit einer Einleitung versehen, München, 1917.

Hamman, A. La philosophie passe au Christ, Paris, 1958.

*Hanson, A. "Theophanies in the Old Testament and the Second Person of the Trinity," Hermathena 65 (1945), pp. 67-73.

Hanson, R. P. C. Allegory and Event, London, 1959.

_____. Tradition in the Early Church, London, 1962.

*_____. Justin Martyr's Dialogue with Trypho, London, 1963.

*Harnack, A. von. Die Ueberlieferung der griechischen Apologeten des 2. Jahrhunderts in der alten Kirche und im Mittelalter, Leipzig, 1882. (Texte u. Unters. I,1).

*_____. Sokrates und die alte Kirche, Berlin, 1900.

_____. Lehrbuch der Dogmengeschichte, Vol. I, Tübingen, 1909⁴.

*_____. "Judentum und Judenchristentum in Justin's Dialog mit Tryphon nebst einer Collation der Pariser Handschrift Nr. 450," Texte und Unters.39 (1913), pp. 47-98.

Harris, R. Testimonies, Part I, Cambridge, 1916; Part II, Cambridge, 1920.

*_____. Justin Martyr and Menander, Cambridge, 1932.

194

*Heard, R. G. "Apomnemoneumata in Papias, Justin and
    Irenaeus," New Test. St. 1 (1954), pp. 122-34.

*Heinisch, P. Der Einfluss Philos auf die älteste christliche
    Exegese: Barnabas, Justin, und Clemens von Alexandria,
    Münster, 1908.

Heinze, M. Die Lehre vom Logos in der griechischen Philoso-
    phie, Oldenburg, 1872.

*Higgins, A. J. B. "Jewish Messianic Belief in Justin Martyr's
    Dialogue with Trypho," Novum Testamentum 9 (1967),
    pp. 298-305.

Hockel, A. Christus der Erstgeborene: zur Geschichte der
    Exegese von Kol. 1,15, Düsseldorf, 1965.

*Hofmans, F. "De profeet Mozes in de Apologie von Sint
    Justinus martelaar," Eph. Theol. Lov. 30 (1954),
    pp. 416-39.

*Holte, R. "Logos spermatikos: Christianity and Ancient
    Philosophy according to St. Justin's Apologies," Stud.
    Theol. 12 (1958), pp. 109-68.

Hooker, M. D. Jesus and the Servant: The Influence of the
    Servant Concept of Deutero-Isaiah in the New Testament,
    London, 1959.

Hoover, R. W. The term ἁρπαγμὸς in Phil. 2,6: A Contribu-
    tion to the Study of the Sources of Early Christian
    Language and Theology, Th.D. Thesis, Harvard University,
    1968.

*Howton, J. "The Theology of the Incarnation in Justin
    Martyr," Studia Patrist. IX (Berlin, 1966) pp. 231-39.

*Hubik, K. Die Apologien des H. Justinus des Philosophen und
    Märtyrers: Literarhistorische Untersuchungen, Wien,
    1912.

*Hüntemann, U. "Zur Kompositionstechnik Justins. Analyse
    seiner ersten Apologie," Theol. und Glaube 25 (1933),
    pp. 410-28.

Hulen, A. "The 'Dialogues with the Jews' as sources for the
    early Jewish argument against Christianity," Jour.
    Bibl. Lit. 51 (1932), pp. 58-70.

*Hyldahl, N. Philosophie und Christentum: eine Interpreta-
    tion der Einleitung zum Dialog Justins, Kopenhagen,
    1966.

*Idigoras, J. L. Religiöse Toleranz bei den christlichen
    Apologeten im 2. Jahrhundert (Dissert.), Innsbruck,
    1957.

*Jaeger, W. Early Christianity and Greek Paedeia, Cambridge,
    1961.

*Jehne, W. Die Apologie Justins des Philosophen und Märtyrers (Dissert.), Leipzig, 1914.

Käsemann, E. "Kritische Analyse von Phil. 2,5-11," Exegetische Versuche und Besinnungen, Vol. I, Göttingen, 1960, pp. 51-95.

Karp, H. Probleme altchristlicher Anthropologie: Biblische Anthropologie und philosophische Psychologie bei den Kirchenvätern des dritten Jahrhunderts, Gütersloh, 1950.

*Katz, P. "Justin's Old Testament Quotations and the Greek Dodekapropheton Scroll," Studia Patristica, I (Berlin, 1957), pp. 343-53.

_____. "Ἐν πυρὶ φλογός", ZNW 46 (1955), pp. 133-38.

Kehl, N. Der Christushymnus im Kolosserbrief: Eine motivgeschichtliche Untersuchung zu Kol. 1,12-20, Stuttgart, 1967.

*Keller, W. Die Logoslehre von Heraklit bis Origenes, Stuttgart, 1958.

Kelly, J. N. D. Early Christian Doctrines, London, 1958.

*Keresztes, P. Justins und Tertullians Apologien. Eine rhetorische Untersuchung (Dissert.), Graz, 1963.

*_____. "The Literary Genre of Justin's First Apology," Vigil. Christianae 19 (1965), pp. 99-110.

*Keseling, P. "Justins 'Dialog Gegen Trypho' (c. 1-10) und Platons 'Protagoras'," Rheinisches Museum für Philologie 75 (1926), pp. 223-29.

*Klein, G. "Der Synkretismus als theologisches Problem in der ältesten christlichen Apologetik," Zeit. Theol. Kirch. 64 (1967), pp. 40-82.

*Koester, H. Septuaginta und synoptischer Erzählungsstoff im Schriftbeweis Justins des Märtyrers (Habilitationsschrift), Heidelberg, 1956.

_____. Synoptische Überlieferung bei den apostolischen Vätern, Berlin, 1957.

_____. "Νόμος Φύσεως: The Concept of Natural Law in Greek Thought," Religions in Antiquity, Essays in memory of E. R. Goodenough, ed. by J. Neusner, Leiden, 1968, pp. 521-41.

*Kominiak, B. The Theophanies of the Old Testament in the Writings of St. Justin (Dissert.), Washington, D.C., 1948.

*Krikones, C. Ὁ λόγος καὶ ἡ περὶ αὐτοῦ διδασκαλία τοῦ φιλοσόφου καὶ μάρτυρος Ἰουστίνου, Thessalonike, 1970.

196

Krinetzki, L. "Der Einfluss von Jes. 52,13-53, 12 par auf Phil. 2,6-11," Theol. Quartalschr. 139 (1959), pp. 157-93, 291-336.

Lachemann, E. R. "A propos of Jes. 7:14," Journ. of Bible and Religion 22 (1954), p. 43.

Lagrange, M. J. "L'Ange de Iahvé," Rev. Bibl. 12 (1903), pp. 212-25.

*_____. Saint Justin, Philosophe, Martyr, Paris, 1914.

La Piana, G. "Ancient and Modern Christian Apologetics," HTR 24 (1931), pp. 1-27.

Larsson, E. Christus als Vorbild: Eine Untersuchung zu den paulinischen Tauf- und Eikontexten, Uppsala, 1962.

*Le Blanc, J. "Le Logos de Saint Justin," Annales de philosophie chrétienne 148 (1904), pp. 191-97.

Lebreton, J. Histoire du dogme de la Trinité, Vol. I, Paris, 1919[4]; Vol. II, Paris, 1928[5].

*Leclercq, J. "L'idée de la royauté du Christ dans l'oeuvre de saint Justin," Année théologique 7 (1946), pp. 83-95.

Lentzen-Deis, F. "Ps. 2,7, ein Motiv früher hellenistischer Christologie," Theologie und Philosophie 44 (Freiburg, 1969), pp. 342-62.

*Lietzmann, H. Justinus des Philosophen und Märtyrers Apologien, München, 1912.

*_____. "Justinus der Märtyrer," Pauly-Wissowa Real-Encyclopädie des class. Altert., Vol. I, Stuttgart, 1919, cols. 1332-37.

Linton, O. "Interpretation of the Psalms in the Early Church," Studia Patristica IV (Berlin, 1961), pp. 143-56.

Loewenich, W. V. Das Johannesverständnis des zweiten Jahrhunderts, Giessen, 1932.

Lohmeyer, E. Kyrios Jesus: Eine Untersuchung zu Phil. 2,5-11, Heidelberg, 1961[2].

*Loofs, F. Theophilus von Antiochien Adversus Marcionem und die anderen theologischen Quellen bei Irenaeus, Leipzig, 1930 (Texte u. Unt. 46.2).

_____. Leitfaden zum Studium der Dogmengeschichte, 1. und 2. Teil, Halle-Saale, 1951-53.[5]

*Lortz, J. "Das Christentum als Monotheismus in den Apologien des zweiten Jahrhunderts," Festgabe für A. Ehrhard, Bonn, 1922, pp. 301-27.

*Martindale, C. C. Justin Martyr, London, 1921.

*Massaux, E. "Le texte du sermon sur la montagne de Matthieu utilisé par Saint Justin: contribution à la critique textuelle du premier évangile," Eph. Theol. Lov. 28 (1952), pp. 411-48.

*Meyer, H. Geschichte der Lehre von den Keimkräften von der Stoa bis zum Ausgang der Patristik, Bonn, 1914.

Michaelis, W. Zur Engelchristologie im Urchristentum, Basel, 1942.

Michel, O. Der Brief an die Hebräer, Meyer Komm., Göttingen, 1966.

Mitros, J. H. "The Norm of Faith in the Patristic Age," Theol. Stud. 29 (1968), pp. 444-71.

*Moffat, J. "Two Notes on Ignatius and Justin Martyr," HTR 23 (1930), pp. 153-59.

*Monachino, V. "Intento practico et propagandistico nell' apologetica greca del II secolo," Gregorianum 32 (1951), pp. 5-49; 187-222.

Müller, M. Untersuchungen zum Carmen adv. Marcionitas (Dissert.), Würzburg, 1936.

Nock, A. D. Conversion. The Old and the New in Religion from Alexander the Great to Augustine of Hippo, Oxford, 1933.

_____. Early Gentile Christianity and its Hellenistic Background, New York, Harper Torchbook, 1964.

Norden, E. Agnostos Theos, Untersuchungen zur Formengeschichte religiöser Rede, Stuttgart, 1923⁴.

Normann, F. Christos Didaskalos; Die Vorstellung von Christus als der Lehrer in der christlichen Literatur des ersten und zweiten Jahrhunderts, Münster, 1967.

Norris, R. A. God and World in Early Christian Theology, New York, 1965.

*Nussbaumer, A. Das Ursymbolum nach der Epideixis des hl. Irenäus und dem Dialog Justins des Märtyrers mit Trypho, Paderborn, 1921.

*Osborn, E. F. "Justin's Response to Second Century Challenges," Austr. Bibl. Rev. 14 (1966), pp. 37-55.

Pannenberg, W. Jesus God and Man, trans. from the German by L. L. Wilkins and D. A. Priebe, Philadelphia, 1968.

Patterson, L. G. God and History in Early Christian Thought, New York, 1967.

*Paul, L. "Über die Logoslehre bei Justinus Martyr," Jahres-
    bücher für protestantische Theologie, 12 (1886), pp.
    661-90; 16 (1890), pp. 550-78; 17 (1891), pp. 124-48.

*Pautigny, L. Justin, Apologies. Texte grec, traduction
    française, introduction et index, Paris, 1904.

*Pellegrino, M. Gli Apologeti greci del II secolo. Saggio
    sui rapporti fra il christianesimo primitivo e la
    cultura classica, Roma, 1947.

*_____. "Christianesimo e Filosofia in San Giustino
    martire," Scuola Cattolica 87 (1959), pp. 301-03.

*Perler, O. "Logos und Eucharistie nach Justinus I Apol. c.
    66," Divus Thomas 18 (1940), pp. 296-316.

Peterson, E. Εἷς Θεός: Epigraphische, formgeschichtliche
    und religionsgeschichtliche Untersuchungen, Göttingen,
    1926.

*Pfättisch, J. M. "Christus und Sokrates bei Justin," Theol.
    Quartalschrift 90 (1908), pp. 503-23.

*_____. Der Einfluss Platos auf die Theologie Justins
    des Märtyrers: Eine dogmengeschichtliche Untersuchung
    nebst einem Anhang über die Komposition der Apologien
    Justins, Paderborn, 1910.

*_____. Justinus des Philosophen und Märtyrers
    Apologien, Teil I. Text: Teil 2. Kommentar,
    Münster, 1933[2].

*Piper, O. "The Nature of the Gospel According to Justin
    Martyr," Journal of Religion 41 (1961), pp. 153-68.

Plumpe, J. C. "Some little-known early witnesses to Mary's
    virginitas in partu," Theol. Stud. 9 (1948), pp.
    567-77.

Pohlenz, M. Die Stoa: Geschichte einer geistigen Bewegung,
    Vol. I, Göttingen, 1948; Vol. II, Erläuterungen,
    Göttingen, 1949.

Pollard, T. E. Johannine Christology and the Early Church,
    Cambridge, 1970.

*Porter, H. B. "The Eucharistic Piety of Justin Martyr,"
    Anglican Theol. Review 39 (1957), pp. 24-33.

*Posnoff, I. Les Prophètes dans la synthèse chrétienne de
    saint Justin (Dissert.), Louvain, 1949.

*Preuschen, E. "Die Echtheit von Justins Dialog gegen Trypho,"
    ZNW 19 (1919-1920), pp. 102-27.

Prigent, P. Les testimonia dans le christianisme primitif:
    l'Épitre de Barnabée I-XVI et ses sources, Paris,
    1961.

*_____. _Justin et l'Ancient Testament_, Paris, 1964.

*Puech, A. _Les Apologistes grecs du IIe siècle de notre ère_, Paris, 1912.

*Pycke, N. "Connaissance rationnelle et connaissance de grâce chez saint Justin," _Eph. Theol. Lov._ 37 (1961), pp. 52-85.

Quasten, J. _Patrology_, 3 vols., Utrecht-Antwerp, 1962-66.

*Ramureanu. "Conceptia St. Justin Martirul et Filozoful despre auflet," _Studii theologice_ 10 (Bucaresti, 1958), pp. 403-24.

*Ratcliff, E. C. "The Eucharistic Institution Narrative of Justin Martyr's First Apology," _Journ. Eccles. Hist._ 22 (1971), pp. 97-102.

*Rauschen, G. _S. Justini Apologiae duae_, Bonn, 1911[2].

*Reijners, G. Q. _The Terminology of the Holy Cross in Early Christian Literature as Based on Old Testament Typology_, Nijmegen, 1965.

*Reinhold, B. "Trinität und Inkarnation bei den griechischen Apologeten des 2. Jahrhunderts," (Dissert.), Bonn, 1961.

Richardson, P. _Israel in the Apostolic Church_, Cambridge, 1969.

Ringgren, H. _Word and Wisdom: Studies in the hypostatization of divine qualities and functions in the ancient Near East_, Lund, 1947.

*Rivière, J. _S. Justin et les Apologistes du deuxième siècle_, Paris, 1907.

*Robinson, J. A. "On a Quotation from Justin in Irenäus," _Jour. Theol. Stud._ 31 (1930), pp. 374-78.

Robinson, J. M. "A Formal Analysis of Col. 1,15-20," _Jour. Bibl. Lit._ 76 (1957), pp. 270-87.

Robinson, J. M. and Koester, H. _Trajectories through Early Christianity_, Philadelphia, 1971.

*Romanides, J. S. "Justin Martyr and the Fourth Gospel," _Greek Orthodox Theological Review_ 4 (1958-59), pp. 115-34.

*Rossi, S. "Il tempo e l'ambientazione del Dialogus di Giustino," _Giorn. Italiano di Filologia_ 17 (1964), pp. 55-65.

Ruesch, T. _Entstehung der Lehre vom Heiligen Geist bei Ignatius von Antiochia, Theophilus von Antiochia und Irenaeus von Lyon_, Zürich, 1952.

*Sagnard, M. M. "Y a-t-il un plan du Dialogue avec Tryphon?"
    Mélanges Joseph de Ghellinck, Tome I, Gembloux, 1951,
    pp. 171-82.

Sanders, J. T.   The New Testament Christological Hymns:
    their historical religious background, Cambridge,
    1971.
Scheidweiler, F.   "Zwei Anmerkungen zum Engelkult," Zeitschr.
    für Kirchengesch. 68 (1957), pp. 319-21.

*Schmid, W.   "Die Textüberlieferung der Apologie des Justin,"
    ZNW 40 (1941), pp. 87-138.

*_____.   "Frühe Apologetik und Platonismus: Ein Beitrag
    zur Interpretation der Proöms von Justins Dialogus,"
    Hermeneia (Festschrift Otto Regenbogen) Heidelberg,
    1952, pp. 163-82.

*Schneider, H.   "Some Reflections on the Dialogue of Justin
    Martyr with Trypho," Scottish Journal of Theology 15
    (1962), pp. 164-75.

*Scho, J.   Paideia bei Justin dem Märtyrer (Dissert.), Trier,
    1968.

Schubert, K.   "Einige Beobachtungen zum Verständnis des Logos-
    begriffes im frührabbinischen Schrifttum," Judaica, 9
    (1953), pp. 65-80.

Schweizer, E.   Erniedriegung und Erhöhung bei Jesus und
    seinen Nachfolgern, Zürich, 1955, Engl. trans. with
    revision by the author, under the title Lordship and
    Discipleship, London, 1960.

_____.   "Two New Testament Creeds Compared," Current
    Issues in New Testament Interpretation, Essays in
    honor of O. Piper, ed. W. Klassen and F. G. Snyder,
    New York, 1962, pp. 166-77.

*Seeberg, B.   Die Geschichtstheologie Justins des Märtyrers
    (Dissert.), Kiel, 1939.

Seeberg, E.   "Geschichte und Geschichtsanschauung dargestellt
    in altchristlichen Geschichtsvorstellungen," Zeitsch.
    Kirch. Gesch. 40 (1941), pp. 309-31.

*Semisch, C.   Justin der Märtyrer, Eine kirchen- und dogmenge-
    schichtliche Monographie, I and II, Breslau, 1840-
    1842. Engl. trans. by J. E. Ryland (vols. 41 and 42
    of the Biblical Cabinet series), Edinburgh, 1843.

*Shotwell, W. A.   The Biblical Exegesis of Justin Martyr,
    London, 1965.

*Sibinga, J. S.   The Old Testament Text of Justin Martyr:
    I. The Pentateuch, Leiden, 1963.

*Sikora, J.   "Philosophy and Christian Wisdom according to
    Saint Justin Martyr," Franciscan Studies 23 (1963),
    pp. 244-56.

Simon, M. Verus Israel: Étude sur les relations entre Chrétiens et Juifs dans l'empire Romain, Paris, 1964[2].

*Sjöberg, E. "Justin als Zeuge vom Glauben an den verborgenen und leidenden Messias im Judentum," in Interpretationes ad Vetus Testamentum pertinentes S. Mowinckel septuagenario missae, eds. N. Dahl and A. Kapelrud, Oslo, 1955, pp. 173-83.

*Smith, M. A. "Did Justin know the Didache?" Studia Patristica, VII (Berlin, 1966), pp. 287-90.

*Spanneut, M. Le Stoicisme des Pères de l'Eglise de Clement de Rome à Clement d'Alexandrie, Paris, 1957.

Spicq, C. L'Epître aux Hebreux, Vol. I, Paris, 1952, Vol. II, Paris, 1953.

*Stahler, R. Justin Martyr et l'apologétique (Dissert.), Geneva, 1935.

Stegmann, V. "Christentum und Stoizismus im Kampf um die geistigen Lebenswerte im 2. Jahrhundert nach Christus," Die Welt als Geschichte (1941), pp. 295-330.

*Steiner, R. M. La Tentation de Jésus dans l'interprétation patristique de saint Justin a Origène, Paris, 1962.

*Story, C. I. K. The Nature of Truth in "The Gospel of Truth" and in the Writings of Justin Martyr, Leiden, 1970.

Strecker, G. "Redaktion und Tradition im Christus-Hymnus Phil. 2" ZNW 55 (1964), pp. 63-78.

*Theodorou, A. Ἡ θεολογία τοῦ Ἰουστίνου Φιλοσόφου καὶ Μάρτυρος, καὶ αἱ σχέσεις αὐτῆς πρὸς τὴν ἑλληνικὴν φιλοσοφίαν, Athens, 1960.

Thieme, K. Kirche und Synagoge, Olten, 1945.

*Titus, E. L. The Motivations of Changes Made in the New Testament by Justin Martyr and Clement of Alexandria (Dissert.), Chicago, 1942.

Tresmontant, C. La Métaphysique du Christianisme et la Naissance de la philosophie chrétienne, Paris, 1961.

Tull, A. C. The Theology of Middle Platonism of the Second Century, Th.D. Thesis, General Theological Seminary, New York, 1968.

Turmel, J. Histoire des Dogmes, Vol. II, Paris, 1932.

Turner, H. E. W. The Patristic Doctrine of Redemption, London, 1952.

Überweg, F. und Prächter, K. Die Philosophie des Altertums, Basel, 1953[13] (repr. from the 12th edition, Berlin, 1928).

202

*Veil, H. Justinus des Philosophen und Märtyrers Rechtfer-
     tigung des Christentums: Apologie I u. II einge-
     leitet, verdeutscht und erläutert, Strassburg, 1894.

Verbeke, G. L'évolution de la doctrine du pneuma du
     stoicisme à S. Augustin: Étude philosophique, Paris-
     Louvain, 1945.

*Voss, B. R. Der Dialog in der frühchristlichen Literatur,
     München, 1970.

*Vysoky, Z. K. "Un prétendu souvenir autobiographique de S.
     Justin," Listy Filologicke (1938), pp. 435-40.

Waszink, J. H. "Der Platonismus und die altchristliche
     Gedankenwelt," Entretiens sur l"Antiquité classique,
     III (Génève, 1955), pp. 137-79.

*_____. "Bemerkungen zu Justins Lehre vom Logos
     Spermatikos," Mullus (Festschr. Th. Klausner), Jahrbuch
     für Antike und Christentum, Ergänzungsband I, Münster,
     1964, pp. 380-90.

*_____. "Bemerkungen zum Einfluss des Platonismus im
     frühen Christentum," Vigil. Christ. 19 (1965), pp.
     129-62.

*Waibel, A. Die natürliche Gotteserkenntnis in der apolo-
     getischen Literatur des 2. Jahrh., Breslau, 1917.

*Waubert de Puiseau, D. H. De Christologie van Justinus
     Martyr, Academisch proefschrift, Leiden, 1864.

*Weid, P. R. "Some Samaritanisms of Justin Martyr," Jour.
     Theol. Stud. 45 (1944), pp. 199-205.

*Weizäcker, K. V. "Die Theologie des Märtyrers Justinus,"
     Jahrbücher für deutsche Theologie 12 (1856), pp. 60-
     119.

Wilde, R. The Treatment of the Jews in the Greek Christian
     Writers of the First Three Centuries (Dissert.),
     Washington, 1949.

*Williams, A. L. Justin Martyr. The Dialogue with Trypho,
     Translation, Introduction and Notes, London, 1930.

*Williams, G. H. "The Baptism of Theology of Justin Martyr,"
     Orthodoxy and Russian Thought, Essays in honor of
     Fr. G. Florovsky, ed. by T. Bird and J. Blane (Mouton
     Press), The Hague, 1971.

Witt, R. E. Albinus and the History of Middle Platonism,
     Cambridge, 1937.

Wolfson, H. A. Philo: Foundations of Religious Philosophy
     in Judaism, Christianity and Islam, 2 vols.,
     Cambridge, Mass., 1962[3].

*_____. The Philosophy of the Church Fathers, Third
     ed., revised, Cambridge, Mass., 1970.

*Zahn, T. "Studien zu Justin," Zeitsch. für Kirchengesch. 8
     (1886), pp. 1-84.

 Zeller, E. Die Philosophie der Griechen, Leipzig, 1923^5.

HARVARD DISSERTATIONS IN RELIGION

published under the aegis of the

HARVARD THEOLOGICAL REVIEW

by

THE SCHOLARS PRESS

Harvard Dissertations in Religion publishes outstanding dissertations in the study of religion submitted to Harvard University for the Ph.D. or Th.D. degree. Nomination of dissertations for the series is normally by the departments or thesis committees to which they have been submitted. Volumes are reproduced directly from typescript provided by the authors.